THE ORIGINS OF THE GREEK CIVIL WAR

ORIGINS OF MODERN WARS
General editor: Harry Hearder

Titles already published:

THE ORIGINS OF
THE GREEK CIVIL WAR

David H. Close

LONGMAN
London and New York

LONGMAN GROUP LIMITED,
Longman House, Burnt Mill,
Harlow, Essex CM20 2JE, England
and Associated Companies throughout the world.

Published in the United States of America
by Longman Publishing, New York

First published 1995

Transferred to digital print on demand 2001

ISBN 0 582 06471 6 PPR

British Library Cataloguing-in-Publication Data

A catalogue record for this book is
available from the British Library

Library of Congress Cataloging-in-Publication Data

Close, David (David H.)
    The origins of the Greek civil war / David H. Close.
        p.   cm. — (Origins of modern wars)
    Includes bibliographical references and index.
    ISBN 0–582–06472–4 (csd). — ISBN 0–582–06471–6 (ppr)
    1. Greece—History—Civil War, 1944–1949—Causes.   2. Greece—
Politics and government—1935–1967.   3. Greece—History—Civil
War, 1944–1949—Diplomatic history.   4. Kommounistikon Komma tēs
Hellados—Influence.   I. Title.   II. Series.
DF849.52.C56   1995
949.507′4—dc20   94–39794
                                                            CIP

Printed and bound by Antony Rowe Ltd, Eastbourne

Contents

Contents

Editor's Foreword

In his lucid and vivid account of the origins of the Greek Civil War of 1943–1950 Dr David Close deals with a comparatively recent tragedy that has had less attention than it deserves from historians. It belongs to that transitional period between the end of the Second World War and the start of the Cold War. This series has had two volumes devoted to the origins of the Second World War, by Philip Bell and Akira Iriye, and Professor Geoffrey Warner is writing a volume for the series on the origins of the Cold War. But this study of the Greek Civil War fills an important place in our understanding of that post-war period.

David Close's book is the twelfth to be published in the series, but the first dealing with a civil war. If Peter Lowe on Korea and Anthony Short on Vietnam had an element of the civil war about them, both volumes had eventually to concern themselves with participation by the USA and other powers. Two other books concerned with important civil wars are being written for the series; Brian Holden Reid is writing on the American Civil War, and Martin Blinkhorn is writing on the Spanish Civil War. Civil wars are by their nature often more savage than international wars, and have a stronger ideological content. The two factors are certainly related.

When, during the Second World War, Hitler's armies were driven out of countries they had been occupying, they left behind ideological confrontations, which could lead to civil war. This was especially the case in the countries on the northern coast of the Mediterranean. Yet the nature of developments in Greece, Yugoslavia and Italy were strikingly different. In Greece Close shows us that a bitter civil war ensued between Greek political groups whose plans or visions for the future were diametrically opposed to each other. Ideological confrontation led to savage conflict, often descending to torture committed by both sides, though rather more by the right than by the left, if only because the right had more power. In

Yugoslavia there was also civil war, though less prolonged than in Greece, and it is interesting to observe that whereas in Greece Britain – or more specifically Churchill – supported the right, in Yugoslavia he supported the Communists. In Greece Churchill favoured the king, in spite of his unpopularity, and here there was an analogy with Italy, where Churchill also supported the monarchy and the right. But in Italy civil war, with all its horrors, did not result. The Communists, Socialists and Catholics joined forces in the resistance, and, because they were separated from the King and Badoglio by the armies of the great powers, they could eventually establish their supremacy and create the Republic of 1947–8. Greece was less fortunate.

On the question of responsibility – or blame – for the war, Close has some interesting things to say. The Germans, he writes, deliberately 'fomented civil war between Communists and their opponents'. And while there was a 'multiplicity of motives for alignment in the civil war', 'some protagonists, at certain points, pursued policies or took decisions which they could arguably have avoided' . So this war, like other wars, was not 'inevitable'. Political leaders were not always crushed by inescapable historical forces. They could often make choices, and to that extent could subsequently be held responsible if their choices led to immense human suffering. Lord Acton argued with Bishop Creighton that it was for the historian to point an accusing finger at the criminals in history. The historian should be the 'moral arbiter'. If academic historians today are a little shy of being moral arbiters, they can at least gently suggest that certain decisions in history were mistaken, or sometimes wicked.

In that Close excites the interests and raises the emotions of the reader in this fine study, he makes it clear that certain actions were reprehensible, and that often both sides, or all parties, are to blame for the ensuing catastrophe. And yet the tragedy was that, in the words of David Close, 'Civil war was a prospect viewed with revulsion by all except a small minority of fanatics on each side'. As too often, it was the fanatics that called the tune.

Harry Hearder

List of Maps

Preface

In recent years it has become easier to reflect on the causes of the Greek Civil War. With the collapse of the Soviet bloc in the late 1980s, and the general disillusionment with 'actually existing socialism,' the Greek Civil War ceased to seem like the beginning of the contemporary era, but like part of a bygone era, which could be contemplated more dispassionately. In Greece a sign of this change in 1989 was the entry by the Greek Communist Party into a government for the first time since December 1944, and the enactment by this government of a reconciliation law, conceding full equality of status to the Communist-led losers in the civil war. Reconciliation was accompanied, very controversially, by the incineration of an estimated eighteen million police security files on left-wingers, to commemorate the 40th anniversary of the decisive battle of the war. We can only hope that this action marked the end of the large-scale destruction of historical records by the survivors and descendants of the two sides – a crazy and malign way whereby they have until recently continued the civil war.

Meanwhile, interpretation of the events of the 1940s has become easier for other reasons, as scholars have continued to explore the mountain of evidence made available in the 1970s and 1980s by the opening of the British and American archives, and as memoirs and documents have continued to be published in Greece. Several major studies have been published in the last few years; and more are expected soon. In time, also, more of the archives of protagonists in the civil war – the Greek government, the Greek Communist Party, and the British Special Operations Executive – are likely to appear. It has only just become possible to write a book like this one; and the interpretations therein cannot be definitive.

The Greek Civil War presents some fascinating problems of causality.

Greece was economically and strategically so interwoven with the capitalist, maritime powers of Britain and the United States, that it is tempting to argue that the violent suppression of the Greek Communist Party was almost inevitable. The interpretations in this book may indeed appear more deterministic in their implications than previous ones. Yet one cannot neglect the important role of individuals and accidents. Some protagonists, at certain points, pursued policies or took decisions which they could arguably have avoided. The Greek king surely did not have to let Metaxas become a dictator in 1936. The British government surely did not have to support the Greek king in such a provocative way during the German occupation. The Communist leader, Siantos, might have allowed for the possibility of British intervention early in December 1944. Stalin and Tito might conceivably have given the Greek Communist Party more military backing in 1946, when it had a chance of overthrowing the government. Each of these decisions or actions was arguably chosen with some degree of freedom, and had a profound influence on subsequent events.

On the other hand, I will argue that the Greek Communist Party's choices were more restricted than has hitherto been supposed. It has been stated that at certain points the party leaders decided unnecessarily on a course leading to war: in September 1943, November 1944, and February 1946. My interpretation is that, on the information available to them, they had very restricted options at each of these junctures, even the third. The facts as presented in this book also make it hard to accept the widely held view that Britain could have prevented the slide to renewed civil war by restraining its Greek clients in the years 1945–6.

Like all foreign writers on Greek events, I have grappled with problems of transliteration from Greek, and settled in most cases for the Library of Congress system, in the hope that this will help readers to find books in English-language catalogues. But I have used alternative forms of transliteration when these are well known, e.g. Stefanos Sarafis rather than Stephanos Saraphes, King Constantine rather than King Konstantinos.

Unless indicated otherwise, all English-language books are published in London, and all Greek-language books in Athens.

I am indebted to the staff of many libraries, including the National Archives in Washington D.C., the Public Record Office at Kew, the Benaki Museum, the Academy and the British School in Athens, and the Flinders University library. I would like to thank Elizabeth and Stephen for having suffered so patiently the side-effects of my work on this book.

David Close   The Flinders University of South Australia

Abbreviations

Notes are provided for those acronyms which appear in the text separately from the full English title.

AKE   *Agrotiko Komma Ellados* (Agrarian Party of Greece)
AMFOGE Allied Mission for Observing the Greek Elections
ASO   *Antifasistike Stratiotike Organosis* (Anti-Fascist Military Organization of the Army)
DSE   *Demokratikos Stratos Ellados* (Democratic Army of Greece)
EA   *Ethnike Allelengye* (National Solidarity)
EAM   *Ethniko Apelevtherotiko Metopo* (National Liberation Front). Communist-dominated, established in September 1941 in order to resist the Germans and provide social services, it grew until it dominated the country during 1943–4. Became a powerful party in 1945, but was thereafter weakened by right-wing persecution and faded away in 1947.
EDA   *Enaia Demokratike Aristera* (United Democratic Left)
EDES   *Ethnikos Demokratikos Ellenikos Syndesmos* (National Democratic Greek League). The main anti-Communist resistance organization, and a major instrument of British policy. The significant part of it was an association of guerrilla bands established from July 1942 by Col. Napoleon Zervas in his natal area of western Epirus. It expanded with British backing and EAM tolerance to other regions, but after a war with ELAS in October 1943–February 1944 was confined to part of Epirus. It became in 1945 the basis of Zervas's National Party of Greece.
EE   *Ethnike Epanastasis* (National Revolution)
EEAM   *Elleniko Ergatiko Apelevtherotiko Metopo* (National Workers' Liberation Front)

EES	*Ethnikos Ellenikos Stratos* (National Greek Army)
ED	*Ethnike Drasis* (National Action)
EKKA	*Ethnike kai Koinonike Apelevtherosis* (National and Social Liberation). Led by Col. Demetrios Psarros, this was after EDES the most influential anti-Communist resistance organization. The significant part of it was a collection of guerrilla bands which operated from early 1943 in the area of Mount Parnassos in Sterea Ellada. Despite British backing they were repeatedly attacked by ELAS and finally destroyed in massacres of April 1944.
ELAS	*Ethnikos Laikos Apelevtherotikos Stratos* (National Popular Liberation Army). The armed force of EAM, formally established in February 1942, and treated by the Communist Party as its main source of power from about May 1943. After defeat in a long battle against British and Greek troops in the capital in December 1944, ELAS was disbanded in accordance with the Varkiza agreement of February 1945.
ELD	*Enosis Laikes Demokratias* (Union of Popular Democracy)
EOK	*Ethnike Organosis Kretes* (National Organization of Crete)
EON	*Ethnike Organosis Neon* (National Organization of Youth)
ESPO	*Ellenike Sosialistike Patriotike Organosis* (Greek Socialist Patriotic Organization)
ENA	*Enosis Neon Axiomatikon* (Union of Young Officers)
EPON	*Eniaia Panelladike Organosis Neon* (United Greek Youth Organization)
FO	Foreign Office, or Foreign Office papers, Public Record Office
GSEE	*Genike Synomospondia Ellenon Ergaton* (General Confederation of Greek Workers)
HMSO	His (or Her) Majesty's Stationery Office
IDEA	*Ieros Desmos Ellenon Axiomatikon* (Sacred Union of Greek Officers)
IMRO	Internal Macedonia Revolutionary Organization
IFC	International Financial Commission
IRC	International Red Cross
KKE	*Kommounistiko Komma Ellados* (Greek Communist Party)
KOA	*Kommounistike Organosis Attikes* (Communist Organization of Attica)
KOSSA	*Kommounistike Organosis Stratou kai Somaton Asphaleias* (Communist Organization of the Army and Security Organizations)
KUTV	*Kommounisticheskii Universitet Trudyashcshya Vostoka* (Communist University for Eastern Workers)

Abbreviations

ML	Military Liaison
Nars	National Archives and Records Service, Washington, D.C.
NOF	*Narodnii Osvoboditelen Front* (Popular Liberation Front)
OPLA	*Organosis Prostasias Laikou Agonas* (Organization for the Protection of the People's Struggle)
OSS	Office of Strategic Services
PAO	*Panelladike Apelevtherotike Organosis* (National Greek Liberation Organization, formerly YBE). An anti-Communist resistance organization based on army officers and state officials in Macedonia. Its guerrilla groups were destroyed by ELAS in the second half of 1943.
PAS	*Panelladikos Apelevtherotikos Syndesmos* (National Greek Liberation League)
PEEA	*Politike Epitrope Ethnikes Apelevtheroseos* (Political Committee of National Liberation). The provisional government established by EAM, lasting from March to November 1944.
PRO	Public Record Office
SAN	Association of Young Officers
SK-ELD	*Sosialistiko Komma-Enosis Laikes Demokratias* (Socialist Party-Union of Popular Democracy)
SKE	*Sosialistiko Komma Ellados* (Socialist Party of Greece)
SOE	Special Operations Executive
SNOF	*Slavomakedonski Narodnoosloboditelniot Front* (Slav Macedonian Popular Liberation Front)
UNRRA	United Nations Relief and Rehabilitation Administration
USFR	*Foreign Relations of the United States* (see Bibliography)
X	Chi. A resistance organization of regular army officers, it came under the leadership of Col. George Grivas in 1943, recruited several hundred members and devoted itself to fighting against EAM in the capital. During 1945 it recruited members from gendarmes and monarchist associations in many parts of the country, devoting itself to the restoration of the monarchy and destruction of EAM. After March 1946 it survived only as a generic name for local vigilante groups helping the police to persecute the left.
YBE	*Yperaspistai Voreiou Ellados* (Defenders of Northern Greece). A resistance organization founded in 1941, and based on the state administration of Macedonia. It was re-labelled PAO early in 1943.

CHAPTER ONE

Greece after the First World War

DEPENDENCY AND SCHISM

'The encounter between the West and the great non-Western majority of
mankind,' wrote the historian Leften S. Stavrianos, 'seems likely to be
viewed in retrospect as the central feature of modern history.' In Greece
the encounter led from the fifteenth century onwards to increasing acceptance of Western influence, a process which eventually brought the
country into what Nikos Mouzelis described as 'the parliamentary semi-
periphery' of the advanced capitalist countries. Greece by the 1930s
qualified for this description because for nearly all the time since 1844 it
had experienced parliamentary rule; it had made substantial progress
towards industrialization; yet it remained dependent on advanced capitalist
countries in many spheres – economic, military, and cultural. [1]

Dependency stemmed from economic backwardness; and by conventional criteria – low income per capita, low rate of literacy, high rural
unemployment, malnutrition among the majority of the rural population,
and a low average life expectancy – Greece rated as backward by northern
European standards. However it shared at least the first three of these characteristics with the other four Balkan countries, Albania, Bulgaria,
Romania, and Yugoslavia. By another criterion, however – the relatively
high proportion of the population engaged in non-agricultural occupations
and living in large towns – Greece obviously diverged from the rest of the
Balkans. By 1940 48 per cent of the population of 7,330,000 lived by non-
agricultural occupations, and 23 per cent lived in the four connurbations
with over 50,000 people: the metropolis (i.e. Athens and its port Piraeus),
Salonika, Patras, and Volos. The metropolis alone contained 15 per cent
and was far larger than any other Balkan city. The urban population was
relatively receptive to Western technology, clothes, and culture: Athens

and Salonika, for example, were on the electricity grid after 1930. Here, the wealthy and educated lived in a way far removed from that of the villages. These, if defined as having under 1,000 people, still included 48 per cent of the population, and many were remote and primitive, like one in the Pindus mountains, described by an American officer attached in 1944 to the base of the main resistance movement against the Germans: here all the inhabitants slept on the floors of their single-roomed huts; the nearest shop was fifteen hours' walk away; and an old woman, seeing an illuminated light bulb for the first time, tried to blow it out.[2]

Political dependency had been continuous since 1832 when the boundaries and the monarch of the new state were determined over the heads of the Greek people by Britain, France, and Russia. 'A Greece truly independent is an absurdity,' declared the British minister to Athens in 1841; 'Greece is Russian or she is English; and since she must not be Russian, it is necessary that she be English.'[3] From the 1830s onwards, successive monarchs represented the interests of one or more of the great powers, who reciprocated by taking a protective interest in them. The political institutions of the new state – monarchy, legislature, civil service, police, armed forces, law courts, legal code, educational system, and later the trade unions also – were modelled on those of various states of northern and western Europe. Many leading members of these institutions acquired a higher education abroad, including the majority of leading politicians between the First and Second World Wars. The prime minister Elevtherios Venizelos, when modernizing the state in the second decade of the twentieth century, entrusted the organization and training of the army to a French mission, of the gendarmerie to an Italian one, and of the navy and city police to British missions. Governments after the Second World War repeated this practice. This is not to deny that these institutions soon acquired some Greek characteristics – notably their subversion by clientelistic practices – as the foreign missions found to their frustration.

The compulsion, inherited by Greeks from Ottoman rule, to seek powerful patrons was projected beyond national frontiers; and so in the early years of the new state there was a 'British', a 'French', and a 'Russian' party. Dependency was reinforced by geographical position. Greece was small and situated at an international crossroads. It was vulnerable to pressure from the sea, because in the 1930s the five largest cities were ports; it had a large merchant fleet; and imported, mainly or entirely by sea, many of its vital requirements including about a third of its wheat. On ten occasions between 1850 and 1944 the country was blockaded or menaced by warships of Britain, France, or Italy. Of special importance for the 1940s was the traditional interest of Britain in ensuring that Greece was ruled by a friendly regime. Britain's strategic goals were to maintain freedom of communication through the eastern Mediterranean and the Suez Canal; ensure that the Straits of Constantinople were not closed by a hostile power, as indeed they were during the First World War; and protect her interests in the Middle East, which grew after the First World War with the acquisition of protectorates there and her increasing dependence on Middle Eastern oil.

Given Greece's vulnerability to foreign intervention, the international instability which prevailed between 1914 and 1949 was intensely disruptive. Each of the two world wars caused a civil war, and the international tension of the inter-war period shaped domestic politics in various ways. The First World War quickly precipitated what became known as the National Schism, which started as a dispute between the prime minister Elevtherios Venizelos and King Constantine over Greece's alignment. The Cretan politician Venizelos was to modern Greece what Bismarck was to modern Germany. Like a previous prime minister in 1907 he wanted 'both from inclination and from policy to gravitate . . . [towards] the Western powers . . . ',[4] a choice justified by Greece's maritime position. Being responsive moreover to the wishes of businessmen in Greece and the diaspora, Venizelos wanted to continue his programme of modernizing the state on the model of Britain and France, and to bring within its frontiers the large Greek population of western Asia Minor. Constantine rejected this policy as too risky to the political and social structure of the old lands, that is the original kingdom comprising chiefly the Peloponnese and Sterea Ellada. In addition, as the Kaiser's brother-in-law, Constantine admired Germany's military efficiency and political institutions. Either choice was risky yet critical to the country's future. Each leader was idolized by his camp. Venizelos had been head of government, and Constantine actively head of the army, during the Balkan wars of 1912–3 which added Macedonia, Epirus, and Crete to the state.[5]

Venizelos with Entente backing established a revolutionary government with its own army in Salonika the capital of the Greek province of Macedonia in 1916. In 1917 the rebels took over the king's government and army in the south, forcing Constantine to abdicate in favour of his son. Thereupon Venizelos's government purged the army and civil administration of monarchists. These events were accompanied by fierce, small-scale fighting in many parts of the country, as those active on each side persecuted the supporters of the other.[6] For the next eighteen years, the Venizelist and anti-Venizelist camps alternated in power as a result of military coups or general elections, and each transfer of power was followed by a purge of the army and public administration. The Venizelist camp, of which the core was the Liberal Party, became predominantly republican, while the anti-Venizelist camp, of which the core was the Populist Party, tended towards monarchism.

The Schism destroyed consensus about the political system, and politicized the machinery of state. Henceforth each of the camps had a military wing on which it depended for political power. For their part many of the officers were keen for political patronage because of recent changes in the social composition of the officer corps. To enable the country to participate in the Balkan Wars of 1912–3 and in the First World War, governments rapidly expanded the army officer corps, and to this end abolished fees in the training school for officers and enabled many conscripts to become professional officers. Thus many of the officers were without private means, and depended entirely on their salaries for a livelihood. In attempting to defend and further their positions they sought political patrons. The practice, anyway traditional and accepted among officers, of forming political organizations and engaging in political conspiracies became more widespread.[7]

Having brought Greece into the First World War on the winning side, Venizelos secured as a reward Thrace, the west of which Bulgaria had occupied since its seizure from the Ottoman Empire in 1913, and Smyrna with much of western Anatolia, which lie in present-day Turkey. In the face of subsequent Turkish revival led by Kemal Ataturk, only western Thrace proved defensible. Eastern Thrace and western Anatolia did not; and in the so-called Asia Minor Catastrophe of 1922, the Greek army was forced to withdraw from them with masses of civilian refugees.

The Treaty of Lausanne which followed between the Greek and Turkish governments ratified an extraordinarily drastic process of population exchange, as a result of which Greece expelled 380,000 Turkish-speaking Muslims to Turkey, while Turkey expelled to Greece about 200,000 subjects who were Greek Orthodox in religion. In addition, about 1,100,000–1,200,000 Greek Orthodox refugees arrived in Greece of their own accord from 1913 to 1922. The great majority came after the Catastrophe from present-day Turkey, and of these perhaps 50,000 promptly re-emigrated and perhaps 70,000 died soon after arrival.

During and soon after the First World War there had been other migrations. Some 58,500 Greek Orthodox migrants arrived in Greece from the Caucasus region and Russia, and another 46,000 from Bulgaria. During or soon after the First World War, 92,000 Bulgarian-speaking Christians left Greece for Bulgaria; and some of the Koutsovlachs, who were Romanian-speaking, emigrated to Romania. Greece emerged from these upheavals as probably the most homogeneous country in the Balkans, with the overwhelming majority of the population in most provinces being Greek-speaking and Greek Orthodox, and the rest fragmented into many mutually unsympathetic groups. A large percentage of those whose mother tongue was not Greek – such as Albanian-speakers in southern regions or

Koutsovlachs in the Pindus ranges – regarded themselves nevertheless as ethnically Greek.

The ethnic groups of significance for the civil war period lived near the northern frontiers: the slavophones who lived mainly in western Macedonia, and the Albanian-speaking Muslims, or Chams, of western Epirus. The slavophones are usually thought to have numbered 100,000, but may in fact have numbered up to 200,000. Possibly a majority had no distinct national consciousness, but, of those who had, most in the inter-war period identified with Bulgaria, which aspired openly to extend its territory at Greece's expense, and sheltered the Internal Macedonian Revolutionary Organization (IMRO) which periodically raided Greece and encouraged the Slavs' separatism. Western Macedonia remained a powder-keg : to the north lay the Yugoslav and Bulgarian sections of the ancient province of Macedonia, inhabited largely by peoples speaking the same language as the slavophones of Greece; within it were tens of thousands of Turkish-speaking, but in religion Greek Orthodox, refugees who were fearful for their newly acquired lands and so suspicious of Slav expansionism.

The Chams numbered only 19,000, but derived some significance from patronage by neighbouring Albania, which encouraged their separatist feelings. The Romanian-speaking Koutsovlachs, who dwelt in the Pindus ranges and Macedonia, may have been nearly as numerous as the Slav-speakers, but very few had any separatist inclinations as Romania was remote. The Muslim, and mainly Turkish-speaking, population of 86,000 in Greek Thrace played little role in the civil strife of the 1940s because its religion was tolerated under the Treaty of Lausanne and it lacked interest in Greek quarrels. The Sephardic Jewish population of 62,000 was found mainly in Salonika and provoked quite strong anti-Semitism from Greeks. Most were deported to death camps during the German occupation. This group likewise played no significant role in the strife of the 1940s.

The exchange of populations gave added force to the National Schism. After 1923, refugees formed a fifth of the total population. They had lost their property in the Catastrophe, and many suffered a severe drop in status, for example from well-to-do merchants and professionals to poor peasants and workers. As many were distinguished from natives by speech, manners, or poverty, they were targets of resentment and scorn. The over-whelming majority of refugees saw Venizelos as their protector and blamed the Catastrophe on his opponents. Over half settled in the newly acquired territories of Macedonia and Thrace, including probably over 600,000 newly established smallholders, so accentuating the difference between the new and old regions of the country. The non-Greek minorities in rural Macedonia were jealous of the territorial claims of the refugees, and so

5

gave their support to Venizelos's opponents. Further south the refugees tended to form distinct communities both in villages and towns. Of special significance for the future were the extensive and generally poor quarters of the metropolis which they inhabited.[8]

The Catastrophe left an ideological vacuum which before 1922 had been occupied by the Great Idea: the ambition of most politicians to see the state expand so as to include all the ancient Greek diaspora of the Balkans and Asia Minor. In pursuing this aim for many decades, successive governments incurred a financial burden which starved the state and the economic infrastructure of resources. Now there were groups who argued that governments should make good this neglect and turn their backs on irredentism. These groups included Ioannes Metaxas, the right-wing dictator of 1936–41, and, at the opposite pole, the Greek Communist Party.

Economic dependency was reflected in a massive and mounting foreign debt. This burden was suffered also by the other Balkan states after the First World War; but the Greek debt was the heaviest per capita and was of long standing. Since 1897 an International Financial Commission (IFC), representing the creditor countries of which the chief was Britain, had supervised repayments, which in 1932 consumed 35–40 per cent of revenue and 9 per cent of national income. Both the IFC and the League of Nations Finance Committee possessed statutory powers over government finances. Naturally this foreign intervention provoked much resentment, especially during the Great Depression in the 1930s. Another cause of dependency was the reliance of the rapid industrialization in the inter-war period on foreign investment. Much of the industry and communications systems were financed by the Western powers, including for example the tramways, underground railways, water company, and electricity company in the metropolitan area.[9]

The majority of Greece's surface area is rugged, and so of little economic value, but suited to banditry when government authority is shaken. Less than a quarter of the land surface is cultivable, most of it on plains near the coast; and there are few mineral resources. Imports in this period were paid for largely by a limited range of exports to a few countries: two-thirds of them consisted of tobacco, cigarettes, currants, and raisins, of which most in the late 1930s were taken by Germany under a clearing arrangement, so that the proceeds had to be spent in Germany. The major role in Greece's economy of its merchant fleet – the ninth largest in the world – formed a link with the democratic, industrialized powers of Britain, France, and the United States. Eastern Europe and the Soviet Union, on the other hand, bought little of Greek exports and provided almost no investment in the inter-war period.

Still more than the rest of the Balkans, Greece depended on the western powers, chiefly the United States, to absorb its surplus rural population, the result of a rate of population growth which was high even by Balkan standards. About half a million people emigrated to the United States in 1896–1940 (the bulk of them in 1900–20); and by 1930 nearly 200,000 had returned, spreading among poor villagers of mountains and islands the impression that it was a land of wealth and opportunity.[10] Remittances by emigrants did something to pay for the surplus of imports over exports; and so their interruption by the Great Depression and later the German occupation was a severe blow.

THE HYDROCEPHALOUS STATE

Dependency accentuated another characteristic which Nikos Mouzelis has identified in semi-peripheral countries: an overgrown state. The size of the state machine was still more marked than in other Balkan countries. Already in 1870, the number of state officials in relation to population was seven times the British level. In 1936 the number of national government officials was 72,000, and by April 1947 it was 91,000, with an additional 60,000 employed by independent semi-government agencies and local authorities, and about another 30,000 in the gendarmerie. In 1913, the level of tax per head was almost the same as in Britain, although the range of services provided by the government was much more restricted. In the early 1930s taxation had reached a level nearly 30 per cent of national income, twice the proportion in Yugoslavia and Romania, and three times that in Bulgaria.[11]

Originating as it did in the autocracy of a Bavarian ruler of the 1830s, the state became defined as the source of citizens' rights and the creator of the individual's national identity. Thus a Greek was defined as a subject of the Greek state, and seen as having few rights in relation to it. The higher judiciary saw themselves as servants of the state, and upheld the authoritarian and arbitrary powers of successive regimes against political opponents. The state defined the structure and scope of voluntary associations, and was the arbiter of social disputes: hence the extraordinary number and functions of lawyers in Greece.[12] The church itself – of which the overwhelming majority of the population apart from the Muslim minority regarded themselves as members – was an integral part of the state. Newly appointed prime ministers were sworn in by the Archbishop of Athens, and religious teaching was compulsory in schools. Excommunications had to be ratified by the state, which for its part accepted the church's sole control over the celebration and annulment of marriages. The Greek Orthodox Church was less likely than Roman Catholic churches to utter opinions on politics, and most unlikely to criticize the government of the day.[13] The state was the source of what was perhaps the main status distinction in Greece: that between those who had mastered the official and literary form of the language, *katharevousa*, and those who understood only the vernacular demotic. *Katharevousa* was the language of politics, administration, scholarship, the law, and serious journalism; yet the majority of the population could not understand it, and so were dependent on those who had learnt it by completing their secondary education.

The state exerted far-reaching and growing control over economic life, control assisted by the dominating position in the economy of certain institutions. The Federation of Greek Industrialists, the Chamber of Commerce and Industry, and the dominant banks were closely linked with leading politicians. The main employers' organizations were regulated by the government and from 1928 represented in the newly created Senate. Because of their ready access to governments and the main banks, large industrialists could secure subsidies, cheap credits, protective tariffs, low direct taxation, and police action against striking workers. The directors of the Bank of Greece (the bank of issue, established in 1928) and of the long-established National Bank (the main merchant bank) were important political figures. The National Bank was responsible for four-fifths of investment in industry in the late 1930s, the dependence on it of industrialists being increased by the weakness of the stock market.[14] The Agricultural Bank (established in 1929) was perhaps the main source of credit for peasants; and it is likely that its loans were influenced by party bias, as they certainly have been in recent times.

The government maintained a strong influence over industrial relations and over trade unions. From 1911 onwards it asserted the right to ratify even small and local collective agreements, to impose arbitration, and to regulate wages and working conditions. It also maintained a strong influence, through friendly unions, over municipal Labour Centres, from their first appearance in 1910, and over the General Confederation of Greek Workers, when this was established in 1918. The bulk of agricultural cooperatives were also established by the state, largely in the 1920s, serving as a means of channelling credit from the Agricultural Bank.[15] The state also influenced the citizen's means of earning a living through its licensing powers for shops and businesses, and its control over retail prices. These powers increased in the inter-war period with the growth of the police. It is possible by this time that state officials – and through them the politicians who influenced them – had the power to influence the livelihood of the majority of citizens.

In addition the state offered the population a means of socially respectable employment hard to find elsewhere. For peasants prepared to finance their children's education, as many were, state employment offered a means of upward mobility for the family. The emphasis of secondary and tertiary education on rote-learning gave an opportunity for success to children prepared to slave their way to a certificate which would earn them a white-collar job. The state was also a vital source of other benefits, such as pensions, credits, licences to do business, or exemptions from penalties.

The control of the state over the society was far-reaching even by Balkan standards. This fact can be partly explained by the relative size of cities in Greece, because cities required bureaucracies for their governance, and created economic and occupational links between the rural and urban population. It was also due to the utilization of public office by political parties for purposes of patronage. As the struggle between parties was especially vigorous in Greece, the spoils system affected the employment prospects of much of the population. For patronage purposes, politicians extended the state's powers. Thus the police were routinely and extensively used to influence elections. School curricula, even in such a basic essential as the form of the Greek language used, were constantly changed by successive regimes. From 1917 onwards, the armed forces were repeatedly and extensively purged, and bishops and judges were occasionally replaced for partisan reasons. Professional associations – such as those of lawyers, doctors, merchants, and industrialists – were strongly influenced by the governing party.[16]

Power was increasingly centralized in Athens. The erosion of local autonomy was a long-term process, beginning with the establishment of the state in the 1830s, when the new monarchy overrode the autonomy which villages had traditionally enjoyed under Ottoman rule. Thenceforth the nomarch (or prefect) as representative of state authority exercised extensive control over local government. The process of centralization seems to have gathered pace from the end of the nineteenth century, as the expansion of the state gave greater powers of patronage to politicians. The municipal police were suppressed in the 1890s. Central control was extended over the agrarian constabulary in the 1920s and 1930s; while the power of the national police forces, which served as maids-of-all-work for governments, was greatly increased in the same period. Local elections were suspended for long periods – none being held for example from about 1915 to 1925, or from 1934 to 1951 – and the local councillors when elected could be sacked by the government. Certainly by the 1930s and perhaps earlier the most trivial decisions at the local level depended on approval by the prefect or a minister in Athens. The growth of the economic powers of the Athens government was causing widespread discontent: 'the need for decentralisation is everywhere recognised,' reported the British ambassador in 1936, referring especially to the administrative neglect of the major port of Patras. There a British official reported 'the exodus of the best families and the most enterprising elements to Athens or abroad'. The American authority on public administration, Hubert Gallagher, noted as examples in 1947 of the decisions that had to be made in Athens the appointment of a village schoolteacher, permission to start a new business no matter how small and remotely located, and the registration of the sale of the smallest piece of farm land.[17] Control was especially tight over the posting or appointment of officials because these were the common coin of patronage.

To the present day, the overgrown state machine has earned little respect from citizens. The official has traditionally seen himself as a servant not of the public but of the state. In the early twentieth century much of the population, especially in the mountain villages, saw the state and the ruling classes as remote and indifferent. A regional gendarmerie commander in Sterea Ellada in 1947, when explaining why mountain villagers had been seduced by Communist propaganda, observed that the only representatives of traditional elites whom they normally saw were gendarmes, priests many of whom were illiterate, and teachers many of whom were left-wing. Alienation from the state was especially serious in the new lands of Macedonia and Thrace because these were densely settled by the despised refugees. The state machine and armed forces continued – especially under the anti-Venizelist regimes of 1920–2 and 1932 onwards – to be staffed disproportionately by natives of the old lands of the Peloponnese and Sterea Ellada; while the new lands found themselves outside the centres of decision-making.[18]

Because the state machine was used for political patronage, state officials were appointed and promoted for reasons other than efficiency, and tended to be demoralized and divided by constant partisan intervention. Thus the bureaucracy never had the chance to develop professional pride or standards; and the general levels of honesty and devotion to duty were low. Hubert Gallagher noted in 1947 that entrance examinations to the public service were rarely held, and that promotion was strictly by seniority, so that there were no incentives for hard work and efficiency. Andreas Psomas conducted a survey of 300 randomly chosen citizens in 1972 and found that they attributed to state officials such characteristics as 'out-moded', 'slow-moving', 'ill-mannered', 'authoritarian', 'incompetent', 'corrupt', 'legalistic'. These findings were probably just as true of the inter-war period. The numbers of state officials, sinecures, and pensions proliferated from the nineteenth century onwards in order to fulfil the patronage needs of politicians; and they absorbed the bulk of state expenditure. Pensions in the early twentieth century included those paid to the numerous officers and officials purged for political reasons.[19]

A state which had developed in this way was insensitive to society's needs, and in many ways was oppressive and parasitical. It took much from citizens and gave little, especially in the 1910s and early 1920s when it needed larger revenues and more conscripts than ever for successive wars. Conscription could be a serious blow to a peasant family because there were no dependents' allowances; and by the end of the wars of 1912–22, there were many men evading military service or bitterly discontented if in the army.[20] The parasitical nature of the state was especially marked in remoter villages which were usually without schools, doctors, roads or frequent postal services; yet periodically received unwelcome visits from gendarmes and recruiting sergeants, and had their resources drained by taxation and debts. A comprehensive system of social insurance was only beginning to be established in the late 1930s.

Civic education in schools was introduced only in 1931, and, like modern history, reserved for the few youngsters who reached the final grade of secondary school. It consisted of the rote-learning of abstract and obscure formulae, devised to instil unthinking obedience to whatever regime was in power. Little if anything was taught to cultivate respect for the state, or the capacity to participate in democratic politics. Those who were illiterate or barely literate had, as in other countries, little sense of political efficacy. Even in 1940 about a quarter of adults were still unable to write their names, the proportion being twice as high in villages as in cities, and twice as high among women as among men. There seems to have been a sizeable minority of villages without access to primary schools. Of the village schools which existed – the result of a massive building programme between the wars – 5,500 had only one class, and most of these contained at least 80 pupils. As late as 1961 only 10 per cent of the population aged 25 or more had completed secondary education – under half the British percentage which itself was low by northern European standards.[21]

In theory Greece was one of the more democratic countries in Europe, as nearly all adult men had the vote from 1844; but this privilege gave little power to people, probably a majority, who were poor and uneducated, and had difficulty in following national events, in understanding the official form of the language *katharevousa*, or fulfilling the complex procedures needed for electoral registration. These weaknesses made them subject to bribery and police coercion. The politician Evangelos Kalantzes, when working for a parliamentary candidate in rural Evrytania in 1920, practised wholesale bribery reminiscent of eighteenth-century England. In a country with widespread poverty, crowds and thugs were easily rented by politicians. For much of the rural population, democracy meant domination by police and party bosses. The absorption in politics for which Greek citizens were and still are famous consisted in reality of gossip about personalities and the division of spoils.[22] This trait did at least make most of the population strongly averse to any attempt by a dictator to monopolize those spoils; and it is perhaps for this reason that dictatorships in Greece have been short-lived and unpopular.

Thus the state not only failed to inspire a sense of obligation, but also weakened such sense of community spirit as existed, or prevented it from developing. This void left the extended family with its network of 'friends' as the main focus of collective obligation. Various politicians in the 1930s were troubled by the lack of a sense of civic duty compared with other countries. The social democrat Stefanos Sarafis wished that the privileged classes in Greece could display the readiness for sacrifice which he saw among the British aristocracy in the First World War. The conservative authoritarian Ioannes Metaxas regretted the absence of the sense of discipline and corporate loyalty which he saw everywhere in Imperial Germany.

While their interests centred in the metropolis, politicians managed nevertheless to retain much influence over the villages and all regions. No strong peasant party developed as it did in Bulgaria, Romania, and Yugoslavia; nor regionally based parties as in Yugoslavia. A long-standing reason for metropolitan influence was the size of the urban lower middle class which bridged the gap between city and country, and provided the basis for vigorous parliamentary parties which in Greece were longer established than in the rest of the Balkans.

Another link between town and country was the traditionally urban orientation of Greek peasants in the old lands, which made many of them aspire to place their offspring in white-collar jobs. Upward social mobility of this kind required patrons to use *mesa* (personal influence) to help clients secure jobs, pensions, credits, licences, or exemptions. Another traditional characteristic of Greek peasants was commercial orientation, which made many of them ready to incur debt and participate in the cash economy. The resulting chronic indebtedness was worsened by the low world prices for various agricultural products in the inter-war years, and the high prices of industrial goods resulting from protectionist policies in the 1930s. Indebtedness was also due to the land reforms of 1917 onwards, which left masses of newly settled smallholders unable to pay for their land. By 1936 three-quarters of farmers were in debt, owing on average almost their annual net income, their creditors being provincial merchants, local money-lenders, private bank managers, and the Agricultural Bank.[23] Therefore they depended on politicians for relief through credits and moratoria. As for the new lands, they were integrated into national politics by their loyalty to Venizelos and so participated ardently in the National Schism.[24]

The influence of city-based politicians shaped the composition of the main political camps in the inter-war period: the Venizelist and the anti-

Venizelist, and in the 1940s the Communist-controlled National Liberation Front (EAM). Each was a coalition of classes and regions, aspiring to control the centre of power in the capital. However two of the parties also took advantage of the tension between the over-powerful centre and the neglected peripheries of the state. Both Venizelists and Communists at different times appealed to the sense of alienation of the new lands which were under-represented in the state machine. Venizelos established a rebel government in Salonika, the main city of the new lands, in 1916, and his supporters tried to repeat this feat in 1935. The Communist Party attempted something similar in 1947–8. During the 1940s the Communists also took advantage of the alienation from the state of the remoter mountain communities.

SOCIAL STRUCTURE

One reason for the importance of the state as a source of stratification was that other class lines were vague and fluid. Although differences in wealth and status were large, the social hierarchy was finely graduated, and there were important ladders of upward mobility in the church, army, business, and the public service. Access to the last, for those of low status, lay through the educational system, the upper reaches of which were disproportionately large for a country with Greece's level of literacy. There were of course 'good families' in which high status was hereditary. The social elites were quite closely linked, and dwelt mainly in Athens or Salonika, consisting of politicians, judges, academics, bankers, officers, civil servants, and businessmen. Bishops rose through the monasteries and so formed a group apart. Most politicians had practised one or more of these occupations, especially those of doctor, civil servant, officer, and above all lawyer; but they formed a fairly distinct occupation group, partly because many of the more prominent were born to political families, which in Greece were remarkably durable. The clientelistic nature of politics required that they possess private wealth and social influence. There was little difference in social composition after the First World War between the Venizelist and anti-Venizelist camps. Lawyers were especially well qualified by their professions to gain a wide political clientele; and they were extraordinarily numerous in Greece because of the frequency of litigation and the legalistic approach of the state to the resolution of social problems. On the fringes of the social elites were numerous unemployed or under-employed lawyers, doctors, and teachers, who were numerous because these occupation-groups were much sought-after for their social influence.[25]

Most of the urban population could be considered as lower middle class, consisting of small-scale employers and middlemen, retailers and clerical workers, and lower professionals such as teachers and journalists. Much of the working class was employed in transport and communications. Of all those employed in industry, a majority worked in places employing six people or fewer, and only a quarter worked in places with over 100 people. Some of the latter were employed in modern, highly capitalized firms, which co-existed with a mass of poor family workshops.[26]

The bulk of the urban working class was engaged in manufacturing, transport, communications, mining, and trade, and these categories formed only 14 per cent of the economically active population in 1928. The total strength of the urban working class must have been well under 20 per cent, even if one adds family assistants in small workshops and some other categories of manual worker.[27] In absolute numbers these categories increased immensely (probably by at least 100 per cent) in the years 1910–40, when the value of industrial production tripled. But as a proportion of the occupied population the working class did not increase noticeably in the inter-war period, because the rural population was also growing rapidly.

Urban workers had little or no sense of class unity. The urban population was swelling steadily with migrants from the countryside, and so many of the workers were of village origin and had relatives in villages.[28] In this respect the urban refugees from Asia Minor differed: settled as they were in miserable shanty towns in suburbs of Athens, Piraeus, and Salonika, they could not turn for support to rural landholdings or rural relatives. Most workers aspired to acquire businesses or workshops of their own. Their standard of living and their educational level were generally very low. Trade unions comprised only a small minority of the urban workforce and were extremely fragmented; most of them served merely as intermediaries between workers and bosses. As Angelos Elephantes wrote, solidarity between workers was essentially comradeship between individuals, or between those from the same neighbourhood or village.[29]

The bulk of the rural population consisted of independent peasants and their families. Four-fifths of farms were owner-occupied, and four-fifths were under 10 acres. Only 10 per cent of those engaged in agriculture were wage-earners outside the family. There were few estates anywhere of more than 60 acres, and some of those belonged to monasteries.

This extreme fragmentation of land was the result of a series of land reforms which had occurred mainly from 1917 to the mid-1920s. Sweeping land reforms took place throughout the Balkans at this time, necessitated by rural over-population, spurred on by the example of the Bolshevik revolution, and facilitated by the relative weakness of large landowners as a class. In Greece, the reforms were especially thorough because they were driven also by the influx of refugees who had to be given land. Eventually 668,316 refugees were settled on the land. In their conservative intention, the land reforms succeeded. A potentially explosive situation was defused, especially in the plains of Thessaly and southern Epirus, where the status of labourers and tenants on large estates had hitherto been wretched. Henceforth the great majority of the rural population owned their homes and some land. But they possessed very little means to improve the productivity of their land or repay their debts, and had very low cash incomes. The small size of most holdings deprived their owners of capital, and the fragmentation of holdings in scattered plots hindered the use of machinery, fertilizer, or pesticides. Especially difficult was the plight of mountain villagers deprived, by the division of large estates in the plains, of access for their sheep and goats to winter pasture. Successive governments therefore faced the challenge of making peasant agriculture viable, a task that would be attempted in the 1930s partly by a moratorium on debts and partly by tariff protection.[30]

There was an important similarity between the urban and rural populations in that the majority of both were self-employed or worked in small family enterprises. Only one-third of the population were wage- or salary-earners.[31] It was this fact that may have been largely responsible for the low rate of direct taxation that remains to this day a major national problem, although it is normally attributed to the inefficiency of the administration and the partiality of governments to the wealthy.

THE GREEK COMMUNIST PARTY

The Bolshevik revolution inevitably had a profound impact on a country experiencing large-scale war, rapid industrialization, and vast population movements. But for a long time it did more in Greece to frighten the ruling classes than to stimulate an effective Communist party.

Socialist ideas were spread among urban workers by professionals and intellectuals in the last years of the nineteenth century, and became widespread from 1911 onwards, manifesting themselves in an increasing number of militant strikes.[32] Participation in the First World War from 1916 stimulated socialist workers to welcome the Bolshevik revolution for various reasons. The war demonstrated in an especially brutal and humiliating way Greece's dependence on the great powers. Secondly, prolonged mobilization for war caused acute social tensions. By the time of the Catastrophe in September 1922 Greece was suffering from the effects of ten years of almost continuous mass mobilization since the first Balkan War of October

1912. Masses of returning soldiers, deserters, and destitute refugees created a serious problem of public order for the police in many parts of the country. This human tide increased the land hunger of the rural population, and there ensued a series of violent demonstrations and disturbances, with war veterans proving especially radical.[33]

The rapid distribution of land by the government, and the relief efforts of the Refugee Settlement Commission of the League of Nations, satisfied much of the rural discontent in the mid- and late 1920s. There remained though the long-term problem caused by peasant debt. In towns, the nation's participation in the First World War led as elsewhere in Europe to unprecedented labour militancy arising from a shortage of basic necessities, a strong demand for labour, then from post-war economic dislocations. From 1921 to 1925 there was a series of large-scale strikes in the transport and other industries. Thereafter the process of industrialization was boosted by the mass influx of refugees, many of whom possessed managerial and industrial skills, while others provided cheap labour. The early process of industrialization caused great economic inequality in a country with poorly enforced factory laws, weakly organized workers, and no state-sponsored social insurance.

In these circumstances membership of trade unions expanded rapidly: there were 206 unions with 44,230 members in 1917; 560 unions with 167,509 members in 1928. They did not however provide the basis of a strong political force, one reason apparent from these figures being their fragmentation, which reflected the structure of Greek industry. The localism of workers, caused by difficulties of communication, hindered the development of national unions except in some of the transport unions.[34]

Without a cohesive working class to provide an electoral basis, reformist socialists had no hope of competing with other political parties, which, as we have seen, enjoyed extensive influence over the poorer classes, and benefited from a long parliamentary tradition.[35] Socialists and the politicians who sympathized with them were no more able or willing than other politicians to construct party organizations that were based on a programme and loyalty to an institution rather than on loyalty to an individual, and that could attract the services of grassroots volunteers in large numbers. Only the Communists – with their characteristic militance, activism, and discipline – could construct such an organization. As in other industrializing or agrarian countries, they possessed policies and organizations that were flexible enough to appeal to other groups besides the embryonic working class. Once established in Greece the Communist Party made it difficult for socialist parties to grow.

Communists in their autobiographies usually mentioned the spectacle of poverty and injustice as the main cause of their decision to serve the party;

and the party's organizing efforts were directed towards an improvement of social conditions. Social injustice was acute and conspicuous at all levels in Greece, for reasons hinted at already, such as the deprivation and discrimination suffered by refugees, the inequalities which accompanied the early phases of industrialization, and the importance in Greece of personal influence for upward mobility. Tobacco workers in Thessaly, Macedonia, and Thrace were especially likely to support the Communists because they consisted largely of refugees concentrated in big workshops and dependent for their livelihood on uncertain foreign markets. Another reason commonly given for conversion to Communism was the experience or sight of police repression, which as we shall see was the normal response by the authorities to social unrest or serious dissidence. Police repression by the regime of General Theodoros Pangalos (June 1925–August 1926), which turned into a dictatorship, caused many students and social reformers to turn leftwards.[36]

The prestige of Communism and Marxist ideas in the inter-war period attracted various movements for social reform. Many teachers were radicalized by the problems of the poor among whom they worked, and by the archaic character of the educational system, with its emphasis on religious education and classical studies, and its use of *katharevousa*. The influential Educational Association for example split in 1927 on the question of teaching religion and *katharevousa* in schools, a majority of its members taking a reformist or socialist position. Communists, the only party to give a major role to women, participated in the Association of Greek Women for Women's Rights, but in the 1920s were weaker here than the socialists partly because their policies gave priority to the class struggle. In his fascinating sketches of humble Communists in Greece in 1935–6, the Australian journalist Bert Birtles told of a schoolteacher sentenced to exile on an island for teaching Darwin's theory of evolution; a student who was expelled from university for organizing a movement to demand better provision for poor students; two women, one working-class and one a university graduate, who came to Communism *via* a concern for women's rights; and a law graduate who came to it through a general sentiment for social justice.[37]

As R.V. Burks has shown, the spectacle of backwardness in a poor country was especially disturbing to those of its citizens with some education, because they knew more of conditions in rich countries, and were more disposed to think about causes and possible remedies.[38] Communism attracted many of them as the most effective way whereby their country could achieve modernization. It thus satisfied both their sense of patriotism and their ambition, because the establishment of a socialist society offered chances of employment to people like themselves. Especially likely to respond in this way were those who experienced personal frustration, injustice or insecurity, such as unemployed professionals, students, or intellectuals, of whom there were many in Greece because of the traditionally top-heavy character of the educational system. As in other countries, many educated people reacted to the Marxist texts like the fictional student Damianos Frantzes in Georgios Theotokas's novel *Argo*, when first reading Marx's *Communist Manifesto* :

> He trembled before the grandeur of its revelation. His wide and varied reading, before this, had given him many unrelated and jumbled ideas. Now suddenly this little red book created order in this intellectual chaos. [This work gave him] a precious certainty which made him incapable of understanding how anyone could think differently . . .

Presumably for similar motives, an increasing number of students in universities and technical and commercial colleges turned leftwards in the late 1920s. Communists catered for them by maintaining a large and permanent youth organization, being the only party to do so.[39]

The precursor of the Communist Party, the Socialist Workers Party of Greece, was founded in 1918, and in 1920 decided to affiliate with the Comintern. In 1924 it accepted its full programme, Lenin's 'twenty-one points', and called itself the Communist Party of Greece (KKE). The 21 points enjoined that the party must always hold itself ready to resort to illegal activities if it was banned, and to seize revolutionary power on behalf of the proletariat when the time was ripe.[40] In accordance with Comintern instructions, it developed into a party of a type unparalleled in Greece. It included many full-time professionals, while all cadres or officials were selected for their abilities in organization, and were expected to devote their lives to the party. Even the rank-and-file members were selected for their qualities of character, and were expected to devote much effort to tasks such as the distribution of literature, organization of meetings, recruitment of members, and creation of new organizations. Party members were instructed to take the lead in campaigning for higher pay and better conditions for anyone who could be considered under-privileged. In the process they were instructed to create cells in non-party organizations of various kinds: ex-servicemen's associations, organizations of the unemployed, students' groups. Many of the members, especially at higher levels, were inspired by a sense of historic mission which gave them unshakable faith and confidence and made them see their task as a long-term one.[41]

One important reason why the Communists remained nevertheless a marginal force was the continuing hold over voters exercised by the major parties. Another was internal division, caused largely by the international Communist movement. The Comintern encouraged dogmatic traits: the unrealistic pursuit of revolutionary aims through strikes and demonstrations; attacks on reformist trade unions; and *ouvrierisme*, or faith in the industrial proletariat and its supposed qualities, leading to exclusion from influence of many creative intellectuals in Greece, especially those in the Educational Association and Student Fraternity. The majority of party members in the late 1920s came from the urban working class, which as we have seen was very small. As in other Communist parties, quarrels within the Greek one were savage. The militant sectarianism became especially marked when in 1928 the Comintern dictated that members escalate the class war and attack socialists as 'social fascists'.[42]

Another major cause of division was policy towards Macedonia and Thrace. The Bulgarian Communist Party used its special influence in the Comintern (deriving from its size and personal connections with the Communist Party of the Soviet Union) to secure the acceptance of its desired policy on Macedonia and Thrace. This was part of the Comintern's attempt to champion national minorities and so break up the Balkan states which were all (except Albania) re-shaped by the Paris peace settlements after the First World War. The Greek party was always treated by the Soviet Union as of little importance, and was forced in 1924 to accept the Comintern line that the non-Greek minorities in Macedonia and Thrace were oppressed by the settlement there of Greek refugees, and that these regions should become 'united and independent' within a Balkan federation. This policy was naturally very unpopular in Greece, and exposed the Greek Communists immediately to prosecution for treason.

Persecution thenceforth weakened the party organization and led to paranoid suspicions among party members about spies in their ranks. Under the short-lived Pangalos dictatorship of January–August 1926, about 1,000 members were arrested including nearly all the leaders. After the dictatorship the party was semi-legal, able with difficulty to participate in parliamentary elections but unable to maintain a headquarters office. Most or all cadres spent long periods in jail in the inter-war period, Giannes Ioannides (later a co-leader of the party) being arrested fourteen times.[43]

Meanwhile the cadres' lack of intellectual sophistication – in which they seem to have been typical of Balkan Communist parties between the wars – hindered them from applying Marxist–Leninist theory in a fruitful way to Greek conditions. As late as 1927 the texts available in Greek did not include Marx's *Das Kapital* or any of Lenin's works except *The State and Revolution* (and this translation was published only in the United States). The party leaders in fact had little intellectual training apart from that acquired in the Communist University for Workers in the Far East (KUTV) in Moscow. Although its first graduates arrived in Greece in 1924, it was not until 1929 that groups of cadres were sent there annually for six-month courses, participants in which included nearly all politburo members and the majority of central committee members after 1931. Naturally the training received under Stalin's regime did not encourage any independent theoretical work or study for its own sake. The study and discussion that many Communists undertook while in gaol, or while exiled on islands, during the 1930s seems similarly to have been derivative and strictly practical in orientation. These circumstances explain why no significant work of theory or scholarship by a Greek Communist appeared before 1940.[44]

After the Pangalos dictatorship the party developed little, and its membership sank to 1,500 in 1929. By this time if not earlier the party was being subsidized on a massive scale by the Comintern, receiving in total $50,000 in 1929–30. The membership figure is unimpressive even if one bears in mind that it signified more than membership of other parties. To the total of party members one should add a larger number of youth members, candidates for membership, and former members who continued to work with the party, not to mention sympathizers. It is true that in 1929, when the party formed a rival trade union confederation, it took with it 60,000–70,000 unionists, about as many as remained in the official body, the General Confederation of Greek Workers. Thereafter however the proportion of unionists affiliated to the latter increased. The party participated in successive general elections, and in that of 1928 secured the election of ten deputies. Thus the Greek Communist Party fared worse in the 1920s than its Bulgarian and Yugoslav counterparts – that is, until their relative success caused them to be banned and driven underground.[45]

The party was reduced to a dismal state in 1929–31 by a factional struggle between revolutionaries and gradualists. The Soviet authorities intervened in 1931 by summoning 35 of the participants to Moscow and later executing all but two, one of whom was Giorges Siantos, who was to be co-leader with Ioannides of the party during the German occupation. The Soviet authorities now appointed a new and younger politburo, nearly all of whose members had been or soon would be educated in the Soviet Union. Moscow's choice as new leader was the 29 year old Nikos Zachariades.

Considering that he is one of the most influential figures in modern Greek history, it is surprising how little is known of Zachariades's background. What is established is that he was born of fairly well-off and educated parents in the Ottoman empire, his father being an agent buying tobacco for a foreign company. When his father died Nikos left school at fifteen to support his family, and worked among the labourers of various nationalities in the docks and tug boats of Constantinople. Thus he witnessed the downfall of the Ottoman empire and the Entente occupation of Constantinople after the First World War. Later he became secretary of a

Communist youth organization in Constantinople in 1921, and worked as a ship hand in the Black Sea. Leaving Asia Minor after the Catastrophe, he settled briefly in the Soviet Union in mid-1923, enrolling in the Communist University for Workers in the Far East and starting his life-long membership of the Communist Party of the Soviet Union. Arriving for the first time in Greece in May 1924 to join his family, he spent the next five years as a cadre of the Greek Communist Party, then returned to the Soviet Union in 1929, and distinguished himself at the prestigious Lenin University. He apparently impressed Stalin with his abilities and gained his trust, and admiringly adopted Stalin's autocratic and egoistic style of leadership, which flouted the Comintern policy of the 1920s that committees should be freely elected and policy should be freely discussed before adoption. Henceforth he imitated Stalin in his harsh rejection of disagreement and identification of his own opinions with party orthodoxy. Thanks to his prestige as the trusted appointee of Moscow, and his great organizational capacities, he soon dominated the Greek politburo, which became the only organ within which policy was discussed, and assumed the right to appoint regional cadres. Zachariades radically reformed the party's organization, making the party more disciplined and united, and improving considerably its skills in clandestine work.[46]

He also gave the party a stronger sense of direction. At the sixth plenum of the central committee in January 1934, it adopted on Zachariades's initiative its first comprehensive analysis of the Greek economy and society. It was in some ways a perceptive interpretation of Greece's social problems, and inspired a programme which the party would try to implement in the 1940s. Represented at this meeting was the Comintern's executive committee which had helped prepare the statement, and present also were most of those who would lead the party during the German occupation: Siantos and Ioannides, whom we have already mentioned, and also Giannes Zevgos, Metsos Partsalides, Stergios Anastasiades, Miltiades Porphyrogenes, Petros Rousos, Leonidas Stringos, Chrysa Chatzevaseleiou, and Vasiles Nepheloudes.

The committee made the important decision that Greece was not yet ready for a socialist revolution because it had not reached a sufficient level of 'capitalist development' and retained 'significant remnants of semi-feudal relations in the agricultural economy' (referring to the peasants' debt burden and the survival of some large estates). Consequently 'the imminent revolution of workers and peasants in Greece will have a bourgeois democratic character with tendencies towards rapid transformation into a proletarian socialist revolution'. While adoption of the 'bourgeois democratic' goal later facilitated overtures to non-revolutionary parties, it was seen only as a stage towards socialism, the stage allegedly achieved by the

Soviet Union. The leading revolutionary class, the proletariat or industrial working class, was 'young and numerically weak' and had still to win over 'the broader popular masses' and especially 'the poor and middling masses of the farming population' and the oppressed ethnic minorities. The capitalist enemy was allied with some landowners, supported by rich peasants, and backed by foreign imperialist powers, especially Britain and France, on which Greece was economically dependent. To combat Communism the bourgeoisie might try 'fascist' measures, including an appeal to militaristic nationalism, oppression of ethnic minorities, and resort to dictatorship. After seizing power, the Communists would accomplish the following: terminate the country's dependence on capitalist powers by repudiating foreign debts and nationalizing foreign-controlled firms; 'attack private capital' by nationalizing large banks and 'monopolies'; abolish 'feudal survivals' by cancelling usurious debts, introducing steeply progressive taxation, confiscating and redistributing to the landless large estates and monastic land; divide church from state; grant self-determination and if necessary the right of secession to national minorities.[47]

An urgent task which the party faced in 1934 was self-defence against dictatorship. After its experience under Pangalos, the party saw reason to fear the restiveness of military strong men in both political camps, who imitated the style and slogans of fascism. Like other Communist parties, but apparently on its own initiative, the Greek Communists moved away from the sectarian line of the Comintern towards cooperation with other parties.[48]

Their reforms in organization and ideology enabled the Greek Communists to take advantage of the opportunities created by the Great Depression, the effects of which were not felt in Greece until late 1931, but then persisted until 1936: unemployment in several industries including tobacco-sorting; a decline in the markets for exports including tobacco and currants; and a general rise in prices of imports as a result of devaluation and increased tariffs to protect industry. By 1932 some Venizelist voters were drifting leftwards as a result of economic hardship, especially the refugee peasants disgruntled because of their increasing debts and their failure to receive enough compensation for property lost in Asia Minor. Communists appealed to such grievances by emphasizing practical demands: wage increases, improvements in working conditions, debt reduction, progressive taxation, and social insurance.

Communists also benefited from a left-wing trend, which paralleled that in western Europe, among intellectuals, students, and much of the educated public. From the early 1930s interest in current events in the Soviet Union spread beyond socialists. Students in tertiary education became increasingly interested in socialist ideas; and the British ambassador received a report in 1935 that 8 or 9 per cent of university students in Athens belonged to some Communist organization. The growing danger of fascist dictatorship, and the intensification of working-class grievances, made socialists readier to accept cooperation with Communists.[49]

In these circumstances, Communist party membership increased after 1931 until it reached about 15,000 in August 1936. At the general election of September 1932, the party (operating as usual under police harassment) won 5 per cent of the vote and ten seats (out of 250); at that of January 1936 it won 6 per cent of the vote and fifteen seats (out of 300). At the municipal elections in February 1934 it secured large votes in several Macedonian and Thracian towns, and the position of mayor in two of them, Kavala and Serres (both mayors being promptly arrested).[50]

As the party grew the proportion of peasants among its members increased. By 1934 half the members were peasants (perhaps most of them refugees) and 44 per cent were workers, only 9 per cent being factory workers. The leadership was mixed but lower class in membership, in this respect quite unlike that of other parties. Thus the 26 members of the central committee elected in December 1935 consisted of five peasants, six low-status professionals like teachers, and fifteen workers of various kinds including a barber, a carpenter, and the former dock worker and ship hand Zachariades. Refugees were strongly represented in the leadership under Zachariades and included five out of seven members of the politburo in 1935.[51]

In several ways, then, the leading Communists were outside the pale of the Greek 'political world' : their predominantly working-class background, refugee status, irreligion, and orientation to Moscow. When one adds to this blend a common experience of persecution, their bitter and alienated mentality becomes understandable.

THE BOURGEOIS REACTION

In reaction to the growing manifestations of social unrest in the early 1920s, especially the unprecedented series of strikes in 1921–5, most politicians acquired a sense of identity as bourgeois or *astikos*. Because the majority of the population were self-employed and were proprietors of some kind, the bourgeois class was considered by its defenders to be essentially Greek rather than a section of society.

The chief stimulus to bourgeois consciousness was social unrest, which most politicians in both camps saw primarily as a problem of public order rather than one of industrial relations or social welfare. By the late 1920s there was broad agreement among the majority of Venizelist and anti-Venizelist politicians on keeping income tax low, postponing social insurance, repressing industrial unrest, and tolerating harsh working conditions and low wages. For example a twelve-hour day, and the employment of children under fourteen, were common in some industries, in contravention to international laws which Greece had accepted. Politicians of both camps considered these working conditions necessary to encourage foreign investors and maintain the competitiveness of Greek industry, with its archaic equipment and inefficient organization.[52]

This attitude was illustrated by the reaction of Andreas Michalakopoulos's government in March 1925 to a strike of railwaymen, seamen, and tram workers, which lasted seventeen days. Like previous governments faced with major strikes, this one was baffled and alarmed, and reacted with sackings, strike-breakers, and troops. Michalakopoulos was especially anxious to deter strikes by public employees, which on principle he considered 'anarchical'. To express loyalty to the government, the mayors of towns and villages in various provinces, especially the more conservative Peloponnese, organized meetings, while a wide array of professional associations sent resolutions of support. The rectors of the Polytechnic Institute and the University of Athens, like most newspapers, called on the government to suppress this attempt 'to overthrow the social order'. As in Italy three years before, parliamentary politicians were so demoralized by the supposed red peril that they let a would-be dictator try for a time to combat it: General Theodoros Pangalos.[53]

Like the other Balkan states, Greece soon started to persecute its Communist party. Greece had contributed to the allied expeditionary force against the new Bolshevik regime in Russia in 1919, and like other Balkan states did not recognize the Soviet Union until the 1930s. During the 1920s, Greek governments introduced measures for suppressing Communist activities. A nineteenth-century procedure giving state officials the power to deport troublemakers without trial was from 1924 vested in each nome (prefecture) in a Security Commission consisting of the nomarch, public prosecutor, and gendarmerie chief. The Pangalos dictatorship in 1926 extended the procedure to 'all other persons suspected of acting against the public order and the tranquillity and security of the State'. Serious strikes in the 1920s were normally followed by arrests and deportations. By 1928, according to the Communist Party's records, 4,368 of its supporters had been arrested, 481 deported, 817 tortured, and 22 murdered. From at least as early as 1925 the army general staff began, in cooperation with the gendarmerie, to seek out Communists among national servicemen and isolate them in a special unit.[54]

The authoritative expression of bourgeois consciousness was the

Idionym (or 'Special') Law of the Venizelos government in 1929, which was passed with the help of anti-Venizelists against strong opposition by left-wing Venizelists. The speakers advocating this measure made the Communists scapegoats for the various symptoms of breakdown in social order during the 1920s: the army's poor morale towards the end of the Asia Minor campaign, and the industrial and agrarian unrest. Accordingly the law penalized attempts to implement or propagate ideas 'which have the manifest purpose of overthrowing by violent means the established social order or detaching part of the state's territory'. One clause penalized those who provoked industrial disputes. A subsequent version of this law in 1936 penalized the mere 'development' of such ideas. A vital corollary of such laws was that the police and judges, who were ardently anti-Communist and subject to government influence, were left free to decide how to interpret them, and in practice used them mainly against strikers and trade unionists. The social order thus defended consisted of the social hierarchy and all the values which maintained it: private property, Orthodox Christianity, the patriarchal family, and the territorial integrity of the state.[55]

The implementation of the Idionym Law was made possible by recent reforms of the police. Venizelos from 1910 did more than anyone else to make the police the main pillar of the executive. An early reform was the establishment of training schools for all ranks of the gendarmerie in 1906–19, partly under the supervision of a mission of Italian *carabinieri*. The training schools imparted a sense of professional dedication to many of their graduates, who made important contributions to later improvements in the working conditions and the organization of the force. A central criminal records system was first established in 1919 and a network of regional offices created in 1925. By 1935 the records-keeping system which lasted for the next 30 years or more had been established. The first national organization for the purpose of counter-espionage and counter-subversion was created by the Pangalos government in 1925, and replaced in 1929 by the Special Security of Athens, with 190 staff, initially to enforce the Idionym Law. The total numbers of the gendarmerie increased from about 8,500 in 1928 to 12,200 by 1936. Its efficiency, and its authority in the countryside, gradually increased also. For example in 1930, after prolonged efforts, it wiped out the last bandits in the rugged country of the northern Pindus ranges. In the late 1930s the physical obstacles to police authority remained formidable, although they were declining: for example, many villages were inaccessible to motor vehicles, and many police stations lacked telephones.[56]

Meanwhile, to cope with the novel problems of the growing cities, the city police were established in 1920, on Venizelos's initiative and on the model of the British metropolitan police. They reached a strength of 4,200 by 1936, the majority of these being stationed in Athens–Piraeus, and made some progress in combating the special problems of cities such as the supervision of traffic and retail prices.[57] In 1929 their criminological services were strengthened and organized in a national directorate, the General Security. A group within it, having started on its own initiative, in 1928, to study the organization and ideology of Communist parties, prompted the formulation of the Idionym Law. Thereafter the General and Special Security, which had overlapping functions, formed the 'political' police.[58] The police suffered from the penury which was characteristic of Greek officials. Thus a city police constable in 1934 received, apart from uniform, accommodation and rations, much less in pay than an agricultural labourer. For motorized transport, the General Security made do with a few motor bikes and one car, all elderly.[59]

One effect of the strengthening of the police forces was to increase greatly the powers and patronage of politicians in power at the national level. Like the state machine as a whole, the Greek police was extraordinarily centralized, by the standards of other parliamentary systems. The Minister of the Interior customarily interfered in details of personnel and policy of the gendarmerie and, to a lesser extent, of the city police. It was common for personal or partisan motives to determine appointments, transfers, and promotions in the gendarmerie; and this sort of interference seriously hampered its work. For example the gendarmerie were hindered in suppressing banditry in the 1920s by politicians who protected bandits. Because the officer corps was bloated with political appointments the training college for officers closed down from 1928 to 1935. It seems also to have been common for the gendarmerie to be used – and commoner still for it to be requested – by politicians to harass their opponents and interfere in elections. The historian K.S. Antoniou, himself a veteran gendarmerie officer, believed that these practices were systematized with the establishment of the Special Security in 1929. It is clear from the accounts of Greek historians and British observers that political interference by the gendarmerie increased with the intensification of the party struggle from 1932 onwards.[60] Police realized that this partisan manipulation reduced their authority and efficiency, but realized also that their individual careers were governed by it.

Police and Communists were pitted against each other from the start. In combating industrial militants the police in the 1920s and 1930s were in accord with successive governments and with employers. Thus the police were commonly used, sometimes at employers' request, to combat strikes and discipline trade unions. As Communists were especially active in industrial agitation, the police tended, wrongly, to see their hand in most of it. In the clashes which regularly occurred between police and strikers, both sides suffered. The police found it a gruelling task to face angry demonstrators for long periods. On the other hand their prejudice and military mentality often led them to use excessive force. Thus when disturbances caused by economic grievances became more frequent during the Great Depression, British observers considered that the gendarmerie (who remained responsible for order in Salonika and most towns) were largely to blame for violence that occurred in many parts of the country.[61]

After 1929 the number of arrests and deportations of suspected Communists increased sharply in response to industrial unrest, which was exacerbated by the Great Depression and remained widespread until 1936. When the Communist vote at by-elections increased in 1931, most politicians became alarmed and keen to support a vigorous application of the Idionym Law. From 1929 to 1934, 2,357 alleged left-wingers were sentenced under this law or for high treason, implying several times that number arrested, interrogated, and rough-handled. In addition large numbers were deported by Security Commissions; and after 1929 the total number of deportations to islands ran at a rate of several hundred a year.[62]

In response to the growth of the party under Zachariades's leadership, the police refined their procedures for detecting Communist activity, disrupting party organization, and breaking the morale of those arrested. Through their agents police intervened in and inflamed the factional disputes of 1929–31. Under one of Tsaldares's governments in 1932–3 they began the practice of pressing those arrested to sign declarations of repentance (*deloseis metanoias*) as a condition of release. The declarations were commonly required to include the betrayal of colleagues, and inflicted bitter humiliation and a life-long stigma on the victims.[63]

By 1935 there was a bitter conflict between the defenders of the traditional social order and its critics. This was in effect a second national schism which cut across the lines of the first. Both Venizelist and anti-Venizelist camps had hitherto contributed to the battle against Communism, the Venizelists providing more of the leadership and organization, while the anti-Venizelists provided more of the rank-and-file combatants. From 1935 onwards the leading role would be taken by anti-Venizelists and the conflict would intensify. As a result this second schism would broaden, and under the impact of the German occupation become the civil war of the 1940s.

NOTES

1. L.S. Stavrianos, 'The influence of the West on the Balkans', in Charles and Barbara Jelavich, eds, *The Balkans in Transition. Essays on the Development of Balkan Life and Politics since the Eighteenth Century* (Berkeley, 1963), pp. 184–5; Nikos Mouzelis, *Politics in the Semi-Periphery* (1986), pp. xiii–xv.

2. Barbara Jelavich, *History of the Balkans. Twentieth Century* 2 vols (Cambridge, 1983), II, p. 187; Leften S. Stavrianos in C. and B. Jelavich, eds, *The Balkans in Transition*, pp. 200, 211; George T. Mavrogordatos, *Stillborn Republic. Social Coalitions and Party Strategies in Greece, 1922–36* (Berkeley, 1983), p. 293; Angeliki E. Laiou, 'Population movements in the Greek countryside during the civil war', in Lars Baerentzen, John O. Iatrides, and Ole L. Smith, eds, *Studies in the History of the Greek Civil War* (Copenhagen, 1987), p. 94; Costas G. Couvaras, *OSS with the Central Committee of EAM* (San Francisco, 1982), pp. 50–1, 62; Robin Higham, 'The Metaxas years in perspective', in Robin Higham and Thanos Veremis, eds, *Aspects of Greece, 1936–40. The Metaxas Dictatorship* (Athens, 1993), p. 229.

3. Stavrianos in C. and B. Jelavich, eds, *The Balkans in Transition*, p. 199; Theodore A. Couloumbis, John A. Petropoulos, Harry J. Psomiades, *Foreign Intervention in Greek Politics* (New York, 1976), pp. 18–20.

4. S. Victor Papacosma, *The Military in Greek Politics. The 1909 Coup d'Etat* (Kent, 1977), p. 36; Couloumbis et al., *Foreign Intervention*, pp. 39–41.

5. Mavrogordatos, *Stillborn Republic*, pp. 27, 55–64, 127–9.

6. Ibid., pp. 72–3, 284–5.

7. Thanos Veremis, *Oi Epemvaseis tou Stratou sten Ellenike Politike* (1983), pp. 78–81, 230–1; Michael N. Pikramenos, 'The independence of the judiciary', in Higham and Veremis, eds, *Aspects of Greece*, pp. 134–6; Mavrogordatos, *Stillborn Republic*, pp. 62, 120, 132, 269, 305–8.

8. Mavrogordatos, *Stillborn Republic*, pp. 185, 200, 231; D. Pentzopoulos, *The Balkan Exchange of Minorities and its Impact upon Greece* (Paris, 1962), pp. 99, 129–30.

9. Mark Mazower, *Greece and the Inter-War Economic Crisis* (Oxford, 1991), pp. 74, 187; Alkes Regos, *E B' Ellenike Demokratia* (1989), p. 53; A.F. Freris, *The Greek Economy in the Twentieth Century* (1986), pp. 28–9; Angelos Elephantes, *E Epangelia tes Adynates Epanastases* (1979), p. 162; C. Tsoucalas, *The Greek Tragedy* (Harmondsworth, 1969), p. 96.

10. Stavrianos in C. and B. Jelavich, eds, *Balkans in Transition*, pp. 206–7.

11. Mouzelis, *Politics*, pp. 10, 12; Constantine Tsoucalas, ' "Enlightened" concepts in the "dark": power and freedom, politics and society,' *Journal of Modern Greek Studies* 9,1 (May 1991), p. 16; Regos, *B ' Ellenike Demokratia*, p. 109, n. 6; 186, n. 97; FO 370/20390/270, 2, R 6606; H. Gallagher, 'Administrative reorganization in the Greek crisis', *Public Administration Review* 8,4 (1948), p. 253.

12. Adamantia Pollis, 'The state, the law, and human rights in Modern Greece', *Human Rights Quarterly* 9 (1987), pp. 587–614; Tsoucalas, '"Enlightened" concepts in the "dark"', pp. 17–18; Pikramenos in Higham and Veremis, eds, *Aspects of Greece*, pp. 136–7.

13. FO 371/43787/21, R 19472.

14. Mazower, *Greece*, pp. 54, 184; G.T. Mavrogordatos, 'Venizelismos kai astikos eksyngchronismos', in G.T. Mavrogordatos and C. Hadziiossif, *Venizelismos*

kai Astikos Eksyngchronismos (Herakleion, 1988), pp. 12–13.
15. Mavrogordatos, *Stillborn Republic*, pp. 161,168,175; Christos Jecchinis, *Trade Unionism in Greece. A Study in Political Paternalism* (Chicago, 1967), pp. 29–35, 46, 55.
16. S. Verney and F. Papageorgiou, 'Prefecture councils in Greece: decentralization in the European Community context', *Regional Politics and Policy* 2, 1 and 2 (Spring–Summer 1992), p. 117.
17. FO 371/21148/-; Waterlow to Eden, 7 March 1936; 371/20392/-, p. 74; Gallagher, 'Administrative reorganization', p. 257.
18. A. Daskalakes, *Istoria tes Ellenikes Chorophylakes* 2 vols (1973), II, p. 622; Regos, *B' Ellenike Demokratia*, pp. 221–3; Keith Legg, *Politics in Modern Greece* (Stanford, 1969), p. 308.
19. Gallagher, 'Administrative reorganization', p. 253; A. Psomas, *The Nation, the State, and the International System. The Case of Modern Greece* (1978) p. 204.
20. Freris, *Greek Economy*, p. 70; G. Vontitsos-Gousias, *E Aities gia ten Etta, te Diaspase tou KKE kai tes Ellenikes Aristeras* 2 vols (1977), I, pp. 17–20.
21. Konstantinos Logothetopoulos, *Idou e Aletheia* (1948), pp. 146–7; Psomas, *Nation*, pp. 186–9.
22. E. Kalantzes, *Saranta Chronia Anamneseis* (1969), pp. 10–12; Psomas, *Nation*, pp. 196–200; FO 371/15966/237, 247, concerning the 1932 election.
23. Mazower, *Greece*, p. 249.
24. M. Attalides and N. Mouzelis, 'Greece', in M.S. Archer and S. Giner, eds,*Contemporary Europe: Class, Status and Power* (1971), p. 175; Nikos P. Mouzelis, *Modern Greece. Facets of Underdevelopment (1978)*, pp. 99, 101; Mouzelis, *Politics*, pp. 31, 42; Mavrogordatos, *Stillborn Republic*, p. 175.
25. Legg, *Politics*, pp. 302–11; FO 371/43787/20, R 1947 ; 371/43787/20, R 19472.
26. Elephantes, *Epangelia*, pp. 404–5.
27. Mavrogordatos, *Stillborn Republic*, p. 119.
28. Freris, *Greek Economy*, p. 90; Regos, *B' Ellenike Demokratia*, p. 46; R. Koundouros, 'Law and the obstruction of social change: a case study of laws for the security of the apparently prevailing social order in Greece', M.Phil. thesis, Brunel University, 1974, pp. 89, 102.
29. Mazower, *Greece*, pp. 32–3; Elephantes, *Epangelia*, pp. 80, 322.
30. K. Kostes, 'Agrotike metarrythmise kai oikonomike anaptyxe sten Ellada, 1917–40', in Mavrogordatos and Hadziiossif, eds, *Venizelismos*, pp. 152–6.
31. Richard Clogg, *Parties and Elections in Greece. The Search for Legitimacy* (1987), pp. 241–2.
32. Jecchinis, *Trade Unionism*, pp. 37–8.
33. Daskalakes, *Istoria*, I, p. 69; Vontitsos-Gousias, *Aities*, I, pp. 17–20; K.S. Antoniou, *Istoria tes Ellenikes Vasilikes Chorophylakes* 3 vols (1965), III, pp. 1339–40; Elephantes, *Epangelia*, pp. 47, 56–7; Mazower, *Greece*, pp. 49–50.
34. Jecchinis, *Trade Unionism*, p. 43.
35. Elephantes, *Epangelia*, p. 42.
36. Vontitsos-Gousias, *Aities*, I, p. 21; R.V. Burks, *The Dynamics of Communism in Eastern Europe* (Princeton, 1961), pp. 48, 190; Elephantes, *Epangelia*, pp. 75, 363.
37. Bert Birtles, *Exiles in the Aegean. A Personal Narrative of Greek Politics and Travel* (1938), pp. 131–7, 178–9, 300–5; Elephantes, *Epangelia*, pp. 364–6.
38. Burks, *Dynamics*, pp. 63, 71, 190; S. Sarafis, *ELAS. Greek Resistance Army* (1989), p. xlix.

39. G. Theotokas, *Argo* (Estia, n.d.), pt 1, ch. 5, pp. 185–6; Elephantes, *Epangelia*, pp. 362–4; V. Bartziotas, *Exenta Chronia Kommounistes* (1986), pp. 41–2, 44.
40. Elephantes, *Epangelia*, p. 45; Ole L. Smith, 'Marxism in Greece: the Case of the KKE', *Journal of Modern Greek Studies* 3,1 (May 1985), pp. 49–50.
41. Jane Degras, ed., *The Communist International 1919–43. Documents* (1960), II, pp. 174, 189–97, 200.
42. Elephantes, *Epangelia*, pp. 53–5, 82–3, 110, 368.
43. Giannes Ioannides, *Anamneseis. Provlemata tes Politikes tou KKE sten Ethnike Antistase, 1940–5*, ed. A. Papapanagiotou (1979), pp. 29–39; Elephantes, *Epangelia*, p. 60; V. Bartziotas, *Exenta*, pp. 88–9.
44. Elephantes, *Epangelia*, pp. 136, 140–1.
45. W.C. Chamberlain and J.D. Iams, 'Rebellion: the Rise and Fall of the Greek Communist Party', Fifth Senior Seminar in Foreign Policy Term Paper, 2 June 1963, Term Paper, Foreign Service Institute, Department of State, Washington D.C., pp. 44–5; Elephantes, *Epangelia*, p. 80.
46. Demetres Vlantas, *O Nikos Zachariades kai 22 Synergates tou* (1984), p. 11; Petros Antaios, *N. Zachariades. Thytes kai Thyma* (1991), pp. 150–7; Perikles Rodakes, *Nikos Zachariades* (1987), pp. 8–15, 54; Elephantes, *Epangelia*, pp. 86, 112, 143–6; Haris Vlavianos, *Greece, 1941–9. From Resistance to Civil War. The Strategy of the Greek Communist Party* (1992), pp. 194–8.
47. KKE, *Episema Keimena* (1984), IV, pp. 20, 23, 25; there is a summary in G. Alexander and J. Loulis, 'The strategy of the Greek Communist Party 1934–44: an analysis of Plenary Decisions', *East European Quarterly*, 15, 3, Sept. 1981, pp. 379–80.
48. Andrew L. Zapantis, *Greek-Soviet Relations, 1917–41* (New York, 1982), p. 329; Smith, 'Marxism in Greece', pp. 54–5.
49. T. Vournas, 'E Oktovriane Epanastase kai e Ellenike Logotechnia', *Ta Nea*, 21 Oct. 1989, p. 3; FO 371/19507/-, pp. 193–4, Waterlow to Simon, 4 June 1935.
50. Bartziotas, *Exenta Chronia*, p. 94.
51. Elephantes, *Epangelia*, pp. 121–33, 307–8.
52. Mazower, *Greece*, pp. 97, 109, 264; C. Hadziiossif, 'E Venizelogenes antipoliteuse sto Venizelo kai e politike anasyntaxe tou astismou sto mesopolemo', in Mavrogordatos & Hadziiossif, *Venizelismos*, pp. 443–7.
53. T. Veremis, 'The Greek state and economy during the Pangalos regime, 1925–6', *Journal of the Hellenic Diaspora*, 7 (Summer 1980), pp. 43–50.
54. R. Koundouros, thesis, pp. 132, 164; Antoniou, *Istoria*, III, p. 1340; Elephantes, *Epangelia*, p. 296.
55. Koundouros, thesis, pp. 117, 158; Nicos Alivizatos, *Les Institutions Politiques de la Grèce à travers les Crises* (Paris, 1979), pp. 299–301.
56. William Miller, *Greek Life in Town and Country* (1905), p. 249; Daskalakes, *Istoria*, I, pp. 50–2; Antoniou, *Istoria*, III, pp. 1338, 1343, 1363–7, 1390–5, 1412, 1423; FO 371/15237/40, Ambassador's report for 1930; 371/12926/-, pp. 105–8.
57. N.G. Katrabasas, *Astynomia Poleon* (1949), ch. 1; D.G. Katsimangles, *E Istoria tou Astynomikou Thesmou sten Athena, Rome, Gallia, kai Amerike* (1981), pp. 141–2; FO 371/13658/-, pp. 100–1, R.W. Urquhart, report for Nov. 1929.
58. N. Charalambides 'To Mystikon Archeion tou K. Maniadake', *Ethnikos Kyrix*, 23 Oct. 1949, p. 4; *Ephemerida tes Kyverneseos*, Series A, 8 Jan. 1929, pp. 17–29; *Ephemerida tes Kyverneseos*, Series A, 25 Jan. 1936, pp. 269–70.

59. FO 371/19517/-, p. 26; 371/12926/-, pp. 54–5; *Ethnikos Kyrix*, 23 Oct. 1949, p. 4.
60. Antoniou, *Istoria*, III, pp. 1424, 1370, 1389; FO 371/12926/29, n.d. report by Major W.T. Rigg; FO 371/15966/247-8; 371/10772/-, C 9791; 371/18393/22-3, R 1162.
61. Koundouros, thesis, p. 152; Antoniou, *Istoria*, III, p. 1389; FO 371/23770/355-6; 371/20389/125-6, R 3310.
62. Koundouros, thesis, pp. 143–4; FO 371/15232/-, p. 190, C 6557; 371/14391/-, p. 384/2; 371/15237/-, pp. 40–2, Ambassador's report for 1930; Alivizatos, *Institutions*, pp. 278–9, 291–4.
63. Bartziotas, *Exenta Chronia*, pp. 91, 107–110.

CHAPTER TWO
Right-wing Dictatorship, 1935–41

ANTI-VENIZELIST RESURGENCE

During the inter-war period all the Balkan countries adopted authoritarian forms of government, as their monarchs suppressed or restricted parliamentary institutions, which with the partial exception of Greece had never enjoyed much popular support. Amidst an international climate of disillusionment with parliamentary democracy, the Balkan regimes tried to tackle a range of problems, including public indebtedness, the assimilation of new territories and of ethnic minorities, and the economic discontent caused in part by loss of traditional export markets. An additional motive for maintaining authoritarian rule was the need to contain the social tensions exacerbated first by the Bolshevik revolution and later by the Great Depression. Thus the monarchs had conservative motives for their attacks on parliamentarism, and ruled through the traditional machinery of state. As the authoritarian regimes were also repressive, particularly towards Communist parties, they provoked a popular reaction led by Communists during and after the Second World War.

Greece succumbed thrice to dictatorial rule, briefly in 1925–6 and 1935, then from 1936 to 1941. The third dictatorship was by Balkan standards remarkably ambitious in its attempt at regimentation of society and repression of dissent. The appearance of such a regime in a country with a long parliamentary tradition can be accounted for by the severity of the crises which Greece had recently undergone. The problem of determining territorial boundaries in 1915–23 had been intertwined with that of alignment in the First World War and also with the constitutional issue of the monarch's powers. The schism caused by this multiple crisis was exacerbated by the mass influx of refugees, which in the short run strengthened the Venizelist camp, but in the long run strengthened the Communist Party. Serious social tensions were caused from the time of the First World War by the creation of masses of indebted smallholders, and by rapid industrialization in a country which hitherto had been mainly agrarian, though with a strong mercantile sector. These tensions were then exacerbated by the Great Depression.

One way in which the Depression weakened parliamentary institutions was by reviving the National Schism. The immediate effect of the Depression was to widen the latent divisions in the Venizelist camp, despite Venizelos's desperate efforts to hold it together by personal charisma and an appeal to traditional loyalties. A wide range of Venizelist businessmen was hurt economically and alienated from the government by the slump, while being alarmed by the industrial unrest to which it led. So they turned to the anti-Venizelists in the hope of prudent financial management and a defence of property rights. Meanwhile the poorer Venizelists were attracted in large numbers to radical groups: the Agrarian, Agrarian-Labour, and Communist parties. These voters included refugee smallholders discontented by their debt burdens, and by their disappointed hope of compensation for property lost in Asia Minor. Other discontented farmers were currant growers in the Peloponnese and tobacco growers in the north who suffered from the slump in overseas markets. Much of the urban working class was discontented because of growing unemployment, police persecution, and after 1932 by the rise in the cost of living caused by the government's devaluation of the drachma and its protectionist measures.[1]

Given the ferocious character of the National Schism, the anti-Venizelist revival was bound to shake the foundations of the political system. Indeed it began a chain of events leading eventually to the fiercely anti-Communist dictatorships of 1935 and 1936. The short-lived government formed by Panages Tsaldares, leader of the Populist Party and therefore of the anti-Venizelist camp, after the indecisive general election of September 1932, replaced many Venizelist officers in the army and police. Much of the official establishment, including the judiciary, church, and the rank-and-file gendarmes, was already anti-Venizelist as a result of earlier periods of dominance by monarchists. Then the anti-Venizelist victory at the election of March 1933 made Venizelists fear further purges which would destroy the basis of their power. A retired general, Nikolaos Plastiras, felt especially vulnerable because of his primary role in the Venizelist coup of 1922, which had resulted in the execution of six leading anti-Venizelists as scapegoats for the Asia Minor catastrophe. So immediately after the 1933 election, Plastiras attempted another military coup, without authorization by Venizelos or adequate support by Venizelist officers.[2] His failure led to his exile for eleven years, and provoked a further, more extensive purge of officers by the Tsaldares government.

In June 1933, a prominent police officer, the director of the General Security, with the connivance of the director of Special Security (both, naturally, partisan appointees of the new anti-Venizelist regime), organized an attempt to assassinate Venizelos himself. Like the Chicago Mafia the assassins chased his car for a long distance down an Athens boulevard, spraying it with machine-gun fire. Those responsible for the crime were condemned even by many in the police, but were protected by anti-Venizelist politicians. The former royalist general-turned-politician, Ioannes Metaxas, applauded the attempt, thereby competing with Tsaldares for the support of party diehards. Thus the culprits escaped legal penalty, and Venizelists were accordingly embittered.[3]

In various other ways the anti-Venizelist regime used the police against its political opponents during the years 1933–5. Government supporters banned or assaulted political meetings in many places, and the government strained convention by the drastic ways in which it influenced the municipal elections of February 1934. Later in 1934 the government tried by legislation to rig electoral boundaries to an unprecedented degree. It was checked by the Venizelist majority in the Senate, a defence which Venizelists expected to lose in the elections of April 1935.[4]

In their alarm at impending loss of power, Venizelist army commanders obtained the consent of Venizelos to a military rebellion on 1 March 1935. The rebel commanders secured much voluntary support from refugee smallholders in eastern Macedonia and Thrace, as well as from natives of Crete. The anti-Venizelist forces, for their part, got strong support from inhabitants of some of the old lands. Thus the expedition to suppress the revolt, led by General George Kondyles, resembled an invasion of the new lands by inhabitants of the old. The revolt failed, whereupon Venizelos fled abroad, to die in exile a year later.[5]

Such was the sympathy for the revolt among the armed forces and the new lands that with better preparation it might well have succeeded. Its failure therefore provoked a massive purge of public officials, including the forced retirement or expulsion of over one-fifth of army officers and over one-quarter of gendarmerie officers. In total, about 1,800 Venizelist army officers were forcibly retired in 1932–5.[6] Many of those who replaced them were partisan anti-Venizelists, including victims of earlier purges. The police and army were now dominated by extreme anti–Venizelists, determined henceforth to prevent any attempt by their rivals to recover their positions. In Crete the purge departed from the convention prevailing hitherto that the majority of public servants should be Cretan, and the dismissed police officers were prominent in agitation against the government. One politician told a British official in mid-1936 that the police were imposing a 'petty tyranny' in Venizelist districts.[7]

Thus Venizelists, together with agrarians and socialists, experienced the persecution hitherto reserved chiefly for alleged Communists. As a result many of the poorer and more radical supporters of these parties drew closer to the Communists. In response the Communists, who had distrusted Venizelos's party, the Liberals, so much that they revealed preparations for the military revolt, made greater efforts to escape from their ghetto and attract Liberal supporters. In the general election of June 1935, the Communists increased their vote to the inter-war record of 9.6 per cent by forming a United Front and receiving the votes from the divided Liberal parties, which abstained. The Communist Vasiles Bartziotas recalled how, in cooperating with Liberal youth groups in Salonika in July 1935, 'we found for the first time a common democratic language, a common basic aim – the defence of the Republic and the struggle against the restoration of the monarchy of the Glucksbergs [the Greek dynasty] and against fascism. . . '[8] The alliance led for a time to a national front of Liberal and Communist organizations in September 1935. Most Liberal politicians soon afterwards withdrew from the front, partly in response to Venizelos's instructions, and managed to retain nearly all their supporters in the general election of January 1936. In this election the Communists allied only with some socialist groups and an agrarian group in a General Popular Front which received 5.6 per cent of the vote and secured fifteen seats.

Liberal supporters were encouraged however to continue cooperation with Communists by the pact between the senior Liberal in parliament, Themistocles Sophoules, and the leader of the Communist parliamentary group Stylianos Sklavainas, on 19 February 1936, which caused a sensation when the Communists revealed it on 2 April. The Communists supported Sophoules's election as Speaker of the parliament (a stepping-stone to the position of prime minister) as part of an agreement on a comprehensive restoration of civil liberties, including the repeal of the Idionym Law and the dissolution of the Special Security.

The quest for allies which the Communists thus began on their own initiative was sanctioned by the Seventh Comintern Congress of July–August 1935, where Ioannides represented the Greek Communists. The Congress sanctioned the Popular Front policy of alliance with all other democratic parties, socialist and bourgeois-liberal, to resist fascists and reactionaries, or in other words the dictatorial right. Zachariades proceeded to apply the decision to Greek conditions in the fourth plenum of the central committee in September and the sixth party congress in December. These bodies interpreted the policy logically as including defence of national soil against aggression by Fascist Italy or Nazi Germany. To align the party still further with national feeling, the congress dropped support for Macedonian secession, in favour of support for equality of rights for all minorities.[9]

During the summer of 1936 the Communists were clearly poised for a breakthrough in rural areas as a result of their agreement with a bourgeois politician, Ioannes Sofianopoulos. From May onwards various agrarian groups in all parts of the country were preparing for a congress in September, which Sofianopoulos was organizing to establish the United Agrarian Party. The Communist Party, in accordance with the decision of its sixth congress, began to dissolve its rural cells and merge them with this incipient party.[10] The Communists were also acquiring allies among trade unionists. Their own trade union federation cooperated with the General Confederation of Greek Workers in a nation-wide general strike on 13 May 1936 in protest against the shooting by police of strikers in Salonika, and planned another on 5 August in protest against the government's restriction of collective bargaining. Thus the Communist Party looked forward to a realignment which might eventually bring to it a majority of Venizelist voters, while leaving most of the Venizelist politicians to move into alliance with the anti-Venizelists. In reaction to this apparent trend, and in alarm also at the increase of industrial unrest during 1936, even the more socially radical Venizelists like George Papandreou, Alexandros Mylonas, and Alexandros Papanastasiou attacked Communism, and supported at least some of the tough measures taken against strikes by the government of Ioannes Metaxas, who became prime minister in April.[11]

Anti-Venizelists for their part felt alarmed by the new alliance which they labelled 'Venizelo-communism'. Their camp, which had for long been conservative in its support of the political practices and dominant groups in the old lands, now also became increasingly conservative in its defence of property rights and in the intensity of its opposition to Communism. The most notable acts of brutality by gendarmes or soldiers against economically motivated demonstrations occurred mainly in the predominantly Venizelist new lands, for example in Herakleion, Crete, on 5 August 1935 and in Salonika on 9 May 1936. In the first seven months of 1936 there were according to official figures 247 strikes, many of them accompanied by demonstrations which were attacked by gendarmes or soldiers.

The government's sympathizers as usual blamed Communists for instigating the events, although it seemed obvious to British and American diplomats that their motivation was mainly economic. But as Communist influence increased, the alarm of bourgeois politicians increased disproportionately. Thus in May 1935 a former director of a political unit of the police, General George Fessopoulos, published articles exposing alleged Soviet intrigues in Greece. Indeed the British ambassador thought it likely that Greece had been marked out by the Comintern because of its political and economic disorder.[12] Late in 1935 and in 1936 senior army officers supplied successive governments with persuasive evidence of extensive

Communist infiltration of the army, chiefly through the annual intake of national servicemen. At least as early as 1935 army training manuals inculcated anti-Communism into recruits and officer cadets. On 18 May 1936 the Populist Party mouthpiece, the national daily *Kathemerine*, published a posthumous article by Tsaldares asserting that the National Schism had been superseded by the confrontation between Communists and those defending traditional Greek values of country, religion, family, and morality. Accordingly the Populist Party manifesto of June did not mention the dead Venizelos. This social conservatism proved attractive to many of Venizelos's business supporters amidst the unprecedented industrial unrest of 1935–6.[13]

Thus the anti-Venizelist camp attracted powerful allies by taking the lead against Communism. It might have consolidated its position as a ruling party had it not, at this point, destroyed itself by splitting into a parliamentary and a dictatorial wing.

PARLIAMENTARY DEMOCRACY IN CRISIS

Facing a powerful combination of enemies, and flanked by restive militants in his own camp, Tsaldares could not afford the luxury of constitutional practices in 1935. The general election which his government proceeded to hold in June, just after the lifting of martial law necessitated by the Venizelist uprising, was according to the British ambassador Sir Sydney Waterlow 'described on all hands as the most corrupt and unreal of modern times', and recalled pre-1909 days as far as 'grafting, menaces and manipulation of votes are concerned'. The police enforced a law for compulsory voting by herding villagers to the polling booths.[14] Anticipating these conditions, the Venizelist or Liberal parties boycotted the election, leaving their opponents virtually to monopolize the new parliament. Not even this victory satisfied the anti-Venizelist militants, now impatient for a restoration of the monarchy. To avert an imminent plebiscite which they feared might not yield the desired result, some officers led by General George Kondyles, supported by Generals Alexandros Papagos, Konstantinos Plates, and Georgios Reppas, ousted Tsaldares in October. They then formed a dictatorship which arrested thousands of political opponents, both on the left and centre-left, and held a plebiscite in November which it rigged systematically and scandalously. Soldiers took a prominent part in the plebiscite, both coercing voters and casting multiple votes.[15]

The plebiscite succeeded in restoring the monarchy, but not in entrenching the dictatorship. George II had spent his twelve years of exile in London and acquired influential friends in the Foreign Office,[16] and so became an important link from then until his death in 1947 between Greece and Britain. He was initially predisposed in favour of British constitutional practices, and disinclined to be the puppet of Kondyles. So he restored a semblance of constitutional rule by sacking Kondyles, proclaiming a general political amnesty for those imprisoned and exiled since March, and appointing a caretaker government, under the Professor of Law Konstantinos Demertzes, with the purpose of holding fair elections by proportional representation. It was typical of the prejudices general among politicians and the king that none, it seems, thought to include in the amnesty the 700–800 allegedly Communist exiles on islands, many of whom had been arrested before the Venizelist revolt in March. Many of them went on hunger strike in an attempt, partially successful, to gain release. The government's desire to restore constitutional practices was, moreover, flouted to some extent by the police, who intervened extensively against the Venizelists' opponents in the general election of January 1936.[17]

The election result destroyed any chance of a stable, parliamentary government. The Venizelist and anti-Venizelist camps won about the same number of seats, so that the fifteen Communist deputies held the balance of power. For several months party leaders tried to agree on a coalition government. Not only did each of the main blocs lack a parliamentary majority, but each suffered also from lack of a recognized leader and consequent fragmentation. The capacity of the main parties to form a government was weakened still further by the death early in 1936 of several leading politicians : Kondyles, Tsaldares, Demertzes, and above all Venizelos, who had dominated the scene for the previous 26 years. Papanastasiou died later in the year.

The chronic individualism and opportunism of Greek politicians now showed itself at its worst. Even so a government with a parliamentary majority might well have emerged from their horse-trading had it not been for one other factor: the veto by the anti-Venizelists in the army and gendarmerie, led by Kondylists organized in the Military League, over the readmission of Venizelists to their ranks, which for Venizelist politicians was an essential condition for joining a coalition. The Military League was represented in the Cabinet by the generals Papagos as Minister of the Army and Plates as Deputy-Minister. While unwilling to accept their pretensions, George II agreed with their opposition to the Venizelist officers whom he saw simply as mutineers.[18]

While politicians failed to form a government, the country faced an awesome combination of problems. Having been an ally and beneficiary of the Entente in the First World War, Greece was threatened by the rearmament and expansion of Nazi Germany and by Fascist Italy's growing territorial ambitions. The threat was especially serious because of the territorial claims of Greece's northern neighbours. Especially threatening was Bulgaria's constant desire to recover the Thracian territory which it had held in 1913–19. In addition the Yugoslav government had a latent ambition to acquire Aegean territory; and Italy's satellite, Albania, had grounds for a claim on northern Epirus because of the existence there of Albanian-speaking Muslims. Meanwhile Greece's armed forces were in disarray as a result of a long-term fall in government revenues and the disruptions caused by repeated purges since 1933. On another front, strikes and demonstrations showed no sign of abating in mid-July 1936: in fact a bad grain harvest promised to intensify them.[19]

The paralyis of government in the face of these problems led to a crisis of faith in parliamentary democracy, which was shared to varying degrees by many politicians, journalists, and businessmen, besides army officers. This crisis existed to some extent in most countries of Europe and all those of the Balkans. An underlying cause was the loss of nerve by traditional elites who faced challenges to their authority by new social forces and economic dislocations stemming from the First World War. Thus politicians had to tackle tasks for which they were insufficiently prepared by background or training: intervention in industrial disputes, protection of workers' conditions, social insurance, aid to smallholders, support for industries hurt by the Depression. From the mid-1930s there was in addition the rather more familiar task of mobilizing public support for defence.[20] Political instability stemmed from the weakness of party organizations and the eternal competition between politicians for patronage resources and status. The reliance of a majority of politicians on poor rural voters, whom they controlled with a mixture of patronage and intimidation, cushioned them to some extent from the need to confront new social problems. Communist parties by contrast were systematically confronting these problems, which is one reason why they were formidable. So the Communist bogy provided bourgeois politicians with a scapegoat for their own failures.

By now the faith of many people in democracy was weakened still further by the seductive examples of the fascist dictatorships and of the Soviet Union. The fascist dictatorships advertised their achievements in restoring national pride and social discipline; while the Soviet Union advertised its ability to mobilize the country's resources to achieve economic modernization and social justice.

In the Balkans, parliamentary institutions were further weakened by the failure of the state to acquire popular respect, and by the enforced exclusion of Communists from political life. In Greece the state machine depended for efficiency on a dynamic head of government; and there was a serious hiatus of such leadership between the resignation of Venizelos as prime minister in November 1932 and the accession of Metaxas in April 1936. Panages Tsaldares, who was prime minister for most of the intervening period, was skilful in parliamentary debate and manoeuvres, but weak and indecisive as a head of government. Under him there was a noticeable decline in the efficacy of the state administration in many spheres.[21] It failed for example to confront the problems posed by over-production of currants, the fluctuating and generally low prices of tobacco, the decline in real wages, and the appalling conditions of urban workers. The efficiency of the gendarmerie was impaired by partisan purges, which accounted to some extent for its bias and excessive violence.

The most notorious of these excesses was the killing of twelve people and the wounding of at least 32 in a peaceful demonstration resulting from a strike by tobacco workers in Salonika on 9 May 1936. Most of the public sympathized with the strikers, a verdict later endorsed in effect by the government through the leniency of the sentences passed in 1938 on the workers arrested. The British Consul-General concluded that 'the police acted with unnecessary brutality, as was their custom', blaming the local chief of gendarmerie for the fact that hardly a meeting had occurred in Salonika in the previous two years without violence. Shortly after the killings the author Yannis Ritsos commemorated them by publishing, in the national Communist newspaper *Rizospastes*, his since-famous poem *Epitaphios*, the name of which was taken from the dirge of the Virgin Mary with which all Orthodox Christians were familiar. Ritsos's work typified the sympathy for the underdog which had for a long time been shown by prominent writers.[22]

Most politicians in both camps drew the very different conclusion that the executive needed to be strengthened, and indeed a growing number believed in the need for dictatorship. On 25 April 1936 an overwhelming majority of parliament authorized Metaxas, who was known for his belief in dictatorship, to govern by decree while parliament adjourned until 30 September. The leading bourgeois politicians of both camps admitted the faults of the political system in their memorandum to the king on 24 May 1937, after the establishment of the dictatorship, by accepting a majority voting system in parliamentary elections, the suppression of strikes, banning of the Communists, the prevention of political interference in the armed forces, and cleansing of the press. In April 1938, after Metaxas had established his dictatorship, the British ambassador reported that 'it is admitted on all hands that an immediate return to parliamentarism would be disastrous'.[23]

Metaxas was supported by only six deputies, but owed his appointment partly to his long-standing personal friendship with the royal family, and partly to his ability to tame the truculent Kondylists in the armed forces, led after Kondyles's death in January by General Alexandros Papagos. They felt nervous about the negotiations between the parties to form a coalition government, because they were vulnerable to reprisals not only by Venizelist politicians but also by Populist followers of Tsaldares whom they had ousted in October 1935. Meanwhile many gendarmerie officers, including those involved in the attack on Venizelos, were vulnerable to reprisals for their excesses since 1933. Leading officers of the army and gendarmerie went to the length of dictating terms to the king through Papagos as Minister of the Army. Papagos virtually ordered the king on 1 February not to appoint Venizelist officers, and on 5 March not to appoint a government dependent on Communist deputies, so expressing officers' alarm at the rumoured pact between Sophoules and Sklavainas.

The king asserted his authority over these over-mighty soldiers by sacking Papagos and replacing him with Metaxas, who immediately secured the submission of the key army commanders, who were divided with regard to Papagos's action. Thereafter Metaxas kept the loyalty of the armed forces by giving them essentially what they wanted: the continued exclusion from the active list of Venizelist officers, with a few individual exceptions; harsh repression of strikers and Communists; and encouragement to officers to devote themselves to the urgent work of rearmament. In April the king appointed Metaxas as prime minister, and the latter consolidated his authority by appointing his supporters as ministers and nomarchs (prefects), prominent among them being former associates in the anti-Venizelist military revolt of 1923.[24] Especially significant was the appointment as Minister of the Interior (controlling the police) of Theodoros Skylakakes, a prominent admirer of fascist dictatorships, and influential among extreme anti-Venizelists in the army. Metaxas also increased substantially the pensions and allowances of the gendarmerie. Thus he forged an alliance with the most militant anti-Venizelists in the army and police.

Metaxas's affiliations explain why he took seriously the warnings from senior army and gendarmerie officers of growing Communist influence. He put a sinister interpretation on the fairly widespread sympathy shown by soldiers for strikers and demonstrators and on the continuance of industrial unrest, which culminated in the announcement by the major trade union federations of a general strike on 5 August. This prospect enabled him to persuade the king that there was a Communist conspiracy which necessitated the suspension of parliament and civil liberties on 4 August. Nevertheless this was certainly a pretext: his real motive was a direct threat to his position as prime minister, in the form of an imminent agreement on coalition by the party leaders.[25]

METAXAS'S TYRANNY

Like the other authoritarian regimes in the Balkans, this one was based on the monarchical state and made no attempt to create a mass party. Metaxas had only six supporters in the parliament of 1936, and concentrated responsibilities in himself and his few followers. He was one of the most inspired and creative of political leaders in modern Greece, but also one of the least likeable. His diaries, which he kept throughout his dictatorship and for much of 40 years before it, reveal a character of political vision and broad cultural tastes, but also of egoism and consuming ambition. He dominated his administration, accumulating portfolios until from November 1938 he held, in addition to that of prime minister, those of foreign affairs, the armed forces, and education, and the deputy ministries of public security, labour, the press, and market control. He also made frequent speeches and tours of the provinces. According to the British ambassador he showed 'almost superhuman disregard, not only of the ordinary pleasures of life, but of things, such as regular meals, which are necessities to most people; from sunrise until late at night he works without interruption . . .'[26]

Not surprisingly, people of independent status could not long endure partnership with this overbearing and suspicious character. After three years, therefore, the key figures who remained in the regime were new men, who owed their importance to him: Konstantinos Maniadakes, the Deputy-Minister for Public Security; Konstantinos Kotzias, the Minister for Athens; Theodoros Nikoloudes, Deputy-Minister for the Press; and Iannes Diakos, who held no portfolio but wielded formidable power as a fixer and go-between.

Metaxas owed his power to George II, who shared with him authority in the army, but otherwise valued the dictator for liberating him from politicians whom he had soon come to despise. Soon after his return he found that he had little taste for government, and indeed showed little sense of obligation to his people. Like his contemporary in Italy, Victor Emmanuel, he let his popularity – limited to begin with – be dragged down by a dictatorship.[27]

The pillar of the regime was the police, which gained extensive responsibilities. It began the regime with large-scale arrests of Communists and left-wingers, and soon recruited informers in vast numbers, even in small villages, especially from people in humble but well-placed positions, like shoe-shine boys and owners of newspaper kiosks and cafés. Political discussion ceased, except between friends and behind closed doors. By a measure of 1938, which remained a basic instrument of state control for most of the time until 1974, the police became responsible for issuing certificates of political loyalty which were required of applicants for any kind of state employment, as well as a wide range of permits, licences, and key occupations including those of journalist and lawyer.

The core of the regime was the political police, consisting of the General Security and Special Security. Maniadakes, backed by the authority of his trusted master, effectively coordinated their work for the first time by holding regular conferences with their directors about strategy for pursuing dissidents. He greatly increased their personnel and resources. The Anti-Communist Unit of the General Security increased from fifteen to about 80 selected men. The Special Security, which also had its anti-Communist unit, increased from its strength of 190 in 1929 to a strength of 445 officers and NCOs, 30 political agents and 1,200 privates, all well equipped. These units could call at will on the rest of the police for mass arrests and disposed of much increased means of transport and funds.

The police served the regime with conspicuous enthusiasm and little dissent. They were now encouraged to harass their traditional enemies – criminals, left-wingers, and strikers – with no more fear of political obstruction. Those police officers with high professional ideals valued their liberation from the traditional curse of political interference, which soon strengthened the force's morale and *esprit de corps*. According to a gendarmerie officer and historian in the 1960s, relations between officers and men improved and became less military in nature.[28] The government showed great solicitude for the police's pay, pensions, equipment, and welfare provisions. Maniadakes also took a close interest in the reform of police training, raising to university level the teaching in the college for gendarmerie officers and establishing a similar college for those of the city police.

Metaxas assigned to the police the grand role of reforming citizens' moral and political values, as he explained to them when he presided over ceremonies such as the graduation of officer cadets. The police participated in the censorship of films; imposed new restrictions on cabarets and bars; and waged a campaign against gambling houses and hashish dens.[29] They evidently found their moral role to be exalted but burdensome. In other respects, the police achieved successful results. The police seems genuinely to have become more efficient in suppressing crime. For example they suppressed animal-rustling in the countryside, an abuse which had persisted hitherto because many of the rustlers were protected by politicians. Foreign observers testified to the police's efficiency in catching the many Italian spies who entered the country in 1939–40.[30]

The army was kept loyal primarily by respect for the king, who busied himself with its training and welfare while condemning political intrigues by officers. Senior officers were bound to the king by their dependence on him to prevent the reinstatement of Venizelist officers, and several were bound also to Metaxas by sentimental ties dating from the 1923 revolt and before, as well as by respect for his formidable ability as a military strategist, stemming from his experience as a senior staff officer in the 1910s. Junior officers were more detached and pragmatic in their attitude towards the regime; and, although predominantly conservative and monarchist, varied somewhat in their political alignments during the enemy occupation of the 1940s. The loyalty of all ranks was increased by the great increase in all types of military expenditure. The scope for dissent was also limited by the intensity of preparation for defence. For senior officers the work was increased by the shortage of skilled personnel created by the purge of Venizelists in 1935. In retrospect, army and naval officers saw the period of the dictatorship as onerous but satisfying because of what was achieved. This achievement was manifest to foreign observers in manoeuvres and parades which showed a progressive improvement in drill, turnout, equipment, and even the physique of troops.[31]

The 'new state' which Metaxas claimed to be creating was really the old one centralized and expanded. From early in his life, Metaxas had identified himself emotionally with state officials, and now showed solicitude for their authority and well-being. For example he invited all public servants to submit their grievances directly to himself. He raised the entry requirements for local officials and improved training procedures for government officials, who consequently showed evidence of greater efficiency. For example foreign businessmen found it easier to get official permits, while ordinary citizens found officials to be more accessible.[32]

The government grew to take on new responsibilities. Seven ministries or deputy-ministries were created, an increase of one-third in the Cabinet's size. State officials seem to have increased by several thousand. The actual (as distinct from legally ordained) strength of the gendarmerie increased during the first four years of the regime from 12,200 to 14,600, while the legally established strength of the city police, fixed at 4,200 in December 1936, increased thereafter only slightly. After the outbreak of war with Italy in October 1940 the gendarmerie were increased much further in order to perform a varied role in defence.[33]

The traditional centralization of government was carried to extreme lengths. Many if not all local councils were dissolved and replaced by government appointees. One result was that the rural constabulary (responsible only for disputes between peasants about land and animals) passed under the control of nomarchs (prefects). Central control over the teaching profession was tightened. Many teachers were sacked for alleged irreligion or political dissent. University lectures were watched by the police, while school teachers were spied on by the official youth movement. School textbooks were rewritten so as to inculcate the regime's ideals. Control was also increased over the church. Metaxas took drastic measures to secure the election by bishops of his favoured candidate as Archbishop of Athens, head of the church, and reduced the size of the church's governing body, the Holy Synod, so as to increase the government's influence. The government also cooperated with the Holy Synod in founding an apostolic mission, and improving the administration of church property, while trying to raise the educational level of parish clergy.[34]

Control of the national press was totalitarian in thoroughness. The content of newspapers was strictly censored, especially material relating to politics, defence, foreign relations, or economic conditions. As in Stalinist regimes, reference to crime, or even sometimes to natural disasters, was deleted. Newspapers were also compelled to print much adulatory material supplied by the government. Probably more popular was the suppression of libel and scandal which had hitherto been common in much of the press.[35] The government also increased its power over communications through radio broadcasting, which was founded in 1937–8. The government planned to make every commune (the lowest tier of local government) acquire a radio; and the number of radios in the country increased from about 10,000 to about 60,000 in 1936–40.[36]

Metaxas carried further the trend towards corporative organization of the economy which Venizelos had begun. At the apex of the regime was a network of powerful bankers and industrialists who were associated with anti-Venizelism and provided an important source of recruits to the government, as well as finance for favoured projects and help with managing the foreign debt. Examples were Alexandros Korizes, Minister of Health and Social Security until 1939, then Governor of the National Bank, then briefly Metaxas's successor as prime minister. Alexandros Kanellopoulos was the leading manufacturer of chemicals, and head of the official youth movement.[37] The recruitment of bankers and their associates was part of a policy of filling posts by professionals in the appropriate field: a trade unionist as Minister of Labour, an agronomist as Minister of Agriculture, a soldier as Deputy-Minister of the Army, and so on.

The Minister of Labour, Aristides Demetratos, was a former Communist and Secretary-General of the General Confederation of Greek Labour. He now appointed its executive council, and then appointed an official trade union in every trade or industry, while suppressing others and banning strikes. He also introduced the system, maintained in some form by subsequent governments, of forcing workers to pay union dues which were collected and distributed by the government.[38] Metaxas planned to incorporate all peasants similarly in a system of official cooperatives which he established, under a Deputy-Ministry held by Babis Alivizatos, who was also president of the National Confederation of Agricultural Cooperatives and Deputy-Governor of the Agricultural Bank. Metaxas intended the cooperatives and trade unions to be represented eventually in a corporative parliament.[39]

Corporations were to assist in the co-ordination of the economy, an aim which Metaxas proclaimed at the outset of the dictatorship. As Waterlow wrote: 'the aim is to substitute, in all departments of the national life, managed State economy for that anarchy of private interests . . . which successive parliamentary Governments had shown themselves impotent to correct. The slogan is "unity of action through unity of direction . . . " [and] rationalisation is in future to be supreme.'[40] Here Metaxas was influenced by international fashion. In his explicit bias in favour of state regulation of the economy, he aligned himself with other dictators and against the Western democracies, while conveniently overlooking the extent to which the latter were following the same trend.

What Waterlow called 'the mania of the dictatorship for State planning in all spheres' sometimes led to complicated and coercive interference in private enterprise. State intervention also took the form of a ten-year programme of public works announced in April 1937. It included the building of docks, railways, and roads as part of a national plan of communications, as well as schemes of afforestation, irrigation, drainage, and flood protection. All this was to be financed in part by forced loans from private banks and insurance funds. The programme also included the conscription of labour for road-building. Only a small part of the public works were decorative; and detached observers did not notice obvious white elephants.[41]

By centralizing the state and working through the existing social hierarchy, Metaxas tried to regiment the population. His most audacious exercise was to organize the National Organization of Youth (EON) which became effectively compulsory for all school children, and on the government's claim came to include 1,250,000 members (in a population of 7,345,000). It included in its curriculum patriotic and religious instruction, and some political indoctrination. Prominent members of the movement acquired quasi-official status, with privileged access to those in authority and the duty of spying on teachers and parents. The essential fuel of the organization was official pressure and patronage: privileges for the leaders; free uniforms, cinema tickets, and excursions for the rank-and-file; and the requirement of former membership for applicants to jobs. The government extracted contributions to the organization from diverse sources: foreign businesses, army pension funds, and trade unions; while the police helped to compel membership and enforce political conformity.[42] Reports reaching foreign observers show that most adults – at least among the well-to-do – saw the organization as alien and infringing on parental authority. Especially unpopular were the presumptuous behaviour of its officials and the removal of girls from parental supervision. Adults and some members of the organization resented its vacuous propaganda and absurd *Führer*-worship, which was commonly parodied (an indication that the notorious spy network of the organization was not totalitarian).[43]

Mass demonstrations to welcome Metaxas on his provincial tours were carefully organized. Welcoming crowds were produced by the Agricultural Bank's pressure on its numerous debtors, and instructions to banks and businesses to send a specified number of employees, who were given instructions about the applause with which they should greet the 'leader'.[44] For the anniversary of the regime in the capital, groups of people were sent from the provinces with expenses paid, while each householder had to display a flag, each café owner to offer some free drink, and each employer to give employees a bonus; and local councils were told what to say in the greetings telegrams which they sent to the prime minister. Meanwhile the residents of Athens and Piraeus showed their true feelings in a mass exodus to the seaside or the country.[45]

The police under Maniadakes's direction succeeded to an unprecedented degree in suppressing opposition. Maniadakes began immediately to destroy the Communist organization, using the considerable experience possessed by some police officers and discussing with them the best ways to proceed. They assembled a library of Communist publications, and studied Communist theory and organization, on which Maniadakes came to consider himself an authority. The principles of Marxism–Leninism and methods of Communist organization formed part of the basic curriculum of the new or reformed training colleges for police, while some trainees received special training in anti-Communist work.

Within a few months the police used the information which they had secured from spies inside the party, some of whom they had recruited before the dictatorship, especially from those who bore grudges against the party resulting from purges. In September the police arrested Zachariades; in October they seized the archives of the Communist Organization of Athens, and in November those of the politburo, while arresting two party members who would become key informers, Telemachos Mitla and Michales Tyrimos. Mitla immediately revealed much about the Communists' infiltration of the army, including the startling news that ten or more officers had been recruited.[46]

Maniadakes eventually decided that it was more important to extract information from those arrested than to imprison them, and so made general the practice of offering captives their liberty in return for declarations of repentance and denunciations of colleagues. As he proudly told an American diplomat in 1949, no Communist should be released until he had been subjected to 'a grilling that would wring everything' out of him including his life story.[47] Under his direction the police fulfilled this policy with such zeal that they eventually extracted 57,000 public declarations of repentance from alleged Communists – three or four times the total party membership in August 1936. Their methods of persuasion usually included prolonged beatings and interrogations, followed if necessary by solitary confinement, and then by more subtle forms of pressure such as reports of betrayal by colleagues or appeals from family members living in penury because the police prevented anyone from helping them. By 1940 the news from abroad, of the Nazi–Soviet pact and a succession of fascist victories, was very discouraging to Communists. In the circumstances it is remarkable testimony to their faith that at least 1,870 gaoled Communists, including many or most leading cadres, refused to recant.

Although the regime's policy was to avoid political executions, twelve people were plausibly claimed by left-wing sources to have been murdered by agents of the regime, and a total of 64 to have died, most of them from privation; sixteen were said to have suffered mental breakdowns, and about 500 to have fallen critically ill in other ways. Presumably most of these victims were alleged Communists.[48]

Within three years, organized work by Communists had become almost impossible. By the end of 1939 Maniadakes had won over enough senior members to form a bogus central committee (the so-called 'Provisional Executive'), which issued its own edition of the party newspaper *Rizospastes* and won away the loyalty of many members from the real central committee. By late 1940 only six members of the real central committee remained free. As the party later admitted, the regime 'succeeded in breaking up the forces of our Party . . . and, finally, it had accomplished its almost complete disintegration . . . in general those Communists who were not in prison had no connection with each other but were dispersed . . . '[49] The party leadership was unable to consider its response to the growing threat from abroad; although in a way this was an advantage because the Nazi–Soviet pact of August 1939 made a response difficult. The other major Communist parties of the Balkans, the Yugoslav and Bulgarian, also suffered from severe persecution at this time, but were at least able to keep their organizations and hierarchies intact.[50]

The regime was based on a rejection of parliamentary politics; and fewer than a quarter of those holding key positions in the regime were professional politicians, Metaxas being one of them. As the control of the traditional networks of patronage passed from politicians to state officials and their supporters, 'party clientelism was replaced by state clientelism'.[51] Politicians were immobilized by police surveillance, and possibly all of importance were placed under some kind of confinement, usually on an island. Local party bosses were, if not immobilized, enlisted by the regime.

They and their patrons were in any case demoralized and discredited by their failure to provide effective government, and hampered too by the relatively prosperous conditions, with full employment and high prices for agricultural produce, which prevailed during the first three years of the dictatorship. Moreover the growing threat from abroad made it difficult for any politicians except the Communists to think of destabilizing the government or dividing the country. After Italy's annexation of Albania in April 1939 such action became almost unthinkable.

For all these reasons dissident activity was very limited. The only form of activity which might conceivably have threatened the dictator's position was pressure on the king. He never seems seriously to have considered responding to the several appeals which he received from politicians to restore some form of parliamentary democracy; and Metaxas made such appeals increasingly difficult by deporting those likely to make them. Other sorts of activity – demonstrations, circulation of newspapers and leaflets – were very restricted by police vigilance. Only the Communists had the organization needed to do these things on any significant scale: for example they produced newspapers continuously until 1939. Consequently other politicians, representing a wide spectrum of political parties, accepted with more or less reluctance the need to cooperate with them. An anti-dictatorial youth front which formed during 1937 seems to have been the most active political organization. It was accompanied in the summer of 1938 by a front of the parties, which excluded the Communists from its managing committee but relied on the Communists' printing presses and organizers.[52] These bodies were active in universities and polytechnics, cultural associations, and factories, especially in the larger towns.

The conspiracy in 1939 by the minor Populist politicians Antonios Livieratos and Georgios Kartales was more formidable than the foregoing because it recruited a substantial number of army officers. But this and other conspiracies in the army never got further than the swearing-in of recruits and preliminary discussions. Two or three of the conspiracies were betrayed by fellow-officers, and two others were detected by the police. All were in any case doomed by lack of support from most officers.[53] The only open uprising against the regime occurred in Chania in western Crete, in July 1938, when an armed crowd occupied the key points in the town. But the rebels were badly organized and gave up to the authorities before the day was over. Their leaders had contacts with a committee of politicians in Athens who had hoped for simultaneous demonstrations in many other places, so as to impress on the king the dictator's unpopularity. But previous arrests of politicians, and police vigilance, ensured that the Chania revolt was isolated.[54]

THE LEGACY OF THE TYRANNY

The suppression of political life was so unfamiliar and unjustified that it was resented by most of the population, and this resentment contributed greatly to the subsequent polarization of the country during the Axis occupation. In May 1937, Waterlow reported that those accustomed to political discussion were increasingly irritated with press censorship and therefore read the clandestine newspapers circulated by the Communists. The prevailing atmosphere is also illustrated by the case of a friend of a prominent official Evangelos Kalantzes, threatened with prosecution for non-compliance with a police order to display a flag on the anniversary of the regime, a threat removed only after Kalantzes interceded with Metaxas himself. By 1939 the regime was so generally unpopular that British diplomats were worried about the Anglophile king's future.[55]

The hatred was especially strong among Communists, many of whom suffered but survived to fight again. Their attitude is described by one of their active opponents in Athens during the German occupation, Chrestos Zalokostas, who during a brief period of truce had a friendly conversation, on 9 October 1944, with the politburo member Iannes Zevgos:

> Zevgos this evening described the torments of Akronauplia in a way showing that he was psychologically affected by them. The look of resignation depicted on his face originated in his prison ordeals. He was suspicious by nature: all we bourgeois reminded him of the dungeons, and he hated us. My contact with Zevgos made me feel the drama of communism in Greece: Siantos, Partsalides, Paparegas, all the leading cadres, were workers who had suffered the tyranny of the Security Police . . . and found themselves, like Zevgos, suddenly in power. They were constantly driven by hatred. Their chief thought was to gain power in order to seek revenge.

An American officer noted at this time that 'there are very few [senior] Communists in Greece who are not sick men' as a result of their pre-war ordeals.[56] The lesson which Communists drew was that they must prevent any possible repetition of this experience by dominating the population themselves. However they were debilitated by another legacy of Maniadakes: fear of spies and mutual distrust.

They were helped on the other hand by the sympathy which they won by their resistance to the dictator. The Communists had not been strong enough to frighten anyone personally before the dictatorship, and now attracted widespread sympathy by their opposition to it. Many of the sympathizers were presumably drawn from the 57,000 who were made to renounce Communism and from the many others who must have been intimidated by the police in their search for suspects. These sympathizers were drawn mainly from the working class, against whom the police campaign was chiefly directed. In the Venizelist and Communist strongholds of Macedonia and Thrace large-scale arrests continued during much of the life of the dictatorship, and were accompanied by conspicuous brutality. The British ambassador Waterlow was told in 1938 of mass arrests, mainly of working-class people, which had provoked 'amazement and indignation in all quarters' because the offences were so trivial, consisting in many cases of minor assistance to the hungry families of deportees.[57]

In Crete, alienation from the regime among all classes was illustrated by the gendarmes' inability to arrest the leaders of the Chania rebellion. One squad which tried to do so was overwhelmed and disarmed by villagers; and in the end the authorities had to persuade the rebels, through intermediaries, to leave by boat. As Metaxas noted in his diary on 6 May 1939, referring to his youth organization in Crete: 'We make no progress there. Lack of authority. Attitude of schoolchildren is everywhere unfavourable.'[58] Other large sections of the population which were alienated were the Koutsovlachs, Turkophone refugees, and above all slavophones, who were punished by police for speaking their mother tongue in public, and ordered to attend night schools to learn Greek. This persecution was especially widespread among slavophones in western Macedonia, and naturally provoked strong resentment. The victims were bound to be drawn to the Communists, with their traditional defence of ethnic minorities.[59]

In many parts of the country, the old alienation of mountain villagers from the state worsened. A British visitor to a poor and mountainous part of the Peloponnese in 1939, when speaking to peasants, was overwhelmed by complaints directed 'mainly against overtaxation by an overly centralised administration, which allowed no place for the representation of local opinion and regarded any attempt at the expression of a local grievance with suspicion'. A specific and widespread grievance was a draconian decree of September 1937 restricting the pasturage of goats in
mountain fir forests and on common lands, with little provision for compensation for those who might thus be deprived of their livelihood. Although inspired by Metaxas's urge to reverse the process of deforestation, this measure showed the eventual futility of environmental protection without concern for social equity.[60]

Many Communist sympathizers were also created among the educated and the relatively well-to-do. A British observer in Salonika reported in June 1938 that many of those recently arrested belonged to a 'respectable' class not commonly associated with Communism, and that the regime was going far towards the creation of the anti-dictatorial front which it claimed to be combating.[61] In fact, an anti-dictatorial front did exist in the main cities, and many activists of several bourgeois parties became accustomed to cooperation in it with Communists.

Prominent among the sympathizers were students at universities or polytechnics, many of whom displayed their resentment of the dictatorship. For them Marxism–Leninism was forbidden fruit, as one of them, Anastasios Pepones, recalled:[62]

> The charm of marxism affected us all, not just those who were accepted or recruited into left-wing parties . . . We all willingly succumbed to the intellectual excitement aroused by philosophical and sociological analyses, such as those of Marx and Engels, or tough and belligerent propositions such as those of Lenin . . . How did we learn about communism and, with it, Marxism? . . . [From] those who insisted that it remain unknown. . . . They did not talk at all about the other opponents of the dictatorship. They told us only about one enemy: unpatriotic, ungodly, immoral communism. . . . Youngsters in the final classes of secondary school or the first year of university learnt suddenly [after the dictatorship] that the world of ideas was not so monotonous, sterile, dry, and boring as made to appear by slogans or proclamations like this one:
> 'We hear only one father and guide
> The Leader, the Leader . . . '

The regime created a predisposition in favour of parliamentary democracy among many of the politicians who suffered from Maniadakes's police, and some of these politicians were still influential several decades later, like the present (1995) prime minister Andreas Papandreou.

Other consequences of the regime were extreme fragmentation and debilitation of the bourgeois parties. While the dictatorship prolonged the division between Venizelists and anti-Venizelists, it created fresh divisions in the anti-Venizelist camp, much of which was antagonized by Metaxas's tyranny. As a result Metaxas's followers were excluded from government until the 1950s, and the Metaxist candidates in the 1946 election were shunned by other monarchists. Because of their talent and experience, several returned to positions of power in the 1950s, but without Maniadakes, whose success in combating Communism was outweighed by the odium which he incurred in persecuting other politicians. The quasi-fascist trappings of the regime – the pseudo-ideology of the 'third Greek civilization', the youth movement, anthems, emblems, and *Führer* cult – evaporated after Metaxas's death in January 1941. There was no Metaxist movement of importance among the myriad right-wing groups that appeared during and after the German occupation.

The regime left a tangible legacy however in the officer corps of the army and gendarmerie. They, like many other state officials, remembered how Metaxas had given them a sense of moral legitimacy and an example of decisive and efficient leadership, which succeeded in suppressing Communism and in resisting the Italian invasion. This memory was especially influential in the years after the occupation, when the state was threatened by Communist subversion, and the forces defending it were weakened by inept governments and political interference. The size of these officer corps was increased and their members to a large extent renewed. In the gendarmerie, the regime eventually replaced most junior officers, by lowering the retiring age of their seniors by four years, retiring the ill-qualified, and maintaining a steady intake into the training colleges for officer cadets.[63] In the armed forces, training schools for officers, NCOs, and technicians worked at full capacity, while new ones were established in order to meet the needs of rearmament and make good the gaps left by the expulsion of Venizelists. Thus the junior ranks came to consist largely of people trained under the dictatorship. This fact was of great importance for post-war politics. For example the twelve colonels who formed the military dictatorship in April 1967 had been officer cadets under Metaxas.[64] Thus the police and army officers in active service under Metaxas formed a dedicated, efficient and relatively cohesive nucleus in the anti-Communist alliance which took shape from 1943 onwards.

AXIS INVASION

The dictatorship was brought down by the invasion of the Axis powers, Fascist Italy and Nazi Germany. The invasion originated in Mussolini's long-term ambition to dominate the east coast of the Adriatic. When Italy annexed Albania in April 1939, Greece eagerly accepted a British guarantee of territorial integrity, so moving a stage further into military dependence on Britain, 'the power considered . . . to be predominant in the Mediterranean'.[65] Hitler's subsequent series of territorial conquests made Mussolini impatient to achieve a striking success of his own while the opportunity was available, and he was spurred into action by Germany's military occupation of Romania in October 1940. Piqued by Hitler's failure to warn him, Mussolini asserted his independence by ordering an invasion of north-western Greece from Albania on 28 October without pretext, warning, or even any clear territorial aims. The Italian troops were very poorly prepared, and unable to benefit fully from their superiority in armaments, because bad weather restricted their use of aircraft, and rugged terrain restricted their use of tanks. The Greek army, against its own commanders' expectations,[66] repelled the invasion. By 4 November it was advancing, and for the next five months engaged Italian troops far within Albania. Thus Greece's war changed in effect from one of defence to one of irredentist gain.

In the explosion of patriotic feeling provoked by the invasion, Metaxas as war leader gained general respect and popularity. Yet the war spelt doom for his regime, for domestic and foreign reasons. For the sake of wartime unity, and in deference to British influence, he could no longer keep politicians in confinement or exclude all Venizelists from active service in the armed forces. The danger to himself was that his liberal and socialist opponents were even more ardently opposed to the Axis than his supporters, because their motives were ideological as well as patriotic. Their zeal in combating dictatorship was approved by Britain and was bound to turn in time against himself. Journalists and intellectuals had to be constantly told by the censors that the war was against Italy and not against fascism. In deference to the British the government now confined itself to reprimanding them and replacing the word fascist with Italy.[67]

Nearly all the politicians who had been exiled or confined gained release by signifying that they were ready to contribute in some way to the war effort. As usual however the Communist prisoners and exiles were excluded from the general amnesty; and the appeals by the several colonies of deportees and prisoners to be allowed to serve in the war effort were rejected. There was in fact some justification for the government's suspicion, because the Comintern line was opposed to the war once Greek soil was freed. This reservation was however known only to a few cadres. The great majority knew only of the letter which Zachariades wrote from jail on 30 October supporting the war as one of 'national liberation against Mussolini's Fascism'.[68] The government publicized the letter through the press and so inadvertently benefited the Communist Party in later years. Although many of the retired Venizelist officers were now readmitted to active service, only a relatively small number were given combat roles, and perhaps none was given a role of any responsibility. About 1,500 of them were not recalled at all: these were mainly of higher rank, and many of them had great experience which was much needed. Thus even in this crisis the regime discredited itself by its partisan bias.[69]

Although Metaxas himself was well aware of the chasm between the conservative spirit of his regime and the radical spirit of the fascist dictatorships, the similarities were more obvious to his opponents, liberal and Communist.[70] Even Metaxas emphasized that he shared with the fascists their rejection of parliamentary liberalism; and his youth movement and the organized *Führer*-worship were obvious imitations of them. Key members of his government like Maniadakes and Kotzias had openly displayed admiration for Nazi methods. Even in March 1941 – when German invasion seemed likely – Maniadakes told an American journalist that he detested the Soviet Union far more than the Axis powers.[71] Thus it was understandable that Communists should henceforth identify the extreme right in Greece with fascism.

A stronger reason why many officials and army officers under Metaxas

were inclined to seek accommodation with Germany is that, as anti-
Venizelists, they were traditionally Germanophile. It seemed natural then
to acknowledge German military predominance, as did the governments of
Bulgaria, Romania, and Yugoslavia between October 1940 and March
1941. One prominent Germanophile, Metaxas's former Minister of the
Interior Skylakakes, was exiled to an island in June 1940. As a result of the
pre-eminence of Germany in Greece's foreign trade, there were many
businessmen with economic interests in friendly relations with Germany.
Because German agents were widespread in Greece, Metaxas could not
prevent negotiations between them and several leading generals including
the Deputy-Chief of the General Staff Konstantinos Plates, who was dismissed partly for this reason in July 1940. Immediately after Metaxas's
death in January his successor as prime minister had to dismiss an army
commander, Markos Drakos, and two corps commanders, Georgios
Kosmas and Demetrios Papadopoulos, allegedly for wanting to negotiate
with the Axis. The Germanophiles' influence was limited, however, by the
universal recognition in Greece that German domination would be incompatible with Greek sovereignty. For this reason the overwhelming majority
of the public, including Metaxas's supporters, hoped for a British victory in
the war.[72]

The regime began to crumble when the elderly Metaxas died on 29
January 1941, in an atmosphere of impending catastrophe. The unsuccessful Italian attack made inevitable a German invasion, because it drew
British forces into Greece, and so created a threat to the southern flank of
Germany's projected invasion of the Soviet Union. Immediately after the
Italian attack, British troops were sent to Crete in order to garrison a naval
base, while British aircraft were sent to the mainland to support the Greek
army. As early as 5 December 1940, Hitler decided to invade Greece, and
in January, the Bulgarian government agreed to assist the invasion in return
for its coveted territorial gains in Thrace and eastern Macedonia.[73] To assist
in defence, a British Commonwealth expeditionary force arrived in mid-
March, and eventually totalled 63,000 in Greece and Crete. German forces
attacked Greece on 6 April from Bulgarian soil, and others followed a few
days later through conquered Yugoslavia. They rapidly overran the country
as all Greek commanders had expected, making the British
Commonwealth troops flee southwards. On 18 April the prime minister
Korizes committed suicide after his government had disintegrated, and on
the 27th the Germans entered Athens.

The king had by now fled to Crete with a new government. Being now
completely dependent on the British, he deferred to their preferences by
appointing as prime minister a Venizelist banker, Emmanouel Tsouderos,
who had won the confidence of Populists and Liberals in conspiring against

Metaxas. Thus the king terminated the dictatorship, but failed to take the opportunity to reunite the nation by appointing a government representing all major groups or by amnestying the Communists.[74] When Crete in turn fell to the Germans just over a month later, the government with a few Greek and numerous British troops retreated to Egypt, which was at that time dominated by Britain.

Thus the king's government and armed forces fell under British control, while leaving their country leaderless to face its conquerors.

NOTES

1. George T. Mavrogordatos, *Stillborn Republic. Social Coalitions and Party Strategies in Greece*, 1922–36 (Berkeley, 1983), pp. 342–3.
2. Thanos Veremis, *Oi Epemvaseis tou Stratou sten Ellenike Politike, 1916–36* (1983), pp. 163–5.
3. D.H. Close, 'The police in the 4th-of-August regime', *Journal of the Hellenic Diaspora*, 13, 1–2 (Spring–Summer 1986), p. 95.
4. Mavrogordatos, *Stillborn Republic*, pp. 318–22.
5. Ibid., pp. 290–1.
6. André Gerolymatos, *Guerrilla Warfare and Espionage in Greece*, 1940–4 (New York, 1992), p. 28.
7. Close, 'Police', p. 97.
8. V. Bartziotas, *Exenta Chronia Kommounistes* (1986), p. 119.
9. Antonio Solaro, *Istoria tou Kommounistikou Kommatos Ellados* (1975), pp. 89–98.
10. Spyros Linardatos, *Pos Ephtasame sten Tessereis Avgoustou* (1965), pp. 227–8.
11. Mavrogordatos, *Stillborn Republic* , pp. 347–9; Linardatos, *Tessereis Avgoustou* , pp. 227–8; Bert Birtles, *Exiles in The Aegean. A Personal Narrative of Greek Politics and Travel* (1938), p. 304.
12. PRO, FO 371/19507/86-7, Waterlow to Simon, 10 May 1935; 371/21147/190, Waterlow to Eden, 22 May 1937.
13. Constantine Sarandis, 'The emergence of the right in Greece, 1920–40' (unpublished Oxford University D. Phil. thesis), pp. 133–4, 237; E. Nikolakopoulos, *Kommata kai Voulevtikes Ekloges sten Ellada, 1946–64* (1985), p. 103; *Ethnikos Kyrix*, 2 Nov. 1949, p. 1; 3 Nov. 1949, p. 1; 6 Nov. 1949, p. 4
14. Close, 'Police', pp. 96–7.
15. FO 371/19509/274, R 6717, Waterlow to Hoare, 6 Nov. 1935.
16. Gerolymatos, *Guerrilla Warfare*, p. 41.
17. Birtles, *Exiles*, pp. 158–67; Close, 'Police', p. 96.
18. FO 371/20389/-, Waterlow to Eden, 18 March 1936.
19. FO 371/20389/-, Waterlow to Eden, 30 July 1936.
20. Veremis, *Epemvaseis*, p. 229.
21. FO 371/18393/51, R 3452, Waterlow to Simon, 14 June 1934.
22. Close, 'Police', p. 97; 'The Epitaphios of Yannis Ritsos', with introduction by Rick Newton, *Journal of the Hellenic Diaspora*, 13, 1&2 (Spring–Summer 1986), pp. 5–51; D. George Kousoulas, *Revolution and Defeat. The Story of the Greek Communist Party* (1965), pp. 114–16.

23. FO 371/22370/383, 11 April 1938; 371/21147/235-9.
24. Gregorios Daphnes, *E Ellas metaxy Dyo Polemon* (1974), II, p. 429.
25. FO 371/20390/-, Waterlow to Foreign Office, 7 Aug. 1936; Daphnes, *Ellas*, II, p. 431.
26. FO 371/21148/-, to Eden, 23 Dec. 1937.
27. John S. Koliopoulos, *Greece and the British Connection, 1935–41* (Oxford, 1977), pp. 71–6.
28. K.S. Antoniou, *Istoria tes Ellenikes Vasilikes Chorophylakes* 3 vols (1965), III, pp. 1482–7.
29. Ibid., pp. 1480–1; Gail Holst, *The Road to Rembetika* (1976), p. 76.
30. Antoniou, *Istoria*, III, p. 1482; John O. Iatrides, ed., *Ambassador MacVeagh Reports. Greece 1943–7* (Princeton, 1980), p. 278; S.P. Antonakos, *Ntokoumenta* (1983), p. 103; FO 371/21148/270; 371/23770/427; 371/23981/343.
31. Georgios K. Tsolakoglou, *Apomnemonevmata* (1959), pp. 10–11; FO 371/22356/51, H.A. Packer, 29 Jan. 1938; Nars 868.00/-, MacVeagh to Secretary of State, 3 Apr. 1939.
32. Iatrides, ed., *Ambassador MacVeagh*, pp. 93, 99, 138; E. Kalantzes, *Saranta Chronia Anamneseis* (1969), p. 32; private information in Nov. 1985 from Nikos Phloropoulos, who under Metaxas was a divisional head in the Treasury.
33. Close, 'Police', pp. 100–1.
34. FO 371/23776/336, R 12105; anon, *Tessera Chronia Diakyverneseos I. Metaxa, 1936–40* (1940), III, pp. 211–2.
35. Nars, 868.918/8, MacVeagh to Secretary of State, 9 Nov. 1937; 868.00/987, MacVeagh to Secretary of State, 22 Aug. 1936; 868.00/1974, MacVeagh to Secretary of State, 18 Feb. 1939; M.I. Malainos, *Simeiomatario tou Vasile Roumele* (1960), II, pp. 129–30.
36. FO 371/23777/8; *Elevtheron Vema*, 2 Aug. 1940, p. 1; 26 Sep. 1940, p. 2.
37. Nars, 868.00/1033, MacVeagh to Secretary of State, 18 Feb. 1938; 868.00/1040, MacVeagh to Secretary of State, 4 Apr. 1938; 868.00/1108, MacVeagh to Secretary of State, 8 Apr. 1940; FO 371/20390/-, Waterlow to Eden, 19 Aug. 1936; 371/23776/303, Palairet's biographical notes for 1938.
38. Christos Jecchinis, *Trade Unionism in Greece. A Study in Political Paternalism* (Chicago, 1967), pp. 56–7.
39. FO 371/23770/331-2, R 7655; 371/23780/231-3.
40. FO 371/20390/237, R 5447.
41. FO 371/21143/-, Waterlow to Eden, 6 Apr. 1937 ; 371/22359/3; 371/22370/391-2.
42. Nars, 868.00/1092, L.E. Reed to Secretary of State, 10 July 1939; 868.00/1095, idem, 5 Aug. 1939; FO 371/22371/93, E. Warner, 19 Dec. 1938; 371/23781/48-50, J.M. Chaplin, 4 May 1939; *Neolaia* (the EON journal); N.D. Petropoulos, *Anamneseis kai Skepseis enos Palaiou Navtikou* (1970), I, pp. 200–1.
43. Nars 868.00/1092, L.E. Reed to Secretary of State, 10 July 1939; 868.00/1095, L.E. Reed to Secretary of State, 5 Aug. 1939; Petropoulos, *Anamneseis*, I, pp. 200–1; L. Archer, *Balkan Journal* (New York, 1944), p. 57; Nicos Alivizatos, *Les Institutions Politiques de la Grèce à travers le Crises* (Paris, 1979), p. 347.
44. FO 371/22370/401-2, E.M.B. Ingram, memo of 23 June 1938; 371/23770/148, R 3993; S. Linardatos, *Tessereis Avgoustou* (1966), p. 122.

45. Nars, 868.00/1014, MacVeagh to Secretary of State, 21 Aug. 1937; FO 371/23770/275; Nicholas G.L. Hammond, *Venture into Greece* (1983), p. 185.
46. Kousoulas, *Revolution*, p. 127; Nikos Charalambides, 'To Mystikon Archeion tou Maniadakes', *Ethnikos Kyrix*, 9 Oct. 1949, pp. 1–4; 13 Oct. 1940, p. 1.
47. Nars 868.00/9-2849, H.B. Minor to Secretary of State, about an interview with Maniadakes on 27 Sept. 1949.
48. Georgios Vontitsos-Gousias, *Oi Aities gia tes Ettes* (1977), I, pp. 56–9; Linardatos, *Tessereis Avgoustou*, pp. 60–3, 395.
49. Quoted in Kousoulas, *Revolution*, p. 144; Solaro, *Istoria*, pp. 114, 119–23.
50. I. Avakumovic, *History of the Communist Party of Yugoslavia* (Aberdeen, 1964), I, pp. 138, 142; Nissan Oren, *Bulgarian Communism. The Road to Power, 1934–1944* (New York, 1944), p. 167.
51. Alexander Kitroeff, 'The Greek peasantry: from dictatorship to occupation', in Higham and Veremis, eds, *Aspects* (Athens, 1993), pp. 67–8.
52. Linardatos, *Tessereis Avgoustou*, pp. 365–72.
53. Sarandis, 'Emergence', pp. 383–7; A. Gerolymatos, 'The role of the Greek officer corps in the resistance', *Journal of the Hellenic Diaspora*, 11, 3 (Fall 1984), p. 70.
54. FO 371/23370/452-5, Waterlow to Halifax, 15 Aug. 1938 ; Linardatos, *Tessereis Avgoustou*, pp. 328–38, 346.
55. FO 371/21147/200-1, to Eden, 22 May 1937; 371/23770/287, Palairet to Halifax, 5 Aug. 1939; Kalantzes, *Saranta Chronia*, pp. 46–7.
56. Christos Zalokostas, *Chroniko tes Sklavias* (n.d.), pp. 364–5; C. Couvaras, *OSS with the Central Committee of EAM* (San Francisco, 1982), p. 81. Akronauplia, in Nauplia in the north-west Peloponnese, is an old Venetian fortress then used for imprisonment of leading cadres.
57. Close, 'Police', p. 105; FO 371/ 23370/433, 414, E.C. Hole, reports for May and June 1938.
58. FO 371/22371/106; I. Metaxas, *To Prosopiko tou Emerologio*, ed. P. Vranas (1964), vol. D1, p. 372, 6 May 1939.
59. FO 371/21150/60, Waterlow to Eden, 16 Apr. 1937; 371/23770/106, report no. 90.
60. J.M. Stevens in L. Baerentzen, ed., *British Reports on Greece* (Copenhagen, 1982), pp. 27–8; the decree was no. 875, promulgated on 22 Sept. 1937.
61. FO 371/23370/414-6, E.C. Hole to Waterlow, 6 June 1938.
62. A. Pepones, *Prosopike Martyria* (1970), pp. 11–13.
63. A. Daskalakes, *Istoria tes Ellenikes Chorophylakes* (1973), I, pp. 77–8; Antoniou, *Istoria*, III, pp. 1489, 1492; FO 371/12926/29.
64. A. Sakellariou, *Enas Navarchos Thymatai* (n.d.), I, p. 204; Metaxas Papers, file 103, memo by Papagos, 28 Jan. 1939; FO 371/22371/92/7, R 10301; G. Zaharopoulos, 'Politics and the army in post-war Greece', in Richard Clogg and George N. Yannopoulos, eds, *Greece under Military Rule* (1972), pp. 30–2.
65. John S. Koliopoulos, 'Metaxas and Greek foreign relations, 1936–41', in Higham and Veremis, eds, *Aspects*, pp. 88, 96.
66. Tsolakoglou, *Apomnemonevmata*, pp. 12–13.
67. George Seferis, *Cheirografo tou Septemvriou 1941* (1972), pp. 51–2.
68. FO 371/24910/114, Palairet to Secretary of Labour Party, 6 Dec. 1940; Linardatos, *Tessereis Avgoustou*, pp. 404, 410, 433, 438, 442; Kousoulas, *Revolution*, p. 141.
69. Gerolymatos, *Guerrilla Warfare*, p. 194.

70. A point developed in my paper *The Character of the Metaxas Dictatorship. An International Perspective* (Centre of Contemporary Greek Studies, King's College, London, 1990), Occasional Paper no. 3.
71. Nars 868.002/261, C.L. Sulzberger, memo of interview on 6 Mar. 1941.
72. D.N. Philaretos to Metaxas, 9 Oct. 1940, Metaxas Papers (General State Archives, Athens), file 34; ibid., file 43, reports from Maniadakes, Papagos, and Papademas in July 1940; FO 371/29841/90; *Italian Diplomatic Documents*, Ninth Series, vol. V, p. 268; G. Andrikopoulos, *E Rizes tou Ellenikou Fasismou* (1977), pp. 98–9; Metaxas, *Emerologio*, 3 Dec. 1940, vol. D2, p. 541.
73. John L. Hondros, *Occupation and Resistance. The Greek Agony, 1941–4* (New York, 1983), p. 41, 42–6
74. Koliopoulos, *Greece*, p. 278; John S. Koliopoulos, 'Unwanted ally: Greece and the great powers, 1939–41', *Balkan Studies*, 23, 1 (1982), p. 24; FO 371/29840/34, Palairet telegram, 19 Apr. 1941.

CHAPTER THREE

Invasion and Collapse of Authority, April 1941–March 1943

THE OLD ORDER IN DECAY

During the Second World War, the experience of enemy occupation shook the legitimacy of several regimes by undermining their authority, and exposing their inability to protect their citizens. In the longer run, this experience made the conquered peoples receptive to arguments by radicals or revolutionaries that 'the social, political, and economic order' that led to the horrors of enemy occupation was 'morally wrong.'[1] Thus the reaction of many people in conquered countries was to yearn for a radically new order after liberation. This reaction was especially strong where, as in the Balkans, the pre-war state had failed by an especially wide margin to satisfy its citizens' desire for economic development, social justice, and political participation. In Greece, the Metaxas dictatorship appeared to most people to be beyond rehabilitation; the monarchy was extremely unpopular; while the parliamentary system which preceded it was badly discredited. Agreement on an alternative regime was an insuperable problem. In the ten years before the German invasion the emotional and ideological gulf between warring parties – Venizelist, anti-Venizelist, Communist, and Metaxist – had deepened, making impossible any consensus about the system which would follow liberation.

The conquerors' harsh measures destroyed, directly or indirectly, the authority of most of the leading groups in Greek society. Retribution for having opposed Germany in two world wars came at the hands of the German army, which dominated the various and competing authorities which now occupied the country. The *Wehrmacht* handed over the greater part of the country for occupation to the Italian troops, whom all Greeks despised, while itself occupying strategic areas, consisting of the metropolitan port of Piraeus, the northern areas of central and western Macedonia,

Evros the border zone with Turkey, and most of the southern island of Crete. It let its allies effectively annexe some regions: Bulgaria got the north-east from the River Strymon in eastern Macedonia to near the Evros, with much of central Macedonia to follow in 1943. Bulgarian troops settled many of their countrymen in these lands, penalized the use of the Greek language, and drove out over 200,000 Greek inhabitants. Italy's client Albania received the adjoining territory of northern Epirus, and Italy acquired the nearby Ionian islands.

These invaders were indifferent to Greece's political survival as a nation; while most of them, including the German army, displayed total indifference also to the inhabitants' welfare. The German troops immediately after invasion seized 'all public and known private stocks of food, apparel, medical supplies, military matériel, and means of transport': this despite the fact that food shortages were obviously imminent because of disruption caused by the Albanian war. The requisitioning of transport and fuel wrecked the facilities for moving basic necessities within the country. The seizure of raw materials caused most industries to close down or operate at a small fraction of their former capacity. Troops seized valuables from private homes, and, after food stocks had disappeared, made extensive tours of villages to requisition food. In the longer term, the government budget was saddled with occupation costs which at one stage, in 1942, reached 90 per cent of national income, and caused runaway inflation which would accelerate during the occupation and continue long afterwards.[2]

As a combined result of enemy depredations and British blockade, famine soon became severe in most of the country. From 1 October 1941 to 30 September 1942 the death rate in the metropolitan area was over three times that for the same months in 1940–1, and people were literally dying in the streets. From October 1942 the famine was alleviated somewhat by the import of supplies under the auspices of the International Red Cross (IRC). The Germans themselves now became worried by the political unrest caused by economic hardship. So the German government in October 1942 sent a special mission under Hermann Neubacher to Greece which began a policy of cooperation with the Red Cross and organized the import of food. But food shortages remained serious for the rest of the occupation, especially in mountain villages which had little chance of receiving Red Cross relief. There exist some indices of destitution in the cities. The calorific intake of a labourer rarely rose above half the pre-war level even after Red Cross supplies arrived. The purchasing power of wages in relation to food in 1943–4 stood at one-sixth of the pre-war level. Serious also, in the country as a whole, were shortages of many other necessities: clothes, shoes, soap, fuel, building materials, and medical supplies. The loss of population caused by increased deaths and reduced births was later estimated by a demographer as 450,000 in the first two years of the occupation.[3]

The Germans' behaviour ensured that few Greeks willingly collaborated with them, and fewer still with any sense of ideological conviction. Some members of the quisling administrations claimed to be fascists or adhered to fascist groups. One of these was Georgios Merkoures, who was appointed Governor of the National Bank, and another was the prominent minister, General Georgios Bakos, who tried to raise a battalion to fight on the Russian front. But fascism had a restricted meaning in Greece. For example, the largest of the pro-fascist organizations, Greek Socialist Patriotic Organization (ESPO), adopted the buzz-words of family, religion, and country, which were conservative rather than fascist in implication. Although the self-styled fascist groups which had existed before the Metaxas dictatorship reappeared, they remained tiny and uninfluential, and were treated with contempt by most right-wing Greeks and by the Germans themselves. Consequently they were vulnerable to attacks by resistance groups. ESPO for example was seriously weakened in September 1942 by the blowing up of its headquarters during a meeting, with the death of its leader Dr Speros Sterodemas. Few native fascists took an important part in the civil strife later in the occupation.[4]

Economic collaborators were more important. Economic hardship divided the population between the small minority who benefited from the occupation and the great majority who suffered. Among the sufferers pre-war status distinctions tended to be levelled by common need and a common preoccupation with the search for basic necessities. About the beneficiaries one cannot generalize except like Mark Mazower to say that 'there were two positions which helped ensure enrichment − proximity to the dwindling supply of goods, and proximity to power'. The new rich certainly included people of relatively low social status before the war, and many people who earned hatred by exploiting their countrymen's needs. Some made fortunes by having their debts wiped out by inflation; by operating successfully on the highly speculative black market; or by buying cheaply the real estate and valuables which others had to sell to buy food. Indicative of the numbers of *nouveaux riches* who appeared during the occupation were the emergence of 6,500 new business enterprises, many of them industrial, and the sale of 350,000 properties and landholdings to 60,000 buyers.[5]

The resentment created by this social upheaval was naturally extensive. Among the most notorious of those who prospered were food merchants or retailers − both large-scale and small-scale operators − who bypassed the official rationing system in order to make profits on the black market. It was generally believed that government officials up to ministerial levels connived at these activities, and indeed it is difficult to see how else they could have been possible. Merchants and industrialists must have needed official tolerance in the form of orders or authorized supplies from the German authorities, or licences from the government. Generally, those businessmen with substantial capital had a better chance of obtaining such favours. In provincial towns, for example, businessmen or bankers were among the leaders of local society whose cooperation was normally sought by occupying troops. Their homes were likely for example to be selected by officers as billets, so that their connections and influence could be utilized.[6] Those without resources could benefit from the occupation by joining the ubiquitous and hated class of informers. The British officer Nicholas Hammond reported on his visit to Salonika in July 1943 that the Germans employed 'mainly youths, waiters and concierges' in this capacity. In all, the proportion of the population which in some way benefited materially from the occupation was estimated by the Germans at about ten per cent in mid-1943.[7]

To govern the country for them the occupation troops relied mainly on the Metaxist official establishment, and especially on its Germanophile elements. They preferred the collaborationist governments to consist of pliant non-entities, and indeed had little choice because no one with political talent or status was willing to serve them. The first administration was dominated by seven of Metaxas's generals under Georgios Tsolakoglou, who was prime minister until December 1942, followed by the professor of medicine Konstantinos Logothetopoulos until the following April.[8] Tsolakoglou curried favour with Germans and Greeks by formally dissolving the Metaxist youth movement, and prosecuting several of Metaxas's ministers for alleged corruption. But his ideology was very similar to that of Metaxas. In the same spirit Tsolakoglou condemned political parties and revered the words family, religion, country, and social order. Like the next two quisling prime ministers, he identified himself with the official establishment, and impressed on the police their exalted role as representatives of state authority. These appeals to the police became increasingly desperate as order deteriorated in the countryside. Tsolakoglou tried to continue Metaxas's campaign against Communism through the same agencies, the police and Security Commissions.

A major function of the collaborationist administrations was to sustain public officials, few if any of whom seem to have been removed by Tsolakoglou. The salaries of public servants and the pensions and pay of army officers remained essential claims on the state budget, and they eventually had to be raised weekly to stay in advance of inflation, and were partly replaced by food coupons. Despite the heavy burdens on the budget, the numbers of public employees were increased in an attempt to relieve unemployment.[9]

Like quisling regimes elsewhere in Europe, those in Greece justified their existence by the need to maintain essential services and to intercede with the enemy on behalf of their countrymen. As elsewhere this defence rang hollow, because they obviously had little bargaining power against the enemy. Although in their post-war apologias the three quisling prime ministers cited cases of successful intercession – for example on behalf of hostages threatened with execution – these were of little account compared with their failures. Still more damning was the fact that they assisted the enemy in the ruthless extraction of resources from their country. Greek public officials acted in an increasingly predatory and corrupt way in extracting taxation. Meanwhile they lacked many of the patronage resources which had linked pre-occupation regimes with the population, especially the geographically remote rural population: the provision for example of agricultural loans, of adequate salaries to employees, or of permits to do business.[10]

In their attempts to maintain order and public services the collaborationist prime ministers nevertheless earned much sympathy from the traditional ruling classes and from those whose appointment was controlled or influenced by the pre-war government. Most non-Communist politicians acknowledged that the quisling administrations were performing at least some valuable functions, and sympathized with their attempts to maintain property rights and the traditional social hierarchy. Also sympathetic was a range of august institutions influenced by the pre-war regime and obliged to cooperate closely with it: chambers of commerce, manufacturers' associations, and professional associations in the capital and provincial cities.[11]

Many in the official establishment acted patriotically by trying to subvert enemy rule. Metaxas's armed forces and gendarmerie had regarded German aggression as unprovoked and fought courageously enough against it. So most of them saw it as their duty to continue resistance in ways which they thought feasible. Widespread and influential resistance networks soon operated within the administration: National Revolution (EE), based in Athens, and Defenders of Northern Greece (YBE, later to become the Panhellenic Liberation Organization, PAO), based in Salonika. Each recruited hundreds of supporters from senior officials, especially army officers. Huge numbers of junior officials, such as employees of the Agricultural Bank, teachers, police, and army officers on the retired list, deserted later to resistance organizations engaged in revolt against the state.[12]

The police worked strenuously, and often at risk to their own lives, to thwart the attempts by the Italians and Bulgarians to win over ethnic minorities. The occupation forces tried to win the minorities' support by offers of various kinds: food rations, posts in the public service, employment in militia forces. Thus Bulgarian officials tried with limited success to win over the slavophone population of central and western Macedonia; Italians with much success wooed the Muslim Chams of Epirus and with little success the Romanian-speaking Koutsovlachs of the Pindus ranges. Germans wooed successfully the Turkophone refugees from Asia Minor in western Macedonia. In response to these moves, successive quisling administrations tried with little success to induce the Germans not to allow further concessions of territory to their allies or privileges to ethnic minorities. They countered the occupation forces' propaganda; warned members of the minorities not to let themselves be seduced; and kept files on those who were. Later the government and its officials saw an additional threat in the attempts by the Communist-led resistance to win over the slavophones and other minorities with its promise to them of full civic equality. Thus the quisling administrations, and the conservative resistance groups, felt a strong sense of mission to preserve Hellenism in the northern provinces. To this end they continued the assimilationist policy of Metaxas's regime, and appealed to the resentment against the minorities felt by the Greek-speaking population.[13]

Resistance to the Axis was especially hard for the gendarmerie. As in other occupied countries the conquering troops needed the native police in order to identify and locate resisters, maintain order, and extract resources such as food in the countryside. Because they were employed for these purposes the reputation of the gendarmerie in the eyes of most of the Greek population sank still lower: they now compounded their sin of service to Metaxas by that of service to the conqueror.

But the critics of the gendarmerie failed to allow for their vulnerability. If gendarmes refused German orders, loss of livelihood was the least they had to fear: torture, execution, and reprisals against their families were likely penalties. Most gendarmes helped resisters if they could get away with doing so, especially if the resisters were not Communists and sometimes even if they were. Seven hundred gendarmes defected to the main anti-Communist resistance group during the occupation; and an estimated 1,600 defected to the much larger and Communist-controlled one, although perhaps many of the latter were coerced. One index of resistance by gendarmes was the fact that 782 were executed (out of a force which at any time totalled about 14,000) during the occupation.

Few gendarmes served the conquerors willingly. Even the much-hated Special Security, the privileged and closely supervised arm of the executive, had initial reservations about collaboration. The government of the third quisling prime minister, Ioannes Ralles (1943–4), could not find a qualified officer willing to command it, and had to appoint a junior officer dismissed long before for political reasons, besides enlisting many unqualified recruits including convicted criminals. The city police (located chiefly in

Athens–Piraeus) largely avoided collaboration. The chief of its Athens branch Evangelos Evert repeatedly evaded orders to act even against Communist resisters, yet avoided dismissal by Ralles because he was valued by the British, to whose officers he gave secret assistance. The zeal which some gendarmes showed in military collaboration with the Germans later in the occupation, in 1943–4, was mainly due to hatred or fear of Communists. While trying to keep an eye on Communist activities most of the gendarmerie – including at least some in the Special Security – tried to avoid betraying them to the Germans. In particular they tried to keep out of German hands their vital files of Communist party members. This sort of police tolerance was an important condition for the growth of Communist resistance.[14]

Most of the traditional ruling classes did little or nothing to resist the enemy. Most were fairly confident that they would eventually be liberated by Britain, and assumed that there was little point in doing anything in the meantime. Some ministers and leading participants in the Metaxas regime, including Maniadakes and prominent police officials, had fled with the king to Egypt. At least one, Metaxas's confidant Diakos, took with him a fortune which he had acquired during the dictatorship, and which he revealed in a customs declaration which became notorious. The head of the exiled government, Tsouderos, being a banker not a politician, was little known to the public; nor were the people whom he chose as ministers until 1943. The British Foreign Office, like its German counterpart, preferred its client government to be weak. The king because of his aloof character aroused little loyalty even from monarchists in exile, and spent much time in a hotel in London, out of touch with his exiled government. In September 1943 the Archbishop of Athens lamented the exiled government's failure 'to take an active interest in what was happening in Greece'. A further defect, which the British authorities never did appreciate, was the exiled government's lack of legitimacy as a result of the successive coups of 1935–6. In these circumstances, the population, especially the 350,000 veterans of the Albanian war, tended to feel deserted and even betrayed by their political leaders.[15]

The overwhelming majority of professional politicians – estimated by one of them, Komnenos Pyromaglou, at about 800 – stayed in Greece during the first two years or more of the occupation. But very few participated in any sort of resistance or even relief activity, apart from some socialists, agrarians and Communists who had been insignificant in parliamentary politics. Many politicians hoped for favours from the government such as pensions, appointments, and food rations, and found it difficult to engage in any political activity. As a result of suppression by Metaxas, most were seriously out of touch with their agents, parliamentary colleagues, and voters. They could not maintain contact with them because travellers were watched and the media censored. Patronage and influence in the administration – the traditional currency of parliamentary politics – were unavailable because of the continuing suspension of parliament and the debility of the government. The personal prominence of politicians made resistance activity difficult: the police could hardly pretend to the Germans that they did not know who or where they were. If politicians did oppose the enemy, or merely go into exile – and even this move was illegal – they left their families as potential hostages. Two bourgeois politicians who did participate in resistance – George Papandreou and Panagiotes Kanellopoulos – were forced to flee abroad, and several other politicians were eventually placed under house arrest.

Limited as their options were, politicians were seriously discredited by this inactivity. To most of the population, especially to the young, their names meant little or nothing during the occupation. The long suspension of parliamentary life prevented politicians from recruiting fresh talent or learning about their countrymen's changing preoccupations and aspirations.[16]

Army officers in active status, of whom there were about 4,000 in Greece, also found it hard to do much. Although physically at liberty, having been paroled by the Germans, they felt restrained by an order of the king to avoid political activity, which in Greek conditions meant resistance activity. The 40 or so generals and 300 colonels among them were also anchored to the cities by the receipt or hope of government pay and official employment. Like politicians they were handicapped by being well known. Guerrilla activity was something for which – remarkably, in view of Greece's long tradition of patriotic banditry – they had not been professionally prepared. In its attempts to model itself on northern European armies the Greek army had neglected guerrilla warfare still more than the Yugoslav one. As Hagen Fleischer pointed out, the army's translation of Clausewitz's *On War* omitted its chapter on guerrilla warfare. When guerrilla activity spread from late 1942, many officers actually regarded participation in it as incompatible with their professional duties, because it exposed villagers to reprisals without serious prospects of weakening the enemy. Many however did take part in some sort of resistance – such as providing information to the British or helping British Commonwealth troops to escape – in those organizations which operated within the state machine. Many junior officers, and many officers on the retired list – perhaps because they were less well known or less likely to receive official favours – did return to their home villages and form resistance bands, including by mid-1942 over 1,000 officers in the Peloponnese alone. But they did not accomplish much. A growing number of active and reserve officers made the difficult trip to join the exiled government in Egypt.[17]

In general, then, traditional elites failed to offer material help or political leadership to the population at a time of extraordinary anxiety and suffering. Their failure left a vacuum which was quickly filled by the Communist Party.

THE BIRTH OF THE NATIONAL LIBERATION FRONT, EAM

Communist activity revived Phoenix-like immediately after the German invasion. There were at first a few party members at liberty, in rudimentary and dispersed groups. There were also several thousand *delosies* (those who had gained liberty by recanting) who still wanted to work with the party. After the invasion these people came under the direction of a growing number of cadres who escaped from islands or gaols because their guards received no orders to detain them or else looked the other way. Many escapees passed through Athens, and either stayed there or else were ordered to the provinces. A central committee which was generally regarded as legitimate was re-established in July and immediately exhorted members to form front organizations.[18]

Within a few weeks of the invasion party members or *delosies* had, largely on their own initiative, begun to construct front organizations which helped the destitute or prepared for resistance activity. Such bodies sprang up in scattered parts of the country under different titles. In this way what was to become the National Liberation Front (EAM) was built from the bottom upwards. Sectors of EAM established in this largely spontaneous way were National Solidarity (EA) for relief purposes, which was formed as early as May 1941; many guerrilla groups formed later in the year, of which a major purpose was to prevent requisitions by enemy troops; the village councils and tribunals which multiplied from mid-1942; and the neighbourhood committees in Athens which appeared in 1943. The trade union federation the National Workers' Liberation Front (EEAM) was established in Athens in July 1941, while another was established independently in Salonika, reflecting the traditional skill of urban cadres in this type of work. In all these ways Communists responded to pressing needs, and tended to take the most active role, while being helped by non-Communists. When EAM was established as a national umbrella organization in Athens in September, the Communist Party was still in effect leaderless, because the future leaders Giorges Siantos and Giannes Ioannides were still in gaol. The organizations in Thessaly began to be linked to EAM in December, and those in Salonika the following April. As a result of this undirected growth EAM acquired a momentum of its own, which it maintained throughout the occupation. In time, the local organizations exerted pressure for regional and then national bodies to represent them.[19]

Rank-and-file Communists acted promptly because most were experienced in underground work, and few were in doubt about the party's strategy: a continuation of the Popular Front policy adopted in 1935. Even during the two months between the invasion of Greece and the invasion of the Soviet Union there was little scope for doubt because the implication of the Nazi–Soviet pact was that Communist parties would prevent domination of the Balkans by either Britain or Germany. Most party members, as we saw, had been eager to fight in the war against Italy. As for the decision of 1935 to segregate peasants into the United Agrarian Party, this now seemed so dogmatic and irrelevant that it was spontaneously and universally nullified.[20]

The Popular Front policy also remained relevant because the quisling administrations seemed just as obviously 'fascist' in Communist terms as the Metaxas regime, though they served the interests of a different foreign patron and somewhat different groups of capitalists. They seemed similar in personnel and in spirit, similarly repressive and undemocratic, and likewise associated with a plutocratic oligarchy which in turn seemed closely linked with foreign imperialists. Still more in fact than the Metaxas regime, the quisling administrations made obvious the connection between political repression, economic inequality, and foreign domination. The Communists plausibly argued, through their own literature and that of EAM, that the pre-war and occupation regimes reflected the same long-term tendency for governments in Greece to become increasingly repressive and exclusive. Given the continued British backing for George II, and his association with Metaxas, there seemed a real prospect that a monarchical dictatorship would be restored. This diagnosis of past and current political ills was readily accepted by a majority of villagers in EAM territory, as British and American officers found in their extensive surveys during the occupation.[21]

By its role in resistance, the Communist Party turned itself from a sect into a mass party. The process was slow at first: there were reportedly over 12,000 members in December 1942, the majority of them *delosies*, then 56,000 members by mid-1943. Not until September 1943 did the secretariat of the politburo have a clear picture of the organization in all provinces. Then growth snowballed, with over 250,000 members reported by the party in June 1944, and continued rapid growth until after liberation.

The Communists acted without guidance from other Communist parties. They had no contact with the Comintern after the summer of 1939, and received no instructions from the Soviet government before June

1944. Only in 1942 did Communist delegates meet members of the Bulgarian and Yugoslav parties; and not until January 1944 did the Communist leaders have regular radio contact with Tito, the Yugoslav Communist leader. In 1941 at least some cadres were influenced by Mao Zedong's application of Popular Front strategy in China. But foreign examples had little influence except in a general way.

Eventually 670 cadres escaped from Metaxas's gaols and prison islands – some as late as July 1943. About half the remaining 1,200 were in time executed, and some starved in captivity, while the leader Zachariades was deported to Dachau concentration camp. Two of the most capable and experienced of the pre-war cadres escaped to become joint leaders. Giorges Siantos became effectively leader in November 1941, and Giannes Ioannides joined him in July 1942. Siantos, born in 1890 in Thessaly, and known affectionately in the party as 'the old man', had early in life worked as a tobacco sorter; served in the army from 1911 to 1920, becoming a sergeant; and been a member of the politburo for long periods from 1927. Ioannides, born in Bulgaria whence his family fled in 1907, had as a youth worked in shops mainly as a barber; later in the party earned the special trust of the Comintern, which appointed him to the politburo in 1931; and by 1941 was regarded as second in authority to Zachariades.

Their aptitudes were complementary. Popular in the party for his modesty and affability, Siantos had a meagre grasp of theory and suffered a sense of stigma because he had been censured by Moscow for his alleged deviation into left-wing 'fractionalism' in 1929–31. But he was much respected in the party for his common sense. Ioannides appeared to colleagues a more aloof and ruthless character, but was more respected – especially by himself – for his abilities as an organizer and strategist. Siantos became responsible for relations with other parties in EAM and for the guerrilla movement. The more retiring Ioannides became boss of the party machine. Neither enjoyed the same authority as the now legendary Zachariades.[22] The other members of the politburo, and often of the central committee, expected to be consulted about strategic decisions, although later in the occupation senior cadres were usually scattered, and consultation was hampered by the difficulties of communications and travel. For similar reasons the national leaders could not adequately control the activities of local cadres.[23]

Even with greater control over their party, Siantos and Ioannides could not have resolved a basic dilemma facing them: whether to win more allies for EAM, or whether to consolidate Communist domination over it. The Popular Front strategy implied readiness to accept cooperation with the bourgeois politicians as far right as the monarchists who had opposed Metaxas. Abroad the strategy implied readiness to accept cooperation with Britain who was accepted as an ally of the Soviet Union from July 1941. In deference to the massive prejudice that persisted against them, even for example among socially radical Venizelists, the Communist leaders concealed their control of EAM. They differed from their Yugoslav and Albanian counterparts in their attempts to woo bourgeois politicians and in forbidding members of EAM to use Communist slogans and emblems. At the different levels of EAM, Communists usually held only a minority of posts. As a result of these precautions the Communist control seems to have remained little known for much of the occupation in most rural areas, even though it soon became recognized in the political hothouse of Athens. EAM became a party unique in Greek history in achieving mass support while its leaders remained obscure.[24]

Communists continued as late as February 1944 to woo bourgeois politicians and resistance leaders, by offering them prominent positions in EAM or in its armed forces. Thus they continued the tactics which had led in 1936 to the Sophoules–Sklavainas pact, and then to cooperation with other parties against Metaxas. They concentrated on their most effective rivals among resisters; but their offers were accepted only by the Venizelist officer Stefanos Sarafis, by a few former parliamentary deputies, and by three minuscule parties: the Socialist Party of Greece (SKE), the Union of Popular Democracy (ELD), and the Agrarian Party of Greece (AKE). Although including several gifted individuals and intellectuals, these parties had no independent importance, and their following and organization were negligible. The AKE was fragmented and soon became in effect a branch of the Communist Party.

The reluctance of other politicians to join EAM can be explained by their perception of Communist control over it. Sympathetic observers of EAM like the American Greeks Leften Stavrianos and Costas Couvaras, who interviewed its representatives, concluded that Communists formed a small minority of the total members but held most key posts, especially those controlling the armed forces, the police, and administration of justice. As it spread through the country, the centralized EAM organization everywhere preceded and then flanked its apparatus of government. Thus the key figure in each locality was not the president of the elected village council organized by EAM, but the president of the EAM committee – the *ipevthinos* or 'responsible one' who was appointed from above. This official regularly called on the armed squads of the National Popular Liberation Army (ELAS) to enforce his authority, and later too on ELAS reservists and on the militia (*politophylake*)[25]

Initially the main work of the Communists' front organizations was economic relief. At first the beneficiaries of National Solidarity were the casualties of invasion: refugees, demobilized soldiers, and prisoners; but soon they included others as food and other basic necessities became scarce.

National Solidarity spread nation-wide, and its relief work became an important source of EAM's popularity. Later a source of supplies was the IRC, the work of which National Solidarity supplemented by compiling lists of the needy. Another source of supplies consisted of food stores requisitioned by the enemy or hoarded by merchants. Raids on these featured among the earliest acts of resistance and in time extended to warehouses in cities. Thus National Solidarity became a rival to the black market, which it forced the quisling administration to curb. According to its own records, National Solidarity distributed during the occupation twenty million kilos of food; gave temporary shelter to nearly half a million victims of house-burning; and operated 73 hospitals, 671 surgeries, and 1,253 pharmacies.[26]

The trade union federation of EAM was the branch to which the Communist leaders attached greatest importance in the first two years of the occupation. Here they were influenced by ideological bias in favour of wage-earners, and by a typically Greek bias in favour of cities. Thus Siantos said in 1943, 'who holds the towns will hold power over the whole of Greece', and Ioannides said, 'the matter [of control over Greece] would be decided in Athens'. In the second half of 1941 this trade union confederation began to construct an efficient organization among workers in much of the public service, in the railways, and in tobacco-processing where unions had for long been militant.[27]

In April 1942 EAM organized a strike by clerical workers in postal, telegraph, and telephone services, perhaps the first mass protest in German-occupied Europe. Thereafter civil servants continually helped resisters by channelling resources to them, and by leaking information about the economic burdens imposed by the occupation forces. Later in 1942 there were strikes in several provincial towns, and a series of mass strikes in Athens–Piraeus, some accompanied by great demonstrations. At first the strikes were designed to secure economic demands like wage increases, the payment of wages in kind, and the equitable distribution of food stocks. Thus they enforced the efforts of EA to ration food equitably. Then in March 1943 general strikes in the metropolis and several provincial cities forced the occupying authorities to withdraw published plans for conscripting people to work outside the country. Thereafter the conscription of labour even for work within Greece fell to a small fraction of its former level. A few months later there were strikes and demonstrations in Athens against the execution of hostages, and in the north against the extension of the Bulgarian zone of occupation. What enabled many of these strikes to succeed – against violence by police and collaborationist troops – was their scale and paralysis of key services. In one strike for example printing workers prevented the government from publishing decrees against the strikers; in another much of the city police in Athens participated. In demonstrations accompanying one strike the archives of the Ministry of Labour were destroyed, and in another case the prime minister Tsolakoglou was physically coerced.[28]

At the end of 1941 leading Communist cadres in Athens began planning the central direction of a guerrilla army and seeking the help of professional officers. They were hindered by the famine which forced those in Athens to devote much effort to subsistence; but they established the central staff of ELAS in February 1942. Guerrilla activity had already been started in various places, on a small scale, by non-Communists and Communists. It satisfied practical needs: to lead villagers in resisting food requisitions by German or Italian troops; to suppress rural crime, which quickly became a widespread menace to peasants; and to give a lead to villagers who in some places, especially in the Bulgarian zone and in Crete, were disposed to rebel against occupation forces. However caution was dictated by the results of a revolt against Bulgarian authorities which local Communists instigated in many villages in eastern Macedonia in late September 1941. This achieved nothing except to provoke the slaughter of several thousand civilians. For some time thereafter, cadres tried to avoid direct attacks on Axis troops, and concentrated on constructing a civilian organization that could eventually support guerrilla bands.

After preliminary surveys to determine which areas would be suitable, the party leaders in Athens sent a middle-ranking cadre, Ares Velouchiotes, to organize bands of guerrillas (*andartes*) in his native Roumeli in April 1942, and thereafter he dominated the *andartiko* until the party leaders established direct control over it from March 1943. Later in 1942 the party leadership established other bands in the Peloponnese, Thessaly, Macedonia, and Thrace. Initially they won over villagers by organizing resistance to the government's increasingly systematic attempts to impose levies on agricultural produce. Meanwhile a former army officer and representative of the rival resistance group the National Democratic Greek League (EDES), Napoleon Zervas, began guerrilla warfare at British instigation in Epirus. In October ELAS and EDES bands numbered many hundreds, and perhaps some thousands by December, and were making small raids on food stores, police stations, lines of communication, and on units of Italian troops. On 25 November they undertook their first major operation. A combined ELAS–EDES force under British command breached the railway viaduct over the Gorgopotamos river (90 miles northeast of Athens), a feat which greatly encouraged resistance activities throughout the country. Thereafter the guerrilla bands grew fast, and the Communist leadership attached increasing importance to them.[29]

An unplanned result of guerrilla warfare was the reconstruction of local government in the mountains. This was necessary because *andartes* depended for sustenance on the villages among which they moved, while cutting them off from the official administration by forcing state officials to flee. Thus *andarte*-controlled territory or 'free Greece' became divided from German- or Italian-controlled territory, which steadily dwindled from the second half of 1942, and by mid-1943 was reduced to the plains. From October 1942 guerrilla bands began in central Roumeli to encourage each village to elect a council in place of the one appointed by Metaxas's regime, and also to elect a new institution, a people's court. There are indications that, as in other cases of grassroots EAM organization, this process was in some places spontaneous rather than Communist-inspired. Certainly it spread rapidly to other regions, including those controlled by the rival resistance organization EDES. Soon codes of regulations for the new institutions were compiled by the EAM armed force, ELAS, for entire regions.

By early 1943 the ELAS-led *andartiko* was fulfilling popular needs in large areas. The new organs of local government corresponded to local wants and customs, and villagers participated readily in the elective institutions. The community councils were – unlike the pre-war ones – autonomous in most of their activities and so encouraged local initiative. The elected people's courts met a long-felt need for arbitration which was quick, free, accessible, and intelligible because it functioned in the demotic form of the language. Another service which was probably popular was a police which was locally controlled and not an agent of the national government. Village communities provided *andartes* in return with an independent economic base.[30]

EAM's initial message to villagers was a simple and populist patriotism. Guerrilla warfare was presented as a continuation of a series of patriotic liberation struggles such as that in Macedonia at the start of the century. The appeal by EAM to patriotic tradition was also shown in the mass demonstrations in the cities on the anniversaries of the war of independence against the Ottoman empire on 25 March 1821, and of the rejection of Mussolini's ultimatum on 28 October 1940. Spokesmen for EAM pointed out the similarities between their village organizations and those which prevailed in the 1820s.

Examples of the *andartes'* respect for traditional feelings was Ares' initial pretence that he was an army major. Disrespect for the church by Communists seems to have been uncommon and was condemned by the party. According to EAM spokesmen the majority of priests supported them, and some certainly became *ipevthinoi*; while on the other hand there were priests who opposed EAM without reprisal. The authority of the clergy in matters of marriage and divorce was respected. The people's courts were ordered to comply with existing civil and criminal codes.[31]

EAM authorities also respected property rights, as they had to in a rural society dominated by small-scale property owners. Therefore rent was paid to the owners of estates which were allotted for cultivation to landless peasants. Many people who derived their wealth from sheep and goats were grateful to EAM for suppressing brigandage. In time though the tendency was for better-off villagers to be antagonized by EAM's forced taxation, its requisitions, and its defence of wage-earners and landless labourers.[32]

Where the Communist Party (KKE) offended vested interests, for example in advocating the establishment of demotic as the official language and the full equality of women, it was likely to win support in areas vital to it. Both were measures of liberation for large sectors of society. For the uneducated majority of the population, the establishment of demotic removed a barrier to full citizenship. For all women except a small, educated minority, the systematic provision for participation in EAM offered a means of escape from domestic tutelage: a feature almost non-existent in other Greek resistance organizations, and an expression of Marxist–Leninist policy. It enabled masses of uneducated women to undertake, for the first time, responsible work outside the home. Except for the trade unions, the sections of EAM in which women were most likely to participate were those which required their traditional domestic skills: the commissariat, relief, nursing, and teaching. Very few women rose to positions of political or military responsibility. Nevertheless, at least some women participated in every activity, including military combat and political discussion. Consequently, EAM brought about a change in many families that was revolutionary. Women were treated with respect in grassroots organizations; men's monopoly of political discussion was broken, and the peasants' traditional relegation of heavy, menial work to women was condemned. EAM leaders attached much importance to their steps towards the emancipation of women; and conversely it was an important motive for the growing opposition which EAM aroused, especially in villages least affected by modern influences.[33]

Another under-privileged group attracted by EAM consisted of the slavophones, the majority of whom, after mid-1943, turned to EAM because it let them maintain their organization, the Slav-Macedonian Popular Liberation Front (SNOF), their schools and armed detachments, and communicate with compatriots across the frontier. They shared fully EAM's feelings about the Metaxas regime. A British officer reported in 1944 that to 'almost all' the many slavophones near Kastoria this regime was 'a bitter memory'. But SNOF's secessionist inclinations made it an unruly ally for EAM. In October 1944 its armed forces, numbering about 1,300, mutinied against ELAS and departed to Yugoslavia; and in November some of them tried to capture Florina, on the Greek side of the frontier, and clashed with ELAS.[34]

The Communist leaders' greatest sacrifice of principle was to accept British patronage of the resistance and the prospect of British hegemony after the liberation. Here they had to overcome their own repugnance for British imperialism and defer to the Anglophile feelings of apparently the great majority of the population including the non-Communists of whom EAM was chiefly composed. Thus the head of the British Military Mission, C. M. Woodhouse, like his colleagues everywhere, found early in 1944 that the rank and file of ELAS 'with a few fanatical exceptions, are loyal allies'.[35] British prestige was boosted by the BBC broadcasts which were the main source of news about the war, and were more clearly received than German broadcasts.

As EAM acquired broader governmental responsibilities, its programme became more specific and in certain respects more radical. 'The programme of popular democracy', based on the resolutions of the sixth central committee plenum of January 1934, was published in a Communist newspaper in January–April 1943 and then circulated in pamphlet form. Welfare services were free: a wartime necessity because much of the population was destitute, but clearly too intended as the basis of post-war policy. EAM encouraged the recipients of services provided by the quisling government to demand that they too be free: thus it encouraged university students to demand free education. EAM authorities took harsh measures against exploitative employers and landlords, and frequently against food merchants whom they deemed to be profiteers. The taxation imposed by EAM authorities was progressive. Thus agricultural produce was taxed on a graduated scale, with those living at subsistence level being exempted. All these measures were embodied in the legislation of the provisional government which EAM was to establish in March 1944 (of which more in the next chapter). This authority explicitly outlawed the profession of idle rentier; implicitly guaranteed work for all; and decreed a minimum wage. It also proclaimed equal pay and political rights for women. The nationalization of major industries and expropriation of landed estates were left until after the war.[36]

EAM assemblies, especially the parliament convened in May 1944 by the provisional government, were a forum in which long-term plans for economic development were discussed. The interest in economic development extended beyond the ranks of EAM, and was stimulated not only by the Communists' ideology, but also by the propaganda of the western Allies. The student Anastasios Pepones, who opposed EAM, recalled how as a student he was encouraged by British radio broadcasts to look forward to economic and social progress after liberation, presumably to be financed by Western aid. Villagers under EAM were aroused as never before to discuss means of economic development. Some observers report-

ed that instead of complaining about who had stolen whose goats or pota-
toes, they were starting to talk about agricultural manuals, tractors,
hospitals, and schools.[37] Here we have an example of the success of political leaders during the Second World War, apparent also in Britain, in
raising the expectations of participants by their promises of a better world
after the war.

In its inspiring combination of national liberation, social justice, economic development, democratic participation, and gender equality, the
EAM programme invites comparison with those of contemporary
Communist-led movements in Yugoslavia and China, which were precur-
sors of national liberation struggles in the 1960s and 1970s in various
countries of Africa. As in those cases, the programme won immense popular support and inspired dedicated service. This moral strength made
possible the movement's expansion. EAM aroused an enthusiastic response
in all regions, even among people with whom the Communist leaders had
little contact, such as the inhabitants of Evros on the Turkish border and
the exiled army in Egypt. This sense of purpose gave EAM a cohesion and
morale which were an important source of strength, especially noticeable
in conflicts between its forces and other guerrilla groups.[38]

In time EAM's social services attracted many professional people, who
acted in an idealistic spirit of patriotism and service to their fellow countrymen. It recruited some eminent surgeons and educational authorities, who
participated in its social services, and eminent intellectuals and writers, who
were inspired by its social vision. But it recruited few from the highest
ranks of the academic, legal, or clerical professions because these were
closely associated with the anti-Venizelist establishment. This weakness
among established elites and politicians delayed its attempt to establish a
provisional government. The professor, Alexandros Svolos, whom the
Communist leaders eventually persuaded to head this government, suc-
cinctly described EAM as 'young in age, rich in ideals and poor in
experience'.[39]

The higher-ranking army officers, from colonel upwards, who joined
ELAS consisted overwhelmingly of Venizelists in reserve status, because for
them ELAS provided a means of returning to their profession and continuing their opposition to the Metaxist establishment. Eminent figures among
them, such as Sarafis, Bakirtzes, and Mantakas, had adopted social–democratic ideas after the purge of 1935. In the lower ranks of all professions,
especially lawyers and teachers, EAM won much support; and such people
provided the administrative talent vital to EAM's elaborate organization.
There was for example a high-school teacher of literature who single-
handedly built up the EAM organization in the Aegean island of Euboea.
EAM supporters were very numerous indeed among clerical workers and

lower-ranking civil servants, because they were pauperized by inflation and literate enough to respond to EAM's intellectual appeal.

Like the Metaxas dictatorship, EAM mobilized young people down to primary school age, whom it enlisted in mixed-sex movements for youth and children. However it succeeded better than the Metaxas regime in arousing spontaneous enthusiasm, in which patriotism was the major component. As in other countries, young people proved especially ardent in resistance, presumably because they were more idealistic, impressionable, and impulsive than adults, and did not feel that they had so much to lose. For these reasons, EAM attracted many students of universities and secondary schools, including the offspring of wealthy and high-status families.[40]

The success of EAM in organizing white-collar and blue-collar workers, and the opposition to it of the rich and respectable, gave it the character of a class movement in the larger towns. Wealthier employers, industrialists, merchants, and bankers were condemned by Communist and EAM ideology as exploiters and representatives of foreign capitalist interests. They were alienated by EAM's success in trade union organization, its advocacy of progressive taxation, and EAM raids on storehouses of merchants accused of black marketeering. EAM also took over the police's pre-war function of controlling prices of basic necessities. Rich people were commonly subjected by EAM to demands for protection money. In fact some of the largest donors to EAM were businessmen making profits from contracts for the Germans and reinsuring themselves against the risk of German departure. On the other hand, many businessmen through fear of EAM contributed lavishly to the funding of Greek collaborationist troops. When for example these troops paraded through Athens on New Year's Day 1944, they were applauded by inhabitants of the wealthier districts.[41] The difference in social tone between EAM and its opponents in the capital was obvious in street demonstrations. But EAM was in few places a truly proletarian movement, partly because of the absence in Greece of a clear distinction between blue-collar workers, artisans, small employers, small retailers, and café owners. On the margins of the capitalist class were small-scale employers and retailers who belonged integrally to communities dependent on EAM's welfare services and dominated by its methods of coercion. Also favourable to EAM were locally prominent businessmen in some communities dominated by EAM – for example in Sterea Ellada, the Thessalian plains, Euboea, and the eastern Aegean island of Lesbos. In some of these cases, support for EAM apparently became identified with regional loyalty.[42] Communists referred to EAM supporters as 'the popular strata', describing them more specifically as a coalition of higher and lower professionals, artisans, clerical workers, manual workers, and peasants.

COMMUNIST STRATEGY

The Communist leaders faced increasing difficulty in reconciling this radical and militant movement with their need to win bourgeois allies and cooperate with the British. In his speech to the party's national congress in December 1942, Siantos referred to a three-stage strategy, which has been analysed by George Alexander and John Loulis.[43] According to the congress resolution adopted in compliance with Siantos's speech, 'the realization of the immediate political aim of our party – national liberation and solution of the internal problem [i.e. the choice of political system] through popular rule – constitutes at this precise moment the only revolutionary position'. This complied with the Popular Front policy announced by Zachariades in September 1935. The Popular Front now took the form of EAM, which according to Siantos in his speech took advantage of the 'revolutionary tendencies' created by the conditions of the occupation, 'not only among workers and peasants [the main revolutionary classes according to established ideology], but also among the petty bourgeois popular strata, including professional people, technicians, intellectuals and artists'. Siantos presented EAM as dynamic and revolutionary in its potential, and here he was realistic, because it was mobilizing masses of the poorer socio-economic groups in town and country against the wealthy and powerful. Thus Siantos made clear his opposition to the desire of most politicians to restore any of the pre-war bourgeois regimes, and his belief that EAM was a stage towards the rapid achievement of socialism. This was because the current strategy 'opens broadly the road towards the realization of the ulterior strategic aims of our party – the establishment of popular democracy as defined by the sixth plenum of the central committee of January 1934'. Popular democracy was the second stage referred to by Siantos, and had been defined in 1934 as 'a democratic dictatorship of the working class and the peasants with a soviet form' which would carry out an 'intensely rapid' transition from the bourgeois-democratic stage to Siantos's third stage, the 'proletarian socialist' stage of the revolution. To emphasize that he still took the 1934 definition literally, Siantos now reiterated that 'popular democracy . . . constitutes a stage of rapid transition towards socialism, that is the abolition of every kind of economic, political and intellectual servitude'.[44]

In taking Siantos literally, Alexander and Loulis make Communist strategy seem too rigid and simple. They fail to point out that the multi-stage strategy of Marxist parties allowed much flexibility in practice. There are examples in their history in which a theoretically transitional stage continued indefinitely, such as the bourgeois-democratic phase of the German Social Democrats in the early twentieth century, or the socialist phase of the Communist Party of the Soviet Union after the 1930s. At least one leading Communist, Metsos Partsalides, argued later that the Popular Front stage was being similarly prolonged. There was also scope for disagreement about the political system appropriate to the current stage. Should the institutions created by EAM be regarded as the prototype of Popular Democracy and therefore revolutionary? This interpretation was implied by Siantos's speech in December 1942, and by later announcements of party policy, such as the pamphlet by Ioannides's close colleague Demetrios Glenos. This view was also advocated by the secretary of EAM from its inception until August 1944, Thanases Chatzes. Or should EAM be treated merely as a political party which would participate after liberation in a revived parliamentary system? This more moderate, reformist, interpretation was favoured by Ioannides and Partsalides. According to Chatzes's history of EAM, the division between the two lines opened up in May 1943 within the core of the leadership, the secretariat of the politburo. Chatzes complained about Ioannides's attempts to extinguish 'the revolutionary soul' of EAM, and in particular to prevent revolutionary experiments by its organs of local government. Ioannides's view was however commonly expressed by party members: for example the ELAS commanders Thanases Metsopoulos and Giorgios Blanas on different occasions told British liaison officers that it was the agreed policy of EAM. Such a version of EAM policy was necessitated by the Communists' periodic attempts to cooperate with the government-in-exile and its British patrons. Thus the party's leaders were deeply ambivalent about their strategy. The party continued until the Varkiza agreement of February 1945 to waver between the revolutionary and reformist lines.[45]

There was also a difference between the Communist and non-Communist interpretations of the democratic elections which all agreed were to be held after liberation. While non-Communists apparently took democracy as meaning simply freedom from dictatorship, Communists interpreted it in its Leninist sense as consisting of regimented mass participation. While the enemy occupation continued this disagreement did not matter to EAM supporters; and the novelist George Theotokas could say, 'No one can explain what People's Democracy means nor even cares.'[46]

In practice however the revolutionary line prevailed because party cadres tended to treat EAM as a revolutionary system of government. The cadres who planned the construction of its major branches in the early months evidently intended them to displace official institutions. The EAM trade union confederation for example replaced its official pre-war counterpart, and in Salonika occupied the same building. The cadres and their military officers who began to assemble a central staff of ELAS from November 1941 envisaged it from the start as a regular army, which would acquire professional officers and an elaborate hierarchy. As British officers repeatedly complained, such a body did not meet their need for decentralized and flexible guerrilla groups. ELAS officers such as its military commander Stefanos Sarafis countered that the purposes of ELAS included the liberation of Athens and the prevention of a right-wing dictatorship.[47] The village councils and people's courts displaced their official counterparts. The village councils demanded the establishment of regional ones, and these in time demanded a national parliament and government. The provisional government, when it appeared in March 1944, behaved like a legitimate one, with ministers, an official gazette to publish decrees, and a currency. It presided over a comprehensive range of public services: education, health, police, postal and telephone systems, newspapers, agricultural cooperatives, all funded by a regular system of taxation. Communist cadres welcomed its appearance by announcing that 'the people in arms had acquired its revolutionary authority' and arranging discussions among troops of reconstruction after liberation. Ioannides's colleague Demetrios Glenos told the doyen of bourgeois politicians Themistocles Sophoules, in September 1943, that EAM, and its projected provisional government, were there to stay and that other parties would have to join them. Thus the Communist leaders were letting their policy be influenced by the partly spontaneous development of EAM.[48]

Another vital aspect of the Communists' practice was their generally intolerant attitude towards other political groups and towards dissidents in their own ranks. Siantos sanctioned this intolerance in his speech to the national congress in December 1942, when he portrayed the Communists as surrounded by enemies. Thus he claimed that they were obliged to defend themselves against ruthless attacks – sometimes in cooperation with the Germans – by supporters of the king, the government-in-exile and the former Metaxas dictatorship. He also warned the republican politicians that if they persisted in their hostility to the Communists and EAM they were 'consciously or unconsciously strengthening the foreign conqueror, and the vigilant Greek people will know full well how to repay such politicians as they deserve'. Siantos's distrust of bourgeois (i.e. non-socialist) politicians later struck a close and sympathetic observer, Professor Angelos Angelopoulos, as deeply rooted and obsessive. Dissidents within the Communist Party – Trotskyist, Archeio-Marxist, and self-styled leftist – were attacked by Siantos in his speech as 'scum' and 'enemies of the people'. At the tenth plenum of the central committee in January 1944 the Communist leaders were still more suspicious, denouncing politicians and resistance groups outside EAM as associated with the quisling government.[49]

Socialist allies in EAM found the Communists' dogmatism and autocratic ways hard to take. In 1942 some socialists like Dionysios Benetatos withdrew from EAM in protest against Communist dominance and were publicly denounced and libelled by Communists in reprisal. The socialists of note, including Alexandros Svolos and Elias Tsirimokos, seceded in the next three years. Tsirimokos, was quoted as saying in August 1945:

> We have experienced for four years what the KKE means by cooperation in a political coalition . . . We know the secret directions which have for some time been given and which reach prisoners in gaol, how EAM requires this and the KKE requires that and 'don't ask questions' and 'they've deserted to the reactionaries' and 'Svolos is on the wrong lines' and 'Tsirimokos has gone wrong' and 'perhaps he's working for the [British] Intelligence Service' and other such allegations.[50]

The grassroots organizations established by rank-and-file Communists behaved in the same spirit from 1941 onwards. In most localities they tried in time to take over or destroy all rivals within reach, often coming to blows with them. Pretexts were easy to find when enemy informers were indeed ubiquitous, and resistance groups tended to compete for scarce resources levied from the communities among whom they lived. But there was a common mentality underlying these attacks: intolerance derived from Marxist–Leninist ideology, and paranoia engendered by the bitter experiences of persecution before the occupation. Those who before the occupation resisted police pressure to recant did so by virtue of their inner conviction and their discipline. Those who had succumbed to such pressure wanted to avenge their humiliation and prove again their value to the party. Both categories had risen in the party hierarchy by their ruthlessness. These qualities led them to persecute followers who were charged with dissidence, as well as people who tried to withdraw from EAM or who refused to join it. A historian of and former participant in EAM recently described thus the attitude of the Communist leadership to other resistance groups: ' . . . dominated by its one-party viewpoint and by the arrogance of power, [it] did not recognize their existence, or their freedom of action, or their rights, when they had them. Nor – still more to be condemned – did it respect the sacrifices of their best fighters.'[51]

Communists' ruthlessness can be explained also by the lack of theoretical training among most junior cadres – a defect emphasized by both Siantos and Zachariades – which hindered them from seeing the conflict between terror tactics and the Popular Front policy. Another factor, lack of political experience among rank-and-file supporters outside the party, seems to have been a reason for 'the extraordinary severity' which even sympathetic observers found in the people's courts.[52]

The mutual hostility between EAM and other bodies was exacerbated by the breakdown of communications during the occupation. Domestic news ceased to circulate in most of the country except by word of mouth or through the news sheets issued by resistance groups, chiefly EAM. The rank-and-file members of each group knew nothing about other groups save what their leaders told them. The British officer Nicholas Hammond described the surprise of members of an anti-Communist band on finding that their ELAS captors were people similar to themselves.[53]

These features of EAM conflicted with its strategy of seeking the broadest possible range of allies. Invitations to other politicians tended to be accompanied incongruously by threats, like that of Glenos to Sophoules. The formation by EAM of a hierarchy of quasi-governmental organizations made it seem less capable of co-existence with other political parties. The terrorism and violence common among Communist cadres were by early 1943 frightening politicians in Athens and Egypt.

Within two years the German occupation created a situation similar in certain ways to that which existed in much of Yugoslavia. The occupation forces were harsh enough to destroy state authority and wreck the economy, yet could not impose an alternative political and economic order. The outcome was near-anarchy, which left traditional elites bereft of power, but gave ample scope to the organizing abilities of the small Communist Party. This proceeded to create a dynamic organization of a new kind, which soon won fervent supporters and made ardent enemies in many parts of the country.

NOTES

1. L. P. Morris, *Eastern Europe since 1945* (1984), p. 22.
2. Stavros B. Thomadakis, 'Black markets, inflation, and force in the economy of occupied Greece', in John O. Iatrides,ed., *Greece in the 1940s. A Nation in Crisis* (1981), p. 65; John L. Hondros, 'Greece and the German occupation', in David H. Close, ed., *The Greek Civil War. Studies of Polarization* (1993), p. 45; Mark Mazower, *Inside Hitler's Greece. The Experience of Occupation, 1941–4* (New Haven, 1993), pp. 23–5.
3. Close, 'Introduction', and Hondros, 'Greece', in Close, ed., *The Greek Civil War*, pp. 8, 46.
4. Hagen Fleischer, *Stemma kai Svastika. E. Ellada tes Katoches kai tes Antistases* (1988), pp. 359–60; Hondros, 'Greece', in Close,ed., *The Greek Civil War*, p. 45; Hagen Fleischer, 'Contacts between German occupation authorities and the major Greek resistance organizations. Sound tactics or collaboration?', in Iatrides, ed., *Greece in the 1940s*, pp. 52, 350; John L. Hondros, *Occupation and Resistance. The Greek Agony, 1941–4* (New York, 1983), pp. 26, 91, 97; Nars, RG 59, R & A (Research & Analysis), no. 872, report, 26 Apr. 1943; Mazower, *Inside Hitler's Greece*, p. 339.
5. Mazower, *Inside Hitler's Greece*, p. 61; Thomadakis, 'Black markets', and K. Vergopoulos, 'The emergence of the new bourgeoisie, 1944–52', in Iatrides,

ed., *Greece in the 1940s*, pp. 73, 302; C. Hadziiossif, 'Economic stabilization and political unrest: Greece 1944–7', in Lars Baerentzen, John O. Iatrides, Ole L. Smith, eds., *Studies in the History of the Greek Civil War, 1943–9* (Copenhagen, 1987), pp. 32–3.

6. Nikos A. Antonakeas, *Pos Eidon ton Apelevtherotikon Agona kata ta Eta 1941–5* (1945), pp. 28, 34–5; P. I. Papathanasiou, ed., *Gia ton Elleniko Vorra. Makedonia 1941–4* 2 vols (1988), I, p. 104; Angelos Elephantes, *E Epangelia tes Adynates Epanastases* (1976), p. 217.

7. FO 371/37204/25, R 7213; Phoivos N. Gregoriades, *To Antartiko* 6 vols (1964), III, pp. 312–14; Elevtheria, 31 Jan. 1965, p. 15; H. Fleischer, 'Nea stoicheia gia te schese Germanikon archon katoches kai tagmaton asphaleias', *Mnemon* 8 (1980–2), p. 192; Hondros, *Occupation*, p. 145.

8. Fleischer, pp. 118, 354–5, 358, 363; Hondros, *Occupation*, pp. 78, 267; Konstantinos Logothetopoulos, *Idou e Aletheia* (1948), p. 162.

9. Georgios K. Tsolakoglou, *Apomnemonevmata* (1959), pp. 162, 174; Nikolaos A. Anagnostopoulos, *E Euvoia sten Katochen* 3 vols (1950–73), I, p. 281; Laird Archer, *Balkan Journal* (New York, 1944), p. 213; William H. McNeill, *The Greek Dilemma. War and Aftermath* (New York, 1947), p. 44; Georgios I. Ralles, *Koitazontas: Piso* (1993), pp. 295–6.

10. Mazower, *Inside Hitler's Greece*, pp. 110–11.

11. Tsolakoglou, *Apomnemonevmata*, p. 163; Logothetopoulos, *Idou*, p. 33; Antonakeas, *Pos*, pp. 30–2; Georgios Ralles, *O I. Ralles Omilei ek tou Taphou* (1947), pp. 23–4, 78.

12. Papathanasiou, ed., *Elleniko Vorra*, I, pp. 46–7, 312–13; Antonakeas, *Pos*, pp. 11–12; Georgos Margarites, *Apo ten Etta sten Exergese* (1993), p. 159.

13. Lazaros A. Arseniou, *E Thessalia sten Antistase* 2 vols (1977), I, p. 69; Apostolos Daskalakes, *Istoria tes Ellenikes Chorophylakes* (1973), I, pp. 249–50, 265–8, 272, 286–7, 290, 294; Papathanasiou, ed., *Elleniko Vorra*, I, pp. 20–3; Ralles, *Ralles*, p. 141; Stefan Troebst, 'E drasis tes "ochrana" stous nomous Kastorias, Florinas kai Pellas, 1943–4', in Chagen Flaiser (= H. Fleischer) and Nikos Svoronos, eds, *Praktika tou Diethnous Istorikou Synedriou. E Ellada 1936–44. Diktatoria, Katoche, Antistase* (1989), p. 259.

14. Mazower, *Inside Hitler's Greece*, pp. 325, 346; Daskalakes, *Istoria*, I, pp. 52, 289; D.G. Katsimangles, *E Anelixis tou Astynomikou Thesmou kai tes Astynomikes Epistemes sten Elladi* (1974), p. 151; Ralles, *Ralles*, pp. 116–17; Leonidas Spaes, *Penenta Chronia Stratiotes sten Yperesia tou Ethnous kai tes Demokratias* (1970), I, p. 262; Georges Zoides, D. Kailas et al., *St'Armata! St'Armata! Chroniko tes Ethnikes Antistases, 1941–5* (1967), p. 235; FO 371/37204/25, R 7213.

15. Tsolakoglou, *Apomnemonevmata*, p. 159; Procopis Papastratis, 'Ta astika kommata kai e exoriste kyvernese', in Flaiser and Svoronos, eds, *Praktika*, pp. 530–1; P. Papastratis, *British Policy towards Greece during the Second World War, 1941–4* (Cambridge, 1984), pp. 90–1; FO 371/37206/136, R 10450; Margarites, *Apo*, pp. 49–52.

16. Komnenos Pyromaglou, *E Ethnike Antistase* (1975), p. 330; Antonakeas, *Pos*, pp. 30–1, 321.

17. Fleischer, *Stemma*, p. 227; Christos Zalokostas, *Chroniko tes Sklavias* (n.d.), p. 152; André Gerolymatos, 'The role of the Greek officer corps in the resistance', *Journal of the Hellenic Diaspora* 11, 3 (Fall 1984), pp. 70–3; Spaes, *Penenta Chronia*, pp. 272–3; Alexandros Mazarakis–Ainian, *Apomnemonevmata* (1948), p. 652.

18. Antonio Solaro, *Istoria tou Kommounistiko Kommatos Ellados* (1975), pp. 123–4;

KKE, *Deka Chronia Agones, 1935–45* (1977), p. 120; Arseniou, *Thessalia*, I, pp. 21–2.

19. Thanases Chatzes, *E Nikephora Epanastase pou Chatheke* 3 vols (1977–9), I, pp. 68–9, 76–8, 93–4; vol. II, p. 339; Arseniou, *Thessalia*, I, pp. 1–2, 30, 36; Anastasios Pepones, *Prosopike Martyria* (1970), p. 50; Demetrios I. Zepos, *Laike Dikaiosyne* (1945), pp. 1–2; Zoides, Kailas et al., eds, *St'Armata!*, p. 235; Vasiles Bouras, *E Politike Epitrope Ethnikes Apelevtheroseos* (1983), p. 53; KKE, *Keimena tes Ethnikes Antistases* 2 vols (1981), I, pp. 84–5; M. Partsalides, *Diple Apokatastase tes Ethnikes Antistases* (1978), pp. 17–18.

20. Giorgios Katephores, 'Ethnika kai taxika stoicheia sten politike tou KKE', in Flaiser and Svoronos, eds, *Praktika*, p. 501; Arseniou, *Thessalia*, I, pp. 30–1; Chatzes, *Nikephora*, I, pp. 93–4.

21. Lars Baerentzen, ed., *British Reports on Greece* (Copenhagen, 1982), pp. 15, 26–7; Costas G. Couvaras, *OSS with the Central Committee of EAM* (San Francisco, 1981), pp. 22–3.

22. Chatzes, *Nikephora*, I, pp. 148–9, 296–8, 457–8; III, p. 343; Couvaras, *OSS*, pp. 80–2.

23. John C. Loulis, *The Greek Communist Party, 1941–4* (1982), p. 45; Ole Smith, 'The "first round" – civil war during the occupation', in Close, ed., *The Greek Civil War*, p. 69; Giannes Ioannides, *Anamneseis. Provlemata tes Politikes tou KKE sten Ethnike Antistase, 1941–5*, ed. Alekos Papapanagiotou (1970), pp. 25–55, 170, 526; Chatzes, *Nikephora*, I, p. 459; II, p. 203; Arseniou, *Thessalia*, I, p. 30; Peter J. Stavrakis, *Moscow and Greek Communism, 1944–9* (Ithaca, 1989), pp. 7, 11–12, 21–2; Spyros Linardatos, *Tetarte Avgoustou* (1966), pp. 404–6, 414, 425, 433–4, 444; Chrestos Tyrovouzes, *Autodioikese kai 'Laike' Dikaiosyne* (1991), pp. 285, 338.

24. M.E. Phatsea, 'E politike typou kai propagandas tou KKE kata ton B' Pangkosmio Polemo', in Flaiser and Svoronos, eds, *Praktika,* pp. 491–3; Zalokostas, *Chroniko*, p. 150; Thanases Metsopoulos, *To 30 Syntagma tou ELAS* 4th edn (1987), pp. 124, 127; Anagnostopoulos, *Euvoia*, II, p. 326.

25. Leften S. Stavrianos, 'The Greek National Liberation Front (EAM): a study in resistance organization and administration', *Journal of Modern History* 24, 1 (1952), p. 47; Peltekis Papers, Benaki Museum, Athens, file 6, G1, pp. 7–8, reports for late 1943 by British liaison officers, M. Ward and R.P. McMullen, on mountains of the central Pindus and Peloponnese respectively.

26. Fleischer, *Stemma*, p. 145; Zoides, Kailas et al., eds, *St'Armata!*, pp. 75–6, 114, 223, 502; A.E. Laiou, 'The resistance in Evros', *Journal of the Hellenic Diaspora* 11, 3 (1984), pp. 35–6; Pepones, *Prosopike*, p. 59; Thomadakis, 'Black markets', in Iatrides, ed., *Greece in the 1940s*, pp. 76–9.

27. E. Barker, *British Policy in South-East Europe in the Second World War* (1976), pp. 189–90; Ioannides, *Anamneseis*, p. 174; EAM, *Pos Prepei na Doulevei e Gynaika sto EAM* (1943), p. 5.

28. A. Augoustidis, 'EEAM, the workers' resistance', *Journal of the Hellenic Diaspora*, 11, 3 (1984), pp. 61–2, 65; Hondros, *Greek Agony*, pp. 152–3; Zoides, Kailas et al., eds, *St'Armata!*, pp. 107, 111–16; Chatzes, *Nikephora* , I, pp. 135–6.

29. Gregoriades, *Antartiko*, V, pp. 184–5; Zoides, Kailas et al., eds, *St'Armata!,* p. 114; Couvaras, *OSS*, pp. 30–1; P. Lagdas, 'Thymamai ton Are', *Ethnike Antistase* 16 (1978), pp. 40–2; Ioannides, *Anamneseis*, p. 521; Mazower, *Inside Hitler's Greece*, p. 135; Margarites, *Apo*, pp. 156, 163–7.

30. Politike Epitrope tes Ethnikes Apelevtheroseos, *Episema Keimena. Praxeis kai*

85

Apophaseis (n.d.), p. 29; Mazower, *Inside Hitler's Greece*, pp. 269, 270–3; Margarites, *Apo*, p. 203.

31. Fleischer, *Stemma*, p. 233; Couvaras, *OSS*, p. 57; Baerentzen, ed., British Reports, p. 33; Zoides, Kailas et al., eds, *St'Armata!*, pp. 149, 530–1; Stavrianos, 'Greek National Liberation Front', p. 51; J. Tomasevich, 'Yugoslavia during the Second World War', in W.S. Vuvinich, ed., *Contemporary Yugoslavia. Twenty Years of Socialist Experiment* (Berkeley, 1969), pp. 115–16.

32. Nars, RG 226, no. 119202, 5 Mar. 1945; *ibid.*, entry 154, box 40, folder 620, A.M.M. Wines to P. West.

33. Couvaras, *OSS*, pp. 73–5, 120–1; Janet C. Hart, 'Empowerment and political opportunity: Greek women in resistance, 1941–64', unpublished Cornell University PhD dissertation, 1991, pp. 169–70, 182–6, 191–4, 202; Hagen Fleischer, 'EAM 1941–7: an approach for reconsideration', unpublished paper presented to the Lehrman Institute conference at Vilvorde, Copenhagen, 3–5 June 1987; EAM, *Pos Prepei*, p. 33; McNeill, *Greek Dilemma*, pp. 63–4.

34. Evangelos Kofos, *Nationalism and Communism in Macedonia* (Salonika, 1964), pp. 123–47; Stavrakis, *Moscow*, pp. 129–31; Nars, 868.00/1-2245, enclosure to despatch 427, captured Communist correspondence, Leonidas (Stringos) to Ioannides, 4 Nov. 1944; Macedonian HQ to Ioannides; FO 371/43764/-, no. 7185, R 14551, P.H. Evans, 7 Aug. 1944.

35. FO 371/43689/122, R 10409.

36. PEEA, *Episema Keimena*, *passim*; Zoides, Kailas et al., eds, *St'Armata!*, pp. 489–92; Fleischer, *Stemma*, p. 235; Couvaras, *OSS*, p. 30; FO 371/37206/119, R 10449, reported conversation by British officer with Giorgios Blanas (Kissavos), 28 Sept. 1943.

37. Bouras, *PEEA*, p. 58; Pepones, *Prosopike*, p. 147.

38. C. Sakellariou, *E Paideia sten Antistase* (1983), pp. 52–68; A. Kastrinos, 'E Laike Dikaiosyne kai avtodioikise eis sten elevthere Ellada, 1941–5', *Istorike Epitheorese* 1 (1963), pp. 141–2; Chatzes, *Nikephora*, I, pp. 350–1; K. Konstantaras, *Agones kai Diogmoi* (1964), p. 104; Couvaras, *OSS*, pp. 61–2.

39. Nars, RG 84, Athens Embassy General File, R.H. Markham to W. Carroll, 'report on Greek situation as of 1 July 1944'.

40. Pepones, *Prosopike*, p. 57; V. Dedijer, *History of Yugoslavia* (New York, 1974), p. 609.

41. Zalokostas, *Chroniko*, pp. 57, 162.

42. Daskalakes, *Istoria*, II, p. 809; Gregoriades, *Antartiko*, IV, p. 439; Arseniou, *Thessalia*, I, p. 344; II, pp. 228–9; Nars, 868.00/7-2347, despatch no. 17.

43. George Alexander and John Loulis, 'The strategy of the Greek Communist Party, 1934–44. An analysis of plenary decisions', *East European Quarterly* 15, 3 (1981), pp. 377–89.

44. KKE, Deka Chronia Agones, pp. 146, 152, 168.

45. Partsalides, *Diple Apokatastase*, pp. 28–9; Glenos, *Ta Semerina Provlemata tou Ellenismou* (1945), p. 33; KKE, *Keimena* I, p. 535; Chatzes, *Nikephora*, I, pp. 457–9; II, pp. 267–8.

46. Metsopoulos, *30 Syntagma*, pp. 282–3; Partsalides, *Diple Apokatastase*, pp. 25–31; Ioannides, *Anamneseis*, pp. 258–9; Nars, RG 226, no. 63353, 'a circular attributed to the Communist Party of Greece', signed Mentor, dated Jan. 1934; FO 371/37206/119, R 10449, report of talk on 27 Sept. 1943; Theotokas quoted in Mazower, *Inside Hitler's Greece*, p. 295.

47. Arseniou, *Thessalia*, I, pp. 366–70; Metsopoulos, *30 Syntagma*, pp. 104–5.
48. Metsopoulos, *30 Syntagma*, pp.194–5, 212; Chatzes, *Nikephora*, II, p. 195; Bouras, *PEEA*, p. 140.
49. KKE, *Deka Chronia Agones*, pp. 148, 194–5, 215; Giorgios Kasimates et al., eds, *Georgios Papandreou. Koryphaies Stigmes tes Neoteres mas Istorias* (1988), p. 145.
50. Dionysios Benetatos, *To Chroniko tes Katoches, 1941–4* (1963), pp. 14–15, 119–26; Tsirimokos in *Sosialistes*, 13 Aug. 1945, quoted in Papathanasiou, ed., *Elleniko Vorra*, I, p. 141.
51. Petros Antaios, *Vema*, 21 June 1992, p. B6. Other relevant sources are: Chatzes, *Nikephora*, II, pp. 592–4; Stefanos Sarafis, *ELAS: Greek Resistance Army*, translated by Marion Sarafis (1980), pp. lviii–lxiii; Pepones, *Prosopike*, p. 56.
52. Stavrianos, 'National Liberation Front', p. 51; Partsalides, *Diple Apokatastase*, p. 23; Chatzes, *Nikephora*, II, p. 503.
53. Nicholas G.L. Hammond, *Venture into Greece. With the Guerrillas*, (1983), p. 89.

CHAPTER FOUR

EAM Challenges the Old Order, April 1943–October 1944

REACTIONS TO EAM

Within only two years after the German invasion, the Communist Party had accomplished a widespread realignment of long-term significance. Broadly speaking it was the realignment to which it had aspired in the summer of 1936. The party had won over to support of EAM much of the radical wing and many of the poor supporters of the Venizelist camp; while most Venizelist politicians felt a strengthening affinity with anti-Venizelists as defenders of the old social and political hierarchy. This hierarchy felt threatened by EAM, and its defenders were acquiring a sufficient feeling of solidarity to start using the terms *ethnikophron* (of sound patriotic opinions) and *ethnike parataxis* (national camp) to describe themselves. In practice the adjective *ethnikos* replaced the pre-war adjective *astikos* (bourgeois). Venizelist politicians felt immediately threatened because EAM had been progressively winning over their active supporters, the local party bosses and voters, so threatening the politicians' chances of returning to their profession. Urgent action was needed because a German withdrawal from the Balkans now seemed imminent, after the Anglo-American military successes in North Africa and the Soviet successes on the Russian front.

The lesson which the German army drew from EAM's success was that it needed vigorous Greek collaboration. Consequently, in April, the German authorities appointed a prime minister better qualified than his predecessors to win support from bourgeois politicians. Ioannes Ralles differed from his predecessors in belonging to an old political family, and having long ministerial experience and extensive political contacts. He had nevertheless a comparatively small following, and was discredited by his temperamental extremism and association with the unsuccessful dictator of 1935, Georgios Kondyles.[1] But as his wife was a Russian refugee from the

Bolshevik revolution, he was well qualified to lead an anti-Communist crusade, and later justified thus his decision to take office:

> The foundations of our social order were quaking. The state had to prepare for its defence, if it was to live. It was certain that the great empire [Britain], which by sentiment and geographical position had always been the protector of Greece, would not tolerate the rule of criminal and subversive elements.

Most bourgeois politicians would have subscribed to this statement, and later showed sympathy with Ralles's attempt to organize the military defence of the 'social order'.[2]

On assuming office, Ralles aspired to establish his authority after liberation by acquiring his own military forces, and by ingratiating himself with other sections of the nationalist camp and their chosen patron, Britain. He obtained before his appointment the Germans' agreement to let him rearm the gendarmerie, and to organize military units later known as Security Battalions. At the same time, during his term of office, he gave covert help to British officers hiding in Athens, and to various anti-Communist resisters.[3] Although an anti-Venizelist – like most politicians who accepted government office during the occupation – Ralles cooperated in organizing the military forces with some Venizelists, who had indeed been the first to propose them, hoping to use them to prevent the king's return. Notable among these Venizelists were two retired officers, Stylianos Gonatas and the ex-dictator Theodoros Pangalos. Two associates of Pangalos joined Ralles's government: Anastasios Tavoulares as Minister of the Interior and Ioannes Voulpiotes as director of Radio Athens; while another, Vasilios Dertiles, was first commander of the Security Battalions. Thus the new bond of *ethnikophrosene* (sound patriotic opinions) blurred the lines of the National Schism. It is also noteworthy that collaborationist politicians tended to be drawn from pre-war rejects or failures.[4]

The politicians' plan to acquire their own army was thwarted by German and Italian mistrust. When the first Security Battalions began operations in the capital in October, they were like the gendarmerie placed under the command of the Higher SS Police Leader, who had just begun to take a leading role in combating the resistance, and answered directly to Heinrich Himmler. Thereafter most of the battalionists acted under close German supervision. In May 1944 Pangalos, Tavoulares, Gonatas, and Dertiles were arrested, because of their attempts to contact the resistance and the British.

German leadership of the battalions was a serious deterrence to recruitment. At first the majority of officers to be recruited were, like Dertiles, Venizelists lured by reinstatement in active service. Most Venizelist officers were however unavailable because they had instead chosen service in the resistance or in the exiled army. Thus most of the officers recruited during 1944 had been in active service in the army or police under Metaxas. Many of them seem to have been motivated by fear or hatred of Communism, prominent among whom were members of resistance groups and units which had been dissolved by EAM, and Metaxists who suffered especially from EAM persecution. But perhaps the chief motive for recruitment was coercion by Ralles, who deprived officers of pay and pension rights for refusing service. Most of the privates were impoverished workers or peasants who were conscripted, or motivated by need for pay and rations.

It seems nonetheless that most or all of the Security Battalionists believed in the need to fight Communism, and in this belief won sympathy from the majority of traditional politicians, officers in active status, and the wealthier classes in the metropolis. Very few liked the Germans, and most were pro-British, deluding themselves that the British approved of their actions. The Security Battalions were recruited mainly or wholly from the old lands of Sterea Ellada, Euboea, and the Peloponnese, areas where support for the monarchy – and therefore anti-Communism – were traditionally strong, and where at first there was a strong popular demand for protection from EAM. The collaborationist units in Macedonia and Thessaly were of a different type: established by the Germans rather than by the government, lacking social respectability, and most not led by officers.

The Germans soon found the collaborationist troops' local familiarity with people and terrain to be valuable in hunting resisters, and so encouraged their expansion to about 7,000 in February 1944 and eventually to 25,000–30,000 active combatants, including about 1,000 officers. The value of the Security Battallions *strictu senso* (i.e. those in southerly regions) to the Germans is attested by their heavy casualties: according to SS figures for the period 1 September 1943 to 1 September 1944, 637 of them were killed in counter-guerrilla operations. These figures also demonstrate the Germans' success in fomenting civil war.[5]

The armed units in Thessaly and Macedonia seem to have been each based in some town or village. Many of the recruits belonged to ethnic minorities (Koutsovlach survivors of the Italian-inspired 'legion' in Thessaly, Turkish-speaking Christians in western Macedonia); some consisted of Greek-speaking villagers fleeing from EAM/ELAS persecution; and many others consisted of criminals attracted by the ample opportunities for plunder. Several were employed by the Germans to discourage resistance by indiscriminate terrorism: they were aptly described as 'death squads' by Mark Mazower, who described their ghastly activities. Even the largest of these organizations in Thessaly acquired fewer than 500 members; and its members in Volos committed such atrocities that the Germans hanged twelve of them. A band in Salonika was led by an illiterate chauffeur named Dangoulas, 'the beast of Salonika', described by a police officer as 'a disgrace to the city'. Another of the several bands in Macedonia was founded in March 1943 by one of the few Greek fascists Colonel George Poulos, and eventually attained a strength of 800, based near Giannitsa. The other bands included National Greek Army (EES), established in December 1943, under the officer Constantine Papadopoulos, based in Kilkis in central Macedonia, one led by the Turkish-speaking animal dealer Michal Agas, based in Kozane in western Macedonia, and one by another civilian Turkish-speaker, Kitsa Batzak, based in Koukkos, also in western Macedonia. In August 1944 the Macedonian bands formed an alliance which in the hope of British support declared itself linked to the main anti-Communist resistance organization, Zervas's EDES. The groups in this union comprised in total 8,000–9,000 combatants.[6]

The army officers who eschewed collaboration realised that they too needed to bestir themselves to counter the challenge by EAM to the old social order. In May 1943 the former commander-in-chief under Metaxas, Alexandros Papagos, and five other generals formed the Military Hierarchy in order to maintain the existing structure of authority in the army, and encourage officers to engage in resistance activity. Although the Germans arrested these generals in July, the Military Hierarchy survived, under the leadership of Colonel Theodoros Gregoropoulos, and in time enrolled 2,500 officers – possibly a majority of those on the active list who remained in Greece.[7]

From May 1943 onwards, in response to the Military Hierarchy's encouragement, many army officers in active status, and some gendarmerie officers, formed guerrilla bands in the mountains of different parts of the mainland: the Peloponnese, Sterea Ellada, Epirus, and central and western Macedonia. These were joined by hundreds of junior or middle-ranking officers, who preferred to operate if possible near their home village or town, and were disproportionately numerous in the traditionally anti-Venizelist and monarchist Peloponnese because so many of them hailed from there. Many, perhaps most, of these new recruits to guerrilla warfare were primarily interested in combating ELAS rather than the Germans; and it was partly for this reason that they received little help from the British. Another reason was that they were militarily feeble. The political organizations which backed them – National Action (ED) in Athens and the PAO in Salonika – were numerically and financially too weak to provide adequate supplies to guerrillas. The industrialist Chrestos Zalokostas described pathetically the efforts by National Action to raise funds in Athens. The bands themselves lacked civilian organizations to supply them with food, shelter, and information, while many of their leaders lacked understanding of guerrilla warfare. It was partly for lack of an effective alternative that many hundreds of professional officers, who even included a few hundred from the active list, joined the EAM army, ELAS, during 1943.[8]

One form of anti-Communist activity which remained open to officers and officer cadets was feuding in the streets of Athens in some organization such as National Action or X ('Chi') led by Colonel George Grivas, famous in the 1950s as leader of an anti-British terrorist group in Cyprus. In November 1943, 2,000–3,000 young officers or cadets were reported by a British agent to belong to such groups.[9]

Another form of activity lay through the exiled army in Egypt. The professional officers who emigrated to join it numbered several hundred by the end of 1941, and about 2,500 by the end of 1943. From early in the occupation, they divided between monarchist, republican, and pro-EAM associations. The monarchists were in a majority and from the start tended to see as their main role the restoration of the monarchy after liberation. In August 1943 some officers who had recently left Greece formed the Union of Young Officers (ENA) to promote the interests of right-wing or *ethnikophron* colleagues, including republicans, and prevent by all available means a Communist coup in Greece.[10] There emerged a division in the army between *ethnikophrons*, who favoured authoritarian methods against the left, and democrats, who did not. The Greek word *demokratikos* means both republican and democratic, and most democrats were veteran republicans, i.e. Venizelists or Communists. The *ethnikophron* faction was reinforced in 1944 by officers from Greece, notably Konstantinos Venteres, whose resistance bands had been terrorized by EAM/ELAS.

Venteres went to the Middle East to represent various nationalist organizations of Athens at the Lebanon conference (for which see below).[11] He had prolonged combat experience in the wars of 1912–22, had been a personal friend of Elevtherios Venizelos, and was among those forcibly retired for participation in the uprising of 1935. As an officer who combined outstanding professional ability with a sense of mission to combat Communism, he became perhaps the most influential figure on the *ethnikophron* side during the rest of the decade, and appointed other officers who thenceforth took a prominent role in combating the Communist Party. He was appointed chief of the general staff by George Papandreou when head of the exiled government in April 1944, and worked with a growing circle of professionally capable officers who ensured that the exiled army was dominated by dedicated *ethnikophron* officers, and gave the nationalist organizations in Athens what they had hitherto lacked: help and recognition by the British and their client government. The general staff under his leadership seemed to British and American diplomats to be more interested in fighting EAM than the Germans. Venteres' work in purging democratic officers from the exiled army, or reassigning them to unimportant posts, contributed to the resignation from Papandreou's government of some prominent Venizelists, and the deterrence of at least one other from joining it.[12]

Venteres was actively supported by the organized anti-Communists in the national army, and also by British officers who supervised his appointments. At the end of 1944 ENA was renamed the Sacred Union of Greek Officers (IDEA) under the leadership of another Venizelist, Solon Gikas.[13] Venteres secured the appointment of the monarchist Thrasyvoulos Tsakalotos to command the Mountain Brigade, which by July 1944 comprised 2,500 men and became the main unit in the exiled army after a purge, under British supervision, of those who participated in pro-EAM demonstrations and mutinies in April. The other important unit was the Sacred Battalion which by this time numbered 731 men, nearly half of them officers, who were predominantly monarchist. Both units enjoyed friendly relations with British officers and acquired much combat experience before the liberation of Greece. Venteres secured the appointment of Panagiotes Spiliotopoulos as military governor of Attica on behalf of Papandreou in August 1944. Spiliotopoulos was an extreme anti-Communist who had been promoted to command a division in the Albanian war under Metaxas, and was widely believed to have collaborated with the Germans in some way in his brief term as chief of the gendarmerie in 1941.[14] Venteres and his associates sympathized with the anti-Communism of the Security Battalionists, and so saw to the appointment and advancement of many of them after the liberation. All these officers and the conspiratorial organization IDEA were to be important in promoting the *ethnikophron* cause during the civil strife in Greece in 1944–9.

By November 1943, nearly all the guerrilla bands formed by army officers in Greece had been attacked and dissolved by ELAS. Two that remained were EDES, founded in 1941, with its forces chiefly in Epirus, and National and Social Liberation (EKKA), founded in 1942 and with its forces in the strategic massif of Parnassos and Giona north of the Gulf of Corinth, in Sterea Ellada. Each was established by a Venizelist officer and was built up with British help. The leader of EDES, Colonel Napoleon Zervas, had a creditable combat record from the distant past, and became a major instrument of British policy. He was not however an inspiring leader: corpulent, bearded, a hard drinker and keen gambler, he had to be forced by British agents to begin guerrilla activity in July 1942, and proved to be a persuasive rogue, despised by other resistance leaders and even by his British masters for his corruption and opportunism. Brigadier E.C.W. ('Eddie') Myers, first head of the British Military Mission, later remarked that Zervas would have stood on his head if asked by the British. Colonel Demetrios Psarros, leader of EKKA, was a very different character: widely admired for his generosity and selfless patriotism, he was an old friend of Sarafis, like him having taken up social democratic ideas after being expelled from the officer corps for participation in the Venizelist rising of 1935. He made courageous efforts to start guerrilla warfare in Macedonia in 1941.

Both EDES and EKKA started with radical and democratic programmes in an attempt, like EAM, to construct some kind of political organization to support guerrilla activities. British patronage and aid enabled them to survive against ELAS attacks. EKKA was regarded by ELAS bands as an interloper in territory which they had liberated and was twice dissolved at gunpoint by them in 1943, but because of its recognition by the British was allowed on Communist orders to reassemble and later reach a strength of perhaps 800 combatants. EDES reached a total of over 4,000 combatants in October 1943, then after losing most of them in war with ELAS, recovered to reach a peak of 7,000 effective combatants and a few thousand reserves in 1944 (whom the British maintained with two gold sovereigns a month per person).[15] Both organizations lost their original political character, as from about September 1943 they became a haven for right-wing officers and gendarmes who were escaping from or fighting against ELAS.

The least effective representatives of the old social order in 1943 were the mass of politicians who dwelt in limbo between EAM, the quisling government, and the government-in-exile. As a result of suppression by Metaxas, they were alienated also from the army and gendarmerie officers in active status. The long suspension of parliamentary life gave full scope to their traditionally fissiparous tendencies. The senior statesman Themistocles Sophoules tried late in 1942 to form an alliance with EAM; then in March 1943 took the initiative in forming an alliance of political groups which might contain EAM. In September–October these and several right-wing resistance groups formed a still broader alliances the National Greek Liberation League (PAS). At this time, too, varied interest groups – some politicians including Sophoules, several minor resistance organizations, army officers, war profiteers, old-established businessmen and bankers – tried to construct a united front under the popular head of the church, Archbishop Damaskinos. But no effective organization or significant action emerged from their laborious negotiations. The most that the architects of PAS expected to achieve, according to one of them, was to hold 'Athens for 24 hours until the Allies arrive'.[16] They disagreed, among other things, on relations with the monarchy and the Security Battalions. An officer in the main anti-Communist resistance organization in the north, the PAO described the many little nationalist groups in the capital at this time as beset with egoism and *archomania* (determination to dominate).[17] The main significance of their activities was to indicate the fear of EAM now shared by virtually the whole political spectrum from socialists to Metaxists. By January 1944, businessmen tended to seek salvation in the collaborationist Security Battalions, which they cooperated in financing, while politicians swallowed their distrust for the Tsouderos government in Cairo, and looked to it with increasing hope.[18]

By 1944 the ideological opposition to EAM by most representatives of the old order – officers, politicians, businessmen, professional groups, public officials – was becoming increasingly negative. Admittedly many anti-Communists, including some who were socially conservative, promised a fairer society after the war. Given the levelling effect on Greek society of general hardship, all political groups felt obliged to make generous promises of social welfare. Thus monarchist politicians including Konstantinos Tsaldares, nephew of the pre-war leader of the Populist Party, issued a proclamation in September 1943 favouring 'socialist democracy' and vague measures to achieve 'social justice'.[19] In the north the PAO accepted the membership of socialists early in 1943. Some left-wing Venizelists were bolder in their promises: George Papandreou, for example, proclaimed a social democratic programme while in the resistance in Greece and then as prime minister in exile in April. So did Zervas's EDES and Psarros's EKKA. But no organization other than EAM made noticeable preparations to implement its promises, and all neglected them as they became part of an alliance in which the most cohesive and determined element consisted of conservative officers of the army and gendarmerie. Such officers distrusted political programmes as a distraction from their military objectives, and as likely to arouse latent divisions, especially the cleavage between republicans and monarchists. One objective, however, which officers treated as too obviously justifiable to be contentious was territorial expansion at the expense of Greece's northern neighbours, with opposition to EAM's alleged sympathy with Slav secessionists. These nationalist policies attracted enthusiastic support from all sections of the national camp and from the majority of the public. Thus the right began for the first time in Greek history to lay exclusive claim to expansionist nationalism.[20]

The conservatives' lack of programme contributed to their weakness in political organization, of which EDES provides an example. Zervas initially expanded EDES territory by laborious negotiations with local notables, and by recruiting old military acquaintances in various regions. Later he relied on the magnetic attraction of the immense quantities of gold sovereigns, weapons, and other supplies which he received from the British. He held EDES together by his personal authority, of which he was jealous; but lacking political ideals, and bad at choosing subordinates, he failed to construct a cohesive organization. Psarros failed even more dismally to construct either a political or a military organization. He saw his followers go in contrary ideological directions, and could not make them organize in their own defence even when they were threatened by ELAS's final assault.[21] The general political incapacity of the conservatives is shown by the fragmentation of their organizations in the metropolis, and their failure to provide enough material support to guerrilla bands.

Because of their weakness, few in the national camp except the quisling prime minister Ralles managed to help the people in all parts of the country who clamoured for protection against the exactions which EAM imposed, or the reprisals which it provoked. Ralles received appeals for protection from various regions, especially from local notables – such as mayors of village councils, lawyers, party agents, businessmen, state officials – who had either represented the Metaxas regime or, earlier, supported the bourgeois parties. He responded by organizing the Security Battalions, which because of their characteristic tyranny and indiscipline came to be seen by most communities as a curse or at best a mixed blessing.

There remained many villages which had to defend themselves against EAM, often with German-supplied arms and with fortifications, and maintained armed groups designed primarily for self-defence. In the wooded mountains of eastern Macedonia, several of these groups benefited from the capable leadership of the former artillery captain Anton Tsaous and seem to have avoided collaboration with the occupying Bulgarian forces. They were numerous but poorly disciplined and reluctant to accept outside leaders; and it was only at the initiative of a British officer that Greek army officers were brought from Salonika in 1944 to staff them. One officer in these bands asserted that his ELAS rivals derived 'immense superiority' from the assets imparted to them by Communist cadres: strict discipline, mobility, a well-organized supply system, and educated members who could undertake political indoctrination and propaganda.[22]

EAM PREDOMINANT

After the Communist Party's national conference in December 1942, the territorial sway of EAM/ELAS expanded steadily. At this time its influence was still patchy. The spheres of ELAS power in the countryside resembled an archipelago: the islands of influence were numerous and sometimes extensive in the mountains from the Gulf of Corinth northwards and in the Thessaly plains, but sparse in the Peloponnese, Epirus, eastern Macedonia, Thrace, and the islands. By now EAM seemed to form a strong underground movement in most mainland towns, except in the north-eastern regions, where the extraordinary severity of the Bulgarian occupation hampered organization and cut EAM leaders off from the German-occupied Evros zone. By September 1944, however, on the eve of the German withdrawal, EAM/ELAS predominated everywhere except for some of the islands – notably Crete and Corfu – and some enclaves on the mainland – notably western Epirus where EDES held out, and two areas occupied by hostile bands, one in western and one in eastern Macedonia. Even in parts of some larger towns EAM authority was by then organized and open.

The early development of EAM in large towns was presumably due to the Communists' experience in trade union organization, and the facilities there for printed propaganda and other means of mass communication.[23] This reliance on the printed word explains EAM's well-attested success among more prosperous, and therefore more educated, peasants. EAM's appeal to women attracted more support in towns than in villages, partly because in towns women were more likely to work outside the home. Later in the occupation, the centre of EAM power shifted to the mountainous areas where ELAS was based; and ELAS in the mountains evidently relied more on coercion to maintain its authority than did EAM in the cities.

The early expansion of EAM in the Thessalian plains was helped by the radical tradition of peasants who earlier in the century gained their land after struggle against oppressive landlords, and in the process won the sympathies of urban intellectuals. But in the mountains of western Thessaly EAM/ELAS suffered from lack of this tradition, and found, interestingly, that the strong tradition there of patriotic banditry against the Turks was no help to it. In parts of Sterea Ellada further south, the early expansion of EAM/ELAS was clearly assisted by the local connections of the Communist pioneer of guerrilla warfare, Ares Velouchiotes, who proved himself an able leader, successful in investing his reputation with dread and awe. In Macedonia, EAM benefited from slavophone support and also from the Communists' pre-war strength among industrial workers and tobacco workers in towns. In eastern Macedonia and Thrace, the Bulgarian forces were strong and ruthless enough to hamper resistance until 1944 when their authority was weakened by German reverses on the Russian front. An additional obstacle, in Thrace, was the presence of the large Muslim minority, which was largely indifferent to Greek quarrels. In the Peloponnese, the Ionian Islands, and the Cyclades, EAM was hindered by especially strong Axis forces, and also by a monarchist tradition sustained by traditionally close links with the official establishment in Athens.[24]

In none of the islands, it seems, did civil strife break out during the occupation. EAM won extensive support in the eastern Aegean islands of

Samos, Ikaria, Chios, and Lesbos, which were strongly Venizelist because they formed part of the new lands united with Greece in 1913, and were therefore out of sympathy with the Metaxist establishment. Lesbos, moreover, was densely settled by refugees. But in the islands the division between EAM and its opponents seems generally to have been softened by a strong sense of regional community. In the largest island, Crete, the expansion of EAM was hindered by the fact that there, more than generally on the mainland, traditional leaders bestirred themselves relatively early in resistance. So except possibly in the western port of Chania and in the Lassithi plateau in the eastern countryside, EAM was overshadowed by other resistance bands, especially by the National Organization of Crete (EOK), which was established and guided by the British. The non-Communist bands cooperated with the gendarmerie, which had given a lead to resisters by participating vigorously in the battle for Crete in May 1941.[25]

Support by slavophones and by Koutsovlachs made EAM powerful in western Macedonia, but tended to antagonize the refugee smallholders. Their settlement in the 1920s had caused widespread friction over land rights with slavophone natives; and now some of the Slav separatists threatened them openly with expropriation. The 67,000 Turkish-speaking Christians among the refugees were especially anti-Slav, apparently because they had been among the later arrivals, and their property rights were more open to dispute. The customary denunciations by Communists of their ignorance and backwardness suggests also a cultural barrier between them and EAM. However the refugees from the Caucasus region were pro-Russian and so favoured Communism. The importance of communal links was neatly illustrated by the case of the village of Imera, in western Macedonia, which split between two groups, one consisting of Turkish-speaking refugees, and one of Greek-speaking refugees from the Caucasus.[26]

In the industrial towns of Macedonia, and in all regions further south, the Asia Minor refugees provided strong support to EAM. Traditionally the great majority of refugees in town and country had been Venizelist, but they had been radicalized by persecution since 1935, and then by economic hardship under the occupation, to which they were especially vulnerable because of their poverty and social isolation. Having no land to sustain it, the urban refugee population in Macedonia as elsewhere was especially influenced by class feeling. In Athens the refugee and working-class districts like Pangkrati, Kaisariani and New Smyrna overwhelmingly supported EAM, although parts of them were separated only by the narrow, stony riverbed of the Ilyssos from the Kolonaki district which was the heartland of the Greek establishment. In rural Euboea, there were three

distinct groups, Greek-speaking natives, Albanian-speaking but Greek
Orthodox natives, and the Asia Minor refugees, of which only the last provided voluntary support to EAM.[27]

The allegiance of some villages was determined primarily by economic
geography. For example some members of Kalarrytes, in the Pindus ranges,
supported ELAS because they traded with EAM-dominated Thessaly;
while all the inhabitants of Syrako, only 400 yards away across a gorge,
supported EDES because they traded with an EDES-dominated part of
Epirus.[28] On the other hand in the divided village of Karpofora in
Messenia, the choice of sides was determined by a pre-war political division between Venizelists and anti-Venizelists which coincided with kinship
networks. In some cases the choice of sides was caused by long-standing
feuds between families or clans. In others the choice of allegiance was
purely personal. An ELAS officer, for example, mentions one soldier who,
having made a girl pregnant, was forced by his battalion commander to
marry her, and in resentment against this coercion, deserted and became
leader of a hostile group.[29]

The multiplicity of motives for alignment in the civil war produced
kaleidoscopic patterns in which villages of apparently similar character but
opposed loyalties might be geographically intermingled, as occurred in
parts of Laconia or in western Macedonia. Observers, British and Greek,
referred to villages as if each was dominated by one political loyalty or
another, so recognizing the considerable cohesion which village communities normally possessed.[30]

EAM grew rapidly during 1943, and in the process its organization
became more centralized and specialized. The EAM central committee
gradually established its control over appointments to the regional committees on the mainland, and brought under its authority the independently
established branches on the islands. Propaganda was conducted through
newspapers and travelling speakers.[31] Specialized services became active. In
February 1943 the youth branch was established for those aged 15–23, and
was accompanied then or later by a children's branch. A terrorist organization was founded in the same month, initially to protect EAM activists, but
in time to conduct a campaign of assassination against collaborators. In each
village the standard organization consisted of elected committees: one to
manage education, another the distribution of rations, another general
administration, and the people's court. Teachers held conferences and
teachers' colleges were established. In December 1943 the EAM central
committee invited other party leaders to cooperate in forming a national
government, which had been envisaged since May by Communist leaders
and EAM activists.[32] The government known as the Political Committee
of National Liberation (PEEA) appeared in March 1944, and decreed

elections for a parliament, the National Council, which convened for two weeks in May. This government lasted formally until November 1944, and during that time codified EAM's practices in legislation.

The approximate numbers of effective ELAS combatants increased from about 2,000 in February 1943 to 12,000 in June, then to 25,000 in January 1944, and 45,000–50,000 in September 1944, by which date there was in addition an organized force of reservists (mostly unarmed) of about two-thirds this number, and 5,000 police.[33] These forces were made more formidable by hundreds of thousands of participants in EAM, who provided supplies, obstructed supplies to the enemy, and formed a remarkably comprehensive network of intelligence. The number of ELAS combatants increased by about one-third when in some regions it acquired the arms of Italian troops, after the Italian government concluded an armistice with the Allies in September 1943. Otherwise the arms came from those hidden by Greek soldiers after the German invasion, captured from Axis troops, or provided by the British. The last were a small minority, because the British preferred to supply non-Communists and gained a justification for doing so as ELAS began attacking them. Consequently, ELAS was unable to equip many potential recruits.[34] Meanwhile Germany like Britain channelled supplies to anti-Communists. Thus ELAS was threatened from different quarters, and so hindered from increasing its strength so as to acquire more supplies, as Tito managed to do in Yugoslavia.

From at least as early as December 1942 ELAS fought successfully against bodies of Italian troops numbered in hundreds, and it took on larger contingents thereafter. In March ELAS occupied the towns of Naoussa in western Macedonia and Karditsa in Thessaly (each with over 10,000 inhabitants), holding the latter for eight months. By this time, Axis troops were forced to withdraw to the larger towns, and to major roads and railways, and could venture away from them only occasionally and in large groups.[35] Although they kept control of major lines of communication, they could not protect them from frequent ambushes and sabotage. From September 1943, German troops started to respond to these attacks with major, determined campaigns against ELAS, which according to its own records suffered a total of 10,500 casualties during the occupation. The Germans, according to their records, lost 8,383 as casualties or missing from May 1943 onwards. Civilians suffered the brunt of German reprisals, as German figures showed: 21,255 Greeks were killed, 20,000 were arrested, 1,918 hostages executed, and 1,700 villages destroyed during the same period.[36] Not surprisingly, much of the population saw ELAS as a curse.

From March 1943 the Communist leaders devoted increasing attention to the organization and control of ELAS. In that month the politburo member Andreas Tzemas went to the mountains for this purpose, and was followed by many senior cadres and party members. Siantos devoted himself mainly to this work from June. From March 1944 the Communist leadership was located mainly at its army's headquarters.[37] Tzemas had in May 1943 established a GHQ under a troika of himself as representative of EAM, Ares Velouchiotes as chief *kapetanios* (leader of guerrilla bands), and Colonel Stefanos Sarafis as commander responsible for military strategy. This tripartite command was replicated at lower levels, acquiring greater cohesion as many of the professional officers, like Sarafis himself, became Communist Party members. Sarafis had a high reputation among left-wing Venizelists. While fighting in another resistance group he was captured by ELAS in March 1943 and was so impressed by its organization and idealism that he chose to join it. His accession was an important gain because ELAS at that point included only 80–90 professional officers. Sarafis's example, and temporary British recognition of ELAS, attracted many of the other officers. By the end of 1943 ELAS included 1,850 professional officers, of whom about two-thirds − and a still greater majority of senior officers − were retired Venizelists who thus found an opportunity to resume their military careers. These recruits enabled GHQ to announce in August that ELAS had been organized as a professional army in each region of the mainland except the north-east. The same month an officer training school was started, from which in time 1,260 lieutenants graduated. By March 1944, GHQ was linked by telephone with regional HQs north of the Gulf of Corinth, and by radio with the Peloponnese and Athens.[38]

As early as June 1943 the growing ELAS units moved to remoter mountains for safety, and there faced the problem of subsistence. Most of the taxation raised by EAM was devoted to the upkeep of ELAS, which also requisitioned goods on a large scale, although in accordance with set procedures. As Communist authorities admitted, these levies provoked strong resentment, which naturally varied according to the prosperity of the region concerned. According to the hostile, but detailed and plausible, accounts by British and Greek nationalist officers, EAM/ELAS rule in extensive areas, especially of the Peloponnese, resembled a military occupation which was disliked by much of the population. British officers observed ELAS units in most regions, and agreed that they were reserving much of their strength for political purposes, specifically the occupation of the towns after liberation. For example a British officer reported that in September 1943, when ELAS GHQ thought that the Germans were withdrawing from the Peloponnese, it moved its main forces close to the main towns instead of complying with a British request to block the enemy retreat.[39] This concern with political priorities is not surprising as it was shared by the Security Battalions, EDES, and the *ethnikophron* officers in Egypt. All were preparing to compete for political power after the German withdrawal.

As competition intensified between these armed groups, ELAS became an increasingly important source of power to the Communist leaders. Thus their centre of gravity shifted from the towns to the mountains. Indeed in some small towns EAM organization was crushed in 1944 by collaborationist troops with German backing. In Macedonia, for example, the enemy dominated the market towns of Florina, Kastoria, and Kozane in the west, and of Nigrita in the east, while ELAS controlled many of the surrounding villages. The Peloponnese, according to an American officer on 18 August 1944, 'is divided sharply into two camps. In the country districts EAM and ELAS *andartes* hold absolute sway. In the towns and along the coasts, the Sec Bns [Security Battalions] prevail.'[40]

THE START OF CIVIL STRIFE

As the ELAS bands expanded, so did tension between them and other groups. Murders by ELAS of gendarmes, and attacks on police stations, began at least as early as May 1942 and increased thereafter; so that in all regions the gendarmerie was forced by stages to withdraw into larger towns. By December there was severe tension in many areas between ELAS and other resistance organizations, some of which it had forced to dissolve. By February 1943 if not earlier, clashes had become violent. About May there was in one British officer's words 'a state of undeclared war' between ELAS and EDES in Epirus and Thessaly, with each side constantly arresting the other's members. In May and June local ELAS commanders twice dissolved Psarros's group EKKA in the area of Mount Parnassos. ELAS's conflicts with EDES and EKKA made a special impact on the public because the military leaders of these organizations were well known in the cities and were allied with politicians.[41]

These conflicts also influenced relations between the Communists and the British, who had chosen from the beginning of 1943 to give preferential support to EDES, and soon afterwards to EKKA also, with parachute drops of supplies, arms, and money, despite the obvious fact that these organizations were militarily much less effective than ELAS. This kind of support was highly prized by all resistance bands, not just because of the deprivations suffered by most of the population, but also because of the power and the prestige which it brought. The non-Communist bands, as we have seen, were not sufficiently organized to find alternative sources of supplies. The Communists at all levels assumed from the start that Britain was hostile to them, both because it was a capitalist power, and more specifically because of its past and continuing association with the king and his conservative government. The leaders however – especially Ioannides, who took more interest than Siantos in the international situation – could see little hope of avoiding British hegemony over Greece, economic and military. This assumption was based especially on the British patronage of the exiled government and army, and the sole British responsibility, until late in the occupation, for supporting the Greek resistance with supplies. They also noted the Soviet abstention from the administration of liberated Italy from July 1943 onwards, and the complete absence of Soviet interest in Greece until 1944. They were attracted, on the other hand, by the great help which British recognition would give them in their continuing campaign to win political allies and establish their legitimacy.

The representatives of Britain shared, unquestioningly, two beliefs: that it was vital to British interests that a post-war government in Greece should be friendly; and that this government should if possible be democratic. These requirements seemed compatible because of the overwhelming popularity – or at least deference – which Britain enjoyed among all Greeks other than Communists. On other issues the British were divided. Winston Churchill and the Foreign Office despised EAM as Communist-led, and insisted that the king should return after liberation, ignoring the warnings by British representatives in Greece of his overwhelming unpopularity. The British Commander-in-Chief in the Middle East and his staff were willing to arm ELAS because they were primarily interested at this stage in the military efficacy, rather than the political opinions, of Greek resistance organizations. The British officers in Greece – nearly all of whom were responsible to the Special Operations Executive (SOE) – held a position between these two. They first arrived in September 1942, and eventually numbered nearly 400, while American officers of the Office of Strategic Services (OSS) began arriving in September 1943 and eventually totalled about 200. The officers of SOE and OSS were dispersed over nearly all regions. The British officers were nearly all instinctively anti-Communist, but were primarily concerned in 1943 with harnessing the Greek resistance to the British war effort. In May 1943 they urgently needed ELAS's cooperation in Operation Animals, a campaign of attacks on Axis troops and sabotage of communications designed to mislead the Germans into expecting an Allied invasion in Greece instead of Sicily.[42]

As British and Communist interests temporarily coincided, the head of the British mission, Brigadier E.C.W. ('Eddie') Myers, persuaded the Communist leaders in June to agree formally to co-existence with the anti-Communist resistance organizations which the British favoured, EDES and EKKA. The policy was formalized in the so-called 'National Bands Agreement' of 4 July 1943 whereby EDES and EKKA participated with

ELAS in a Joint HQ and allowed recruitment by rival bands in territory which they had hitherto claimed. The short-lived period of co-existence was marred by quarrels and distrust, and applied only in the central mainland provinces of Sterea Ellada, Epirus and Thessaly.

Among regions where conflict continued were Macedonia and the Peloponnese, where ELAS tried to dissolve rival bands before they gained British recognition. Between July and December, ELAS dissolved several bands in southern, western and northern Peloponnese which were led by strongly anti-Communist army officers (in one case by a gendarmerie officer). The skirmishing involved forces which on at least one occasion numbered several hundred on each side. As was usually the case in clashes between resistance bands, the fatal casualties were few but much publicized. ELAS wanted them publicized to intimidate opponents, and continued after the bands were dissolved to hunt some of their leaders in the towns.[43]

ELAS bands attacked those of the PAO in various parts of central and western Macedonia during 1943. Here as elsewhere many survivors of ELAS attacks took refuge in collaboration with the enemy, so satisfying ELAS by fulfilling its accusations. The ELAS attacks began in March and intensified in August, despite repeated attempts by a British officer, Nicholas Hammond, to make peace. In October the last PAO bands were driven into the Aegean peninsula of Macedonia, Chalkidike, and by December virtually all were dissolved. Attacks by ELAS on nationalist bands in eastern Macedonia began in July, starting near crossings of the Strymon, and extending in November eastwards to Mount Pangaion. Meanwhile EAM/ELAS in this region built up its political and military organization, which had hitherto languished as a result of Bulgarian repression.[44]

Tension between ELAS and its rivals was heightened by the results of the discussions in Cairo, from 10 August to 15 September, between six representatives of the resistance (four from EAM or the Communist Party, one EDES, one EKKA), the exiled government, and the British ambassador Reginald Leeper. The resistance delegates presented a demand, supported unanimously by the exiled government, that the king promise not to return to Greece before a plebiscite was held on the constitution. The vital significance of this demand was obvious to all Greeks. Nevertheless it was rejected by the Foreign Office and Churchill in London. As a result of their insistence, the resistance delegation was humiliated by being bundled onto a plane and sent back to Greece. This outcome was a disaster to those influential moderates – such as the minister in the exiled government, Panagiotes Kanellopoulos, the EDES leader Komnenos Pyromaglou, and the socialist member of EAM Elias Tsirimokos – who distrusted both the Communists and the king, while wishing to avoid British tutelage.[45] It kept alive their suspicion that the British government planned to force a client monarchy on the Greek people. The Communist leaders were now convinced that the British were ready to use ruthless measures to destroy them.

Most historians believe that this was a decisive event. Before it there seemed to be at least a hope of stopping the growing civil conflict. An agreement based on a plebiscite before the king's return, and the inclusion of resistance representatives in the exiled government, would have been very popular in Greece, and welcome also to the Communist Party, which had benefited from the National Bands Agreement – by for example the mass accession of professional officers to ELAS – and was thrown into temporary confusion by the breakdown of the Cairo talks.[46] But ELAS aggression in the Peloponnese and Macedonia during the period of the National Bands Agreement indicates that the Communist Party was never interested in co-existence with rival organizations, and would have utilized an agreement with the exiled government to absorb or suppress them.

The return of the delegates from Cairo was followed almost immediately by various events which seemed threatening to the Communists: a report that British agents were trying to form an anti-Communist front in Athens; the first determined German offensive against ELAS; and the claim by Ralles that the newly formed Security Battalions had British approval, an announcement which the Foreign Office delayed two critical weeks in denying. These danger-signs gained in significance from the apparent imminence of an Anglo-American invasion of Greece. Siantos – who had a foot twisted after torture by Metaxas's police – announced at an EAM conference at this time that the range of anti-Communist groups 'want to restore the pre-war situation in our country . . . for me a further experience of prison and torture'. The purpose which the Communist leaders tried with special intensity to achieve between now and February 1944 was to conquer or absorb other resistance organizations. Attainment of this aim would be followed by the formation of a provisional government, representing a broad spectrum of notables. With this end in mind EAM continued to seek fresh allies, especially among Venizelist politicians. The apparent intention was to ensure that the British when they landed in Greece would find no collaborators hostile to the Communist Party.[47]

In the capital, EAM began in September–October to assassinate members of nationalist organizations, and so provoked retaliation by gangs composed largely of officers or officer cadets. Elsewhere the most formidable opponent was EDES, which was using the National Bands Agreement to recruit deserters from ELAS in territory which it claimed. Moreover, during September many anti-Communist officers joined EDES, driven by lack of alternatives as the last bands led by monarchist officers succumbed to ELAS. An attack on Zervas was facilitated by the Italian government's withdrawal from the war in September, enabling ELAS in various regions to gain several thousand rifles from Italian troops who surrendered.[48]

Accordingly the Communist leaders ordered an offensive against EDES on 9 October, an order which resulted immediately in attacks in various parts of Epirus, Sterea Ellada, Thessaly, and Macedonia. This was a deeply unpopular decision with the Greek public, and was viewed with dislike and anxiety by many in EAM. The non-Communists in ELAS, and the army officers in both ELAS and EDES, had little enthusiasm for the fighting. The chief object of ELAS commanders was to dissolve EDES bands rather than kill their members. Consequently the new head of the British Military Mission, Colonel C.M. Woodhouse, reported on 19 October that 'the fighting has been fierce and noisy, but the casualties very small'. The fighting was accompanied by a propaganda war in Athens, with EAM accusing EDES of collaboration (gaining plausibility from the explicit exemption of EDES from German propaganda attacks), and EDES reciprocating with the standard anti-Communist accusations of irreligion, lack of patriotism, and dictatorial aims. During the four months of skirmishing Zervas lost the majority of his followers in desertions, and lost his territories in northern Epirus, western Thessaly, and western Sterea. But he held much of his heartland in central Epirus, thanks partly to British supplies, and still more to a tacit understanding with German troops, who left him in peace while repeatedly attacking ELAS. Consequently the Communist leaders decided early in February 1944 to try to persuade EDES to accept a peaceful merger. At the ensuing negotiations, at Myrofyllo and subsequently at Plaka, the Communists failed also in this aim, because the leaders of EDES and of EKKA remained understandably opposed to absorption in EAM, and were backed by Woodhouse. Faced with this refusal, EAM representatives abruptly decided, on 29 February, to agree to a cease-fire on the basis of the current territorial division. Thus the borders between the two organizations congealed until December 1944, EDES being confined to an area lying mainly west of the central spine of the Pindus ranges, south of the roads running from Metsovo through Ioannina to Igoumenitsa, and north of the road from Arta to Preveza.[49]

COMMUNIST AGREEMENT WITH THE BRITISH

After failing to win over any prominent Venizelist politicians, the Communist Party through EAM announced, on 10 March 1944, a five-member government, the PEEA, under the leadership of Colonel Euripides

Bakirtzes (who had just been won over from EKKA) and also including the former Venizelist general, Emmanuel Mantakas, who had taken a leading role in the Chania uprising of 1938 against Metaxas. This success helped the Communists to win over the socialist constitutional lawyer, Professor Alexandros Svolos, under whose leadership the government was reconstituted on 18 April with a total of ten members who included three professors, two officers, three former deputies, and three leading members of EAM, Siantos, Tsirimokos, and Gavrielides. Siantos was the only known Communist, but Mantakas and Professor Petros Kokkales were secret Communists; while Kostas Gavrielides could always be relied on to cooperate with them, and Elias Tsirimokos was a founding member of EAM. The others, who were not members of EAM, did not act together. The Communists controlled the levers of power through Siantos as Minister of the Interior and Mantakas as Minister of the Army. To the public in Greece this seemed an impressive array of dignitaries and new allies, and its formation served in turn to win allies for EAM.[50] For the Communist leaders the provisional government obviously served a dual purpose: it could, like its recently established counterpart in Yugoslavia, become a revolutionary government, or it could provide a lever to force their entry into the exiled government.

The new provisional government provided what the exiled government had failed to: leadership on Greek soil. Apprehensive of its likely appearance, Tsouderos had already invited some politicians in Greece to come to Egypt to help him to broaden his administration, and among those who responded was George Papandreou. Before Tsouderos could achieve this aim, his authority was destroyed by a movement of political protest in which much of the exiled armed forces participated. The movement was instigated by the Anti-Fascist Military Organization (ASO) led by the Communist Iannes Salas, who had escaped in 1941 after the German invasion from the 'Marxist academy' of Akronauplia prison in Greece, and then established this front organization within the faction-ridden exiled army. The Communist leaders had failed to recognize this army's potential importance, and their only contact with Salas was through their two delegates to Cairo the previous August, who had warned him against provoking the British. Hearing of the formation of the provisional government in Greece, Salas ignored the warning and tried, by inciting protests in the exiled army, to compel the exiled government to share power with representatives of EAM. British officers treated the movement as a mutiny – which technically it was – and tried to suppress it at gunpoint, so causing the protests to spread. Eventually they rounded up and disarmed the mutineers, but not before the king and the British ambassador Reginald Leeper realized the urgent need to give the exiled government greater authority.

At that point Papandreou arrived in Egypt, and impressed them – by his decisiveness, shrewdness, and sense of vision – as the man they needed. Having begun his long political career as provincial governor on behalf of Elevtherios Venizelos in 1915, he held major portfolios in two administrations in the 1920s, and was a successful Minister of Education in Venizelos's administration in 1930–2. After Venizelos's final retirement in 1935 he broke away from the Liberal Party to form his own Democratic Socialist Party. Later he participated in the wartime resistance, being imprisoned by the Italians. Like another Venizelist resister, the army officer Venteres, he left Greece embittered by EAM aggression, and convinced that the Communist Party was trying to establish a dictatorship. His weakness was the small size of his own party, and the jealousy of other politicians which made them unwilling to serve under him when he was appointed as prime minister on 26 April. But he immediately showed his political vision and rhetorical ability in a radio broadcast to Greece, announcing a programme of democratization and social welfare which challenged that of EAM.[51]

Papandreou now cooperated with Leeper in organizing a conference of politicians and resistance leaders which would overshadow EAM and isolate its representatives. In response to invitations issued by the exiled government, 24 people representing fourteen parties and organizations attended, six of these being representatives of the left, including Svolos, the president of the provisional government, and three leading Communists. Many of these participants came from Greece. The whole political spectrum was represented, except for collaborationists and monarchists, the latter because they refused to sit down with Communists. The conference was held from 17 to 20 May in a mountain resort in Lebanon, and was stage-managed by the British. In despatching their representatives, the Communist leaders were continuing their strategy of widening their public support, and assumed that they had a strong bargaining position because of EAM's dominating position in free Greece: thus they directed their delegates to insist on half the ministries including those which controlled the police and army.[52]

Their initial mistake was failure to foresee that the Communist Party's delegates would be isolated at Lebanon, and would not carry their colleagues with them. The delegates of the provisional government were denied by the British even their own means of communication with Greece, and were unexpectedly confronted by a strong prime minister, who immediately began to win over Svolos and his non-Communist colleagues, all of whom were keen for an agreement.[53] The majority of other delegates had like Papandreou been thoroughly alarmed by EAM expansionism in Greece. They believed that the Communist Party was seeking dictatorial power through EAM and was largely responsible for the civil strife in much of the country. The Communist representatives were made especially vulnerable by two recent events: the April mutinies in the exiled army – which were assumed to be incited by the Communist Party – and the horrifying murder of Psarros, leader of EKKA, for which some ELAS commanders were undeniably responsible (see below p. 112). Being in such a weak position, the Communist delegates had to join their colleagues in accepting a resolution submitted by Papandreou which became known as the Lebanon Charter, and provided among other things for the unification of resistance forces under the exiled government. They also accepted a minority of ministries in this government, excluding those controlling the police and army.

The Communist leaders in Greece immediately repudiated the agreement, and for the next two months treated the provisional government as revolutionary, in accordance with the obvious wishes of Communist cadres. The implication of this course, for which they were clearly preparing, was seizure of power by force after liberation.[54]

Papandreou had by personal domination of the Lebanon conference asserted his authority among the professional politicians and recruited enough of them to form a respectable government. Soon afterwards he persuaded the king to defer his return to Greece until after the plebiscite on the constitution agreed to in the Lebanon Charter. Having British backing, Papandreou's government now vied with the provisional government for authority in Greece, and became the rallying point for the national camp.

During this confrontation between two governments, the exiled army was reconstructed as an anti-Communist rump. Almost every unit had dissolved during the April mutinies and the British suppression of them. Now Greek officers under Venteres, as chief of general staff, cooperated with British officers in purging the armed forces of their EAM sympathizers. Eventually about 8,000 of the exiled army – out of a total of about 18,500 – were arrested and interned by British troops for the rest of the war, while from the remainder was recruited what became known as the Mountain Brigade. This, with a Field Artillery Regiment, the Sacred Battalion, and a gendarmerie battalion would form the nucleus of the anti-Communist forces after the liberation of Greece. Thus the Communist Party was seriously weakened in the long term, a blow which it might have avoided had it initially accepted membership of Papandreou's government.[55]

The reasons why the Communist Party eventually abandoned this intransigence were mixed. One was the realization that they could not carry their allies with them. It appears that the great majority of non-Communists in EAM were dismayed by the prospect of war against the British and against the powerful Greek interests aligned with them. Reports of this disagreement within EAM reached Leeper and Papandreou. In addition to the nationalist resistance groups, the extreme anti-Communist organizations like Grivas's X in Athens, and the Security Battalions in the southern provinces, won respectability by claiming that they were serving British ends, a claim lent plausibility by the clearly deliberate failure by the British government, during eight crucial months, to add anything to the weak expression of disapproval of the Security Battalions by the king on 6 January. In fact the British government adopted the recommendation by the senior British liaison officer in Greece, Colonel C.M. Woodhouse, in June that it keep open the way to reconciliation with the Security Battalions.[56]

As liberation from the Germans approached, British influence over the Greek population was reinforced by two overwhelming arguments. One was the urgent need for relief supplies which the British would control and it was hoped supply. The growing civil war from late 1943, and the sabotage of roads and bridges which the Germans perpetrated on departing in September–November 1944, caused still further disruption to the economy already ravaged by occupation. In almost every sector production was seriously reduced by forced movements of people and by lack of such essentials as vehicles, fuel, raw materials, seed grain, draft animals, fertilizers, pesticides, and building materials. Meanwhile the shortage of food, clothing and medical supplies remained generally acute. There were few usable roads or railways left in the country, and few motor vehicles or locomotives to use them. Greece's vast merchant fleet had largely disappeared, having been used up or destroyed in the Allies' service. During the occupation EAM gained influence by organizing relief, controlling distribution of essentials, and curbing profiteers. All could see that after liberation this economic leverage would pass from EAM to the British.[57]

The second new argument for supporting the British was territorial. As the Germans withdrew, it seemed obvious to many including Svolos that Greece would need support from Britain against anticipated territorial claims by her northern neighbours. This argument had special force in the northern provinces where there was vehement resentment of the Bulgarians, which spread to slavophone Greeks who tended to be associated with them. The Communists could not be relied on to protect Greece's territorial integrity because of their subservience to Moscow, which notoriously favoured Bulgarian claims on Greek territory, and their sympathy with the slavophones' claims for minority rights. Moreover the Communists could be, and were, accused of partiality to the Communist parties which were about to take power in Albania, Yugoslavia, and Bulgaria, because of their friendly relations with them. From August, when the autonomous republic of Macedonia was proclaimed as part of a federal

Yugoslavia, there was the added threat of territorial claims by this new territorial unit on Greek Macedonia. The value of British support was to be shown in October when British protest to the Soviet Union secured the withdrawal of Bulgarian troops from Greece.

The dissidents in EAM acquired leadership when Svolos eventually returned from the Middle East, reaching the mountain headquarters of the provisional government on 22 July, and quickly emphasized that, unless agreement was reached with Papandreou, he would resign. It seemed likely that he would take with him four non-Communist colleagues, so wrecking the provisional government.[58] The Communist leaders might have ignored this risk if they had received any encouragement from the Soviet Union; but instead they received repeated discouragements. Just after the announcement of the provisional government in March, the Soviet government pointedly chose to congratulate King George II on the Greek national day and to recognize Tsouderos's government. In June, after much waiting, the Communist delegate to the Middle East Petros Rousos obtained from an official of the Soviet Embassy in Cairo the advice that the provisional government should join Papandreou's government. This advice was brought to the Communist leaders in Greece just before the arrival at a mountain airstrip on 25 July of a mission of eight Soviet officers. The mission asserted that its brief was solely military – specifically, it seems, to spur ELAS into greater military efforts against the Germans, rather than against British-protected EDES. It is probable though that another purpose was the closely related one of warning the Greek Communists to abandon their confrontation with the exiled government. Ioannides recorded that when he mentioned to the political adviser of the mission, Lt-Colonel Chernichev, the possibility of conflict with the British, the latter curtly expressed his disapproval by a grimace. The Soviet representatives made no response even to the requests by the Communists, at this and other times, for military aid. By contrast they were giving large-scale military support at this time to the Bulgarian partisans and to a Romanian division on Russian soil. The Soviet government's attitude can be explained by the hypothesis that during May and June it reached an agreement with Britain on spheres of influence in Romania and Greece respectively. Such an agreement could not have been hard to reach, because neither side showed any strategic or economic interest in the other's sphere. The agreement would be confirmed by Churchill and Stalin in a personal meeting in Moscow in October when they concluded the famous 'percentages agreement' on spheres of influence in the Balkans.[59]

Thus at the momentous meeting of their central committee on 28–9 July, the KKE leaders saw that their strategy would lead to disapproval by the Soviet Union, the collapse of their provisional government, schism in

EAM, and civil war against the traditional social and political hierarchy backed by Britain. The only evidence that exists of these discussions consists of three accounts from memory by, respectively, the politburo member Petros Rousos, the secretary of EAM Thanases Chatzes, and the head of the Communists' Athens organization Vasiles Bartziotas. Although disagreeing in some respects, their accounts show that the dilemma which the party faced was agonizing. According to Rousos all agreed that they could seize power in Greece, but that they probably could not keep it – a calculation apparently overlooked by those historians who assert that the Communists missed an opportunity to seize power after liberation.[60] Thus few if any disagreed with the eventual decision to send representatives to the exiled government on condition that Papandreou resign. When Papandreou declined thus to save the Communist leaders' face, they saw no option but to accept agreement anyway. Thus they abandoned their implicit claim that the provisional government was revolutionary; and early in September six ministers representing the left – again without their own radio contact with their base in Greece – joined Papandreou's government, which had meanwhile been high-handedly transferred by the British to a spot near the base of General Henry Maitland Wilson, the Supreme Allied Commander in the Mediterranean, at Caserta near Naples.

The Communist leaders made their retreat more palatable to supporters by two simultaneous orders directed to ELAS. One, apparently in response to a request by the Soviet mission, was to put all units 'on a war footing' for a final offensive against the Germans during their retreat which was now undeniably imminent. The second was to move strong forces near the capital so as to occupy it when the Germans withdrew. The delegates sent to join Papandreou's government were intended to reassure the British that they need not send troops to Greece, so leaving EAM in control of the country during a plebiscite and elections to a constituent assembly after the Germans withdrew. The Communist leaders saw the continuing danger that the British might intervene by force to restore the pre-war political system. Their qualms were forcefully expressed by the politburo representative in Papandreou's government, Iannes Zevgos, who privately wondered on 18 October: 'Will History condemn us for disarming the people and imposing the reactionaries on them? Will they criticize us like Ebert and Noske?'[61]

But for the meantime the Communist Party enjoyed the best of both worlds. On the one hand, it benefited by rapprochement with the British, which attracted new supporters and led to a formal denunciation by the British of the Security Battalions on 6 September. This was a serious blow to the Security Battalions' morale and public support. The new legitimacy of EAM dismayed conservatives who feared a Communist takeover with

British tolerance.[62] EAM justified their fears by moving in most parts of the country towards a *de facto* seizure of power and the destruction of its remaining Greek opponents.

NATION-WIDE POLARIZATION

The Plaka agreement of February 1944 merely reduced the intensity of civil conflict in one region while it became more intense in other regions of the mainland. The agreement was in any case incomplete as it included no territorial demarcation, and left scope for disputes during the rest of the year at various points along the borders between EDES and EAM. Except for a flare-up of fighting in June, the disputes consisted of small-scale skirmishing with few casualties among combatants and little transfer of territory.

More serious was the war between EAM's local military leaders and Psarros's organization EKKA further east. Because of its small size and location, EKKA was more vulnerable to attack, and was made more vulnerable still by the activities of those of its members who were officers linked to the Military Hierarchy of officers of the regular army. At the end of February, 68 of them, led by Evthymios Dedouses, issued a manifesto of loyalty to the king. There followed a series of violent clashes between their members and ELAS. Two colleagues of Psarros, Euripides Bakirtzes and Konstantinos Langouranes, saw that EKKA's position was hopeless and joined EAM. Psarros, characteristically, refused to abandon his followers to the vengeance of ELAS, and sought survival by accepting nearly all ELAS's demands except the dissolution of his military organization. Eventually one of the three top ELAS commanders, Ares Velouchiotes, in knowing defiance of party policy, authorized an ultimatum which was followed by an attack by 4,500 of ELAS against 350 of EKKA at the village of Klema in the small hours of 17 April 1944. Psarros and 150–200 of his comrades were killed, most of them after surrender and by sadistic methods. Among those who conducted interrogations with torture just before or during the massacre were Ares and another ELAS commander Colonel Zoulas. There followed, for several months thereafter, a purge of alleged sympathizers with EKKA and EDES in what had been EKKA territory. According to a prominent EKKA member, the eventual death toll included over 400 of his fellow combatants. Siantos recognized the murder of Psarros as a disaster, because accounts of it from witnesses spread immediately to Athens and the Middle East. Moreover, many members of EKKA, notably Dedouses, survived to continue their fight against Communism with understandable fervour.[63]

In eastern Macedonia, between the rivers Strymon and Nestos, the survival of nationalist guerrilla bands was apparently helped by the delay in the growth of EAM in the Bulgarian zone of occupation. A series of battles between them and ELAS groups from July 1943 to January 1944 left the nationalist groups dominating the forested and mountainous country approximately north of a line between Drama and Xanthi, and the wooded, marshy plains from the Nestos as far east as Komotene in Thrace. In January several bands in the northerly part of this area complied with a proposal by a British officer that they establish a joint HQ under Anton Tsaous, who received and distributed British supplies dropped by parachute. From June 1944 the bands were staffed by a growing number of army officers of PAO and EDES. By August 1944 the Anton Tsaous bands had acquired a total membership of about 3,000 (according to Sarafis), which increased further after the Bulgarian withdrawal as army officers and former collaborationists joined them.[64]

Anton Tsaous seems to have had no contact with the armed bands in western Macedonia, which sought German rather than British patronage. In the regions of Katerine, Kozane, and Ptolemaïs, villagers who were mainly or entirely Turkish-speaking refugees from Asia Minor seem to have owed their survival against repeated ELAS attacks to acceptance of arms from the Germans, and to fortification of their villages. Their total number of armed combatants was estimated by Sarafis in mid-1944 at about 6,000 and by a British officer in October at 8,000. The Turkish-speaking villagers started at the end of 1942 to accept arms from the Germans for protection against ELAS, and in the winter of 1943–4 were made by the Germans to participate in their campaigns against ELAS. Prominent among their leaders were Michal Agas and Kitsa Batzak, civilians who like Anton Tsaous took Turkish *noms de guerre*. Michal Agas headed an organization in Kozane which imposed taxation, ran a school which taught German, and included a propaganda department under a lawyer. From February 1944 onwards ELAS attacks reduced greatly the number of these fortified villages, burning many of them, and then subjecting their inhabitants to propaganda. Of an original 52 fortified villages in the Kozane region, only 28 remained by April, but many of these still survived in August. Further north, in the areas of Argos Orestikon, Kastoria, Florina, Amyntaion, and Edessa there were several slavophone villages originally won over by Bulgarian officers which held out, with arms supplied by Germans, against repeated ELAS attacks.[65]

In Athens–Piraeus, street fighting between nationalist and EAM gangs continued until the German withdrawal. Foremost on the nationalist side was Grivas's organization X which was tolerated and possibly armed by the Germans, and even before the German departure fortified a base near the ancient temple of the Theseion under the Acropolis. The number of armed combatants of ELAS in Athens–Piraeus rose from 1,600 in April–May to 5,500 at the time of the German departure in October. By this time there was an ELAS unit billeted in each of the many districts dominated by EAM/ELAS, and their streets were openly patrolled by the young toughs of these units armed with sten guns. Terroristic assassinations were carried out by a special unit, members of which were by August disguising themselves in German uniforms and conducting a vendetta against all army officers, presumably because they were prominent in the Security Battalions and in groups like X. In September Zalokostas wrote that 'EAM is murdering on average two of our lads each day – officers, students, officer-cadets'. He added that of the 500 cadets in the regular army's training college for officers, in 1940, 215 had now been killed.[66]

Most of the civil strife in 1944 was between ELAS and the collaborationist forces. The Security Battalions accompanied German troops in frequent raids on EAM-dominated districts of Athens–Piraeus, and from March 1944 were frequently resisted by force. The conflicts reached their peak of intensity in August, when many thousands of people were arrested after the encirclement by Germans and collaborationists of selected districts. Meanwhile in Salonika the followers of Poulos, Dangoulas, and others cooperated likewise with the Germans against the working-class districts of Salonika, while these or other forces had from at least as early as November 1943 helped the Germans in operations in western and central Macedonia. Several hundred of these collaborationists consisted of slavophones originally recruited with the help of Bulgarian officers. From the start of 1944 Security Battalions accompanied Germans in extensive sweeps of the Peloponnese and Euboea, regions crucial to the Germans because they seemed most exposed to Allied invasion. Collaborationist forces repaid attacks on themselves by burning houses and executing hostages in large numbers, and commonly conducted interrogations with torture. In Euboea and in western Macedonia, they were guilty of extensive looting and arbitrary terror. EAM/ELAS retaliated with a campaign of assassinations which included much-publicized attacks on the families of collaborationist troops and gendarmes. In the first half of 1944 EAM agents assassinated the prefect of Euboea (who was a general active in organizing the Security Battalions), the sub-prefect of Patras, and the Minister of Labour, and kidnapped four other prefects. According to German records, in June 1944 five–ten people each day (presumably Greeks) were being killed by EAM assassins.[67]

In extensive areas (such as Athens–Piraeus and the towns of Thessaly) EAM/ELAS was seriously weakened by the initial offensives launched by Germans and collaborationists at the end of 1943 and the start of 1944, but then recovered – in part by recruiting refugees from their offensives and benefiting from the odium which they provoked. Fighting between ELAS and collaborationist troops reached its zenith in most places in July–September, just before the German evacuation.[68]

It seems that most of the bands which participated in civil strife in 1944 had local ties of some sort. For example they recruited inhabitants of the areas in which they normally operated, while army officers gravitated to their natal localities. Conflict took the form in many areas of destructive and bloody feuds between neighbouring villages: these feuds were widespread in Laconia, western Macedonia, western Sterea and eastern Epirus. Some villages were divided, such as Karpofora in the south-west, where the feud between two factions accounted for ten lives between March and August 1944.[69]

It is clear from German casualty figures, and from descriptions by observers, that the most numerous sufferers in civil strife were unarmed villagers in the disputed zones, who were vulnerable to reprisal attacks, confiscation of goods, and intimidation by both sides. Especially wretched was the fate of those subjected to local tyrants – such as the collaborationists Poulos in western Macedonia or Liakos in Euboea, or the Communists 'Robespierre' in western Sterea or 'Odysseus' in Evros – who ruled by terror, with frequent arrests, torture, and execution of suspects. A British officer reported from an EAM execution centre somewhere in Sterea Ellada on 4 September 1944 that 'owing to the stench of rotting corpses, it is impossible to pass near a place by my camp. Lying unburied on the ground are naked corpses with their heads severed.' In western Sterea Ellada and Epirus, another British officer reported that the 'sadistic crimes and mutilations were revolting' during the civil war between ELAS and EDES in October 1943 to February 1944. An ELAS officer described one of Poulos's interrogation centres in Chelidona in western Macedonia, a school building with blood stains on the walls where torturers had wiped their hands.[70]

LIBERATION

German troops began to withdraw from the south and Aegean islands at the start of September 1944, and the last of them crossed the northern frontier on 4 November. Their withdrawal was accompanied by the descent of ELAS forces from the mountains in order to harass the German retreat and to occupy the plains and towns. They proceeded to destroy what vestiges remained of the traditional state, dissolving the gendarmerie and burning police archives in the towns, and establishing EAM government in all its ramifications. EAM authority was also established at this time in several Aegean islands. The Communists kept the provisional government in existence until early November; and elections were held for its local authorities late in October as decreed by Siantos as its Minister of the Interior.[71]

A similar process was occurring almost simultaneously in the rest of the Balkans. On 20 August the Red Army launched an offensive against Romania, and in the next two months liberated that country, as well as Bulgaria and – in cooperation with Tito's Partisan forces – eastern Yugoslavia also. Romania and Bulgaria thus fell under the effective control of the Soviet forces, while Yugoslavia and Albania were taken over by Communist-dominated front organizations commanding guerrilla armies similar to ELAS. The Communist parties of all those countries grew rapidly, and began to harass and persecute other parties. Thus was demonstrated the truth of Stalin's remark to Tito in April 1945: 'This war is not as in the past; whoever occupies a territory also imposes on it his own social system. Everyone imposes his own system as far as his army can reach. It cannot be otherwise.'[72]

In Greece, it was not clear to anyone, during the German retreat, that the Red Army would halt at the Greek frontier, or that the British would dispatch substantial forces. Thus the obvious course for the Communist leaders was to consolidate their power, regardless of their agreement with Papandreou's government in exile. Immediately after their central committee meeting of 28–9 July they ordered an intensified campaign of assassinations and arrests in the capital, trying thus to ensure that their most dangerous opponents were cowed or put out of action before the Germans departed.[73] They were opposed by Venteres's colleague Colonel Panagiotes Spiliotopoulos, who on 1 August secretly assumed the post of military governor of Attica on behalf of Papandreou's government, and appointed as his chief of staff the leading officer in the Military Hierarchy, Theodoros Gregoropoulos. Both were respected by regular army officers in active status, and secured the cooperation of about 3,000 of their colleages, and of the anti-Communist organizations, in their preparations to hold the capital after the Germans' departure. The public officials of Ralles's quisling government also prepared to transfer loyalty to Spiliotopoulos. As the gendarmerie were divided and discredited by their collaborationist activities, Spiliotopoulos relied especially on the chief of the city police, Evangelos Evert. On 23 September and again early in October Spiliotopoulos's supporters, notably members of X, evaded EAM patrols in order to bring into Athens shipments of arms that had been organized by Venteres overseas. The first and perhaps second shipment were transferred mainly to the city police.[74]

Spiliotopoulos could not however prevent EAM from taking control of outlying suburbs during September as the Germans withdrew to the centre and gave up their attacks. EAM domination of the capital became increasingly open. Assassinations by its agents continued at least to the middle of the month. On the 23rd some EAM supporters briefly seized the government radio station and announced that EAM/ELAS was about to liberate the country. Soon after 17 September, Spiliotopoulos saw with despair that the garrison commanders whom he had just appointed made their peace with EAM, while the chief of gendarmerie was preparing to do so after desertions by his men. Spiliotopoulos's authority was saved when it was confirmed by Papandreou in a broadcast on 29 September. Soon afterwards, with Ralles's consent, the gendarmerie and city police formally acknowledged Spiliotopoulos's authority, and the Security Battalions surrendered to him.[75]

The Communist leaders faced the consequences of recognizing the exiled government when they heard of the Caserta agreement on 26 September between their representatives, the government, and British authorities. Sarafis and the two other Communist representatives at Caserta had to agree to the arrival in Greece of British forces in support of Papandreou's puppet government; to place ELAS together with other Greek armed forces under the overall command of General Ronald Scobie, acting on behalf of this government; to keep regular ELAS forces out of the metropolitan region and out of EDES territory; and to leave to the government the trial of the hated collaborators. The decisive argument used by Papandreou against the Communist representatives was that their refusal would break up his government. The Communist leaders in Greece reacted with shock and confusion to news of the agreement; but shrank from a return to their defiant stand in July. Siantos, flanked by the Soviet representative Popov, broke the news to ELAS troops that they would not make their coveted triumphal march into the capital. But he and five politburo colleagues did what they could to strengthen their control over the capital by continuing large-scale arrests – in defiance of the government and the Caserta agreement – and continuing to send in arms. Meanwhile strong forces of ELAS regulars were stationed near the capital; and EAM/ELAS benefited from temporary British recognition of its authority in most of the country, including nearly all provincial towns.[76]

The Germans on withdrawing from the provinces left collaborationists garrisoned with ample supplies of weapons, while also leaving depots of arms within reach of ELAS, so deliberately fomenting civil war.[77] Finding themselves surrounded by ELAS, and without their German commanders, many of the collaborationist troops suffered from low morale and poor discipline; and the conscripts among them were probably keen to desert. Thanks to mediation by government representatives or British officers some of these garrisons surrendered peacefully, to be held in confinement thereafter under British supervision. But some refused to surrender to ELAS, and were attacked and defeated with heavy losses on both sides, notably at Kalamata, Meligala, Pyrgos, and Mistra in the southern and western Peloponnese in September and October. These battles were credibly reported to have been followed by indiscriminate massacres of 600 civilians at Pyrgos and of 1,600 at Meligala. Among those captured at Meligala were the prefect, the public prosecutor, and gendarmerie commander of Messenia, who were apparently among a group of fourteen prisoners who were lynched in a public square in Kalamata by friends and relatives of their victims: 'a gruesome spectacle' according to an American observer. Thus were requited the executions of about 1,500 people by collaborationists in this area during the occupation. After liberation, in the Peloponnese as a whole, at least 375 gendarmes and Security Battalionists were killed before British officers and government representatives could end the fighting.[78]

In Macedonia, the British and the government were still weaker; and ELAS commanders, believing the worst of British intentions, ignored Scobie's order to treat collaborators as members of EDES. Various accounts (Greek and British) show that several hundred collaborationist fighters were killed during October and November in battles in western and central Macedonia in or near Krya Vryse, Koukkos, Salonika, Servia, Kilkis, and Nigrita. In the largest of these battles, at Kilkis on 3 November, according to an ELAS account, about 9,000 collaborators fought against 6,000 of ELAS. Most of the collaborationist troops were killed or captured. Here the killed included Kitsa Batzak and Dangoulas. At Krya Vryse on 11 October 50 collaborationists were killed and 400 captured. At Koukkos on 17–18 October 130 collaborationists were killed and 77 captured. At Nigrita on 12–13 November, 500 collaborationists were killed and 120 captured. Near Servia, on 24–5 November, Michal Agas's followers, who had hitherto been shielded by British recognition, suffered an attack on 24–5 November with the loss of 120 men.[79]

In these battles ELAS captured large quantities of arms and ammunition, while also acquiring those left in their way by the retreating Germans. Their arms now included nearly 100 field guns. These gains did much to remedy the desperate shortages from which most ELAS units had hitherto suffered, and enabled them to arm many new volunteers.

Thus the German occupation ended with the population polarized in nearly all parts of the mainland between EAM and its opponents. It seemed obvious to relatively detached observers that each side commanded the loyalty of a large part of the population. But EAM was far more united and disciplined than its enemies. In most regions on the mainland this polarization had resulted in mutual hatred and considerable violence, which had reached new heights in the few months preceding the German withdrawal. It was in this situation, on 18 October, that George Papandreou's government disembarked from a British warship and drove ceremonially into the capital, having been preceded by British troops.

It was clear that control of military power would be a critical problem facing his government; and it was not at all clear that this problem would be settled in favour of the British and their anti-Communist clients. The British forces now in Greece were only of a token character, and still apparently fewer than the modest contingent of 6,000 which the British Cabinet had decided in August to send. Small as these figures were by comparison with ELAS strength, they were still smaller when compared with the Red Army divisions which now controlled much of the Balkans, and were helping native Communist parties ideologically in agreement with the Greek party to move into commanding positions. In these circumstances, EAM seemed to have reasonable prospects of establishing its power peacefully, provided that it avoided overt provocation of the British. Since the Atlantic Charter promulgated by Churchill and Roosevelt in August 1941, the Western Allies had reiterated their devotion to the principle of self-determination of nations; and it seemed hardly conceivable that the British government would use force to impose its clients on the main resistance group of an allied country.

It is worth comparing the Greek situation with that of other countries where British, or Anglo-American, forces competed for influence at this time with a Communist-led resistance movement. In Yugoslavia, Italy, and France, the experience of enemy occupation had discredited the pre-war regimes and created conditions favourable to radical resistance movements, including movements led by Communists. But the Communist parties in Italy and France had to acknowledge the power of other organized mass parties, socialist and christian democrat. These Communist parties suffered from the further disadvantage that Anglo-American troops invaded in great strength and so made impractical any thought of a Communist coup. Therefore Communists had to accept the prospect of participation with other mass parties in a pluralist political system. The Communist parties of Yugoslavia and Greece, by contrast, faced no serious competition from other parties because the latter were poorly organized and bankrupt of ideas. In Yugoslavia, the Communist Party could establish a formidable resistance movement early in the German occupation because it had not, like its Greek counterpart, been pulverized by the pre-war regime, and soon after the German invasion of April 1941 could take a prominent role in the mass revolt by Serbs and Montenegrins against oppression by Germans and by their Croat collaborators. By the time that the British sent sizeable military missions and large-scale supplies into Yugoslavia, in 1943, the

Communists under Tito had established an independent power-base, and had no need, like the Greek Communists, to accept British tutelage. The British then decided to help the Yugoslav Communists because they were the only effective resistance movement and because the British had no vital interest in Yugoslavia. By October 1944, the Communist-led People's Liberation Movement had established a position in Yugoslavia even stronger than that of EAM in Greece, and secured Soviet approval in moving to crush what was left of rival parties.

In other liberated countries of eastern Europe, invasions by Soviet forces made an independent revolution unthinkable. Greece, however, was not invaded by large Allied forces at this time because it lay outside any theatre of war. In Greece, moreover, conflict between political groups was particularly violent and widespread under the German occupation. Thus it was only here that the German withdrawal created the conditions for widespread and prolonged civil war.

NOTES

1. FO 371/18393/9; John O. Iatrides, ed., *Ambassador MacVeagh Reports* (Princeton, 1980), p.55.
2. Georgios I. Ralles, *O I. Ralles Omilei ek tou Taphou* (1947), p. 42; Georgios I. Ralles, *Koitazontas Piso* (1993), pp. 288–9, 299, 339, 345.
3. Ralles, *Piso*, pp. 41, 113, 117.
4. Dionysios Benetatos, *To Chroniko tes Katoches, 1941–4* (1963), pp. 144–6.
5. Sources include J. L. Hondros, *Occupation and Resistance. The Greek Agony,1941–4* (New York, 1983), pp. 81–3; Procopis Papastratis, *British Policy towards Greece during the Second World War* (Cambridge, 1984), pp. 209–10; André Gerolymatos, *Guerrilla Warfare and Espionage in Greece, 1940–4* (New York, 1992), pp. 321–2; Nars, RG 226 P.I.C. Paper no. 55, 'Greek Security Battalions', no. 83476, anon (c. July 1944) ; RG 226, nos. 71905, 52590; FO 371/43694/71, R 16802; Ralles, *Ralles*, pp. 56, 65, 123; Chrestos Zalokostas, *Chroniko tes Sklavias* (n.d.), p. 288; Hagen Fleischer, 'Nea stoicheia gia ten schese Germanikon archon katoches kai tagmaton asphaleias', *Mnemon* 8 (1980–2), pp. 189–203; Apostolos Daskalakes, *Istoria tes Ellenikes Chorophylakes* (1973), I, p. 184.
6. Mark Mazower, *Inside Hitler's Greece* (New Haven, 1992), pp. 334–9; *Elevtheria*, 26 Jan. 1965, p. 5; 29 Jan. 1965, p. 5; Georges Zoides, D. Kailes, et al., eds, *St'Armata! St'Armata! Chroniko tes Ethnikes Antistases* (1967), p. 462; Nars, RG 226, no. 83476; FO 371/43694/201, telegram, 11 Oct. 1944.
7. Thanases Chatzes, *E Nikephora Epanastase pou Chatheke* 3 vols (1977–9), I, pp. 376–9; Theodoros Gregoropoulos, *Apo ten Koryphe tou Lophou* (1965), p. 262; Zalokostas, *Chroniko*, p. 102.
8. B.G. Baltogiannes, *Ethnike Antistase EOEA–EDES: Ole e Aletheia* (1986), p. 156; André Gerolymatos, 'The role of the Greek officer corps in the resis-

The Origins of the Greek Civil War

tance', *Journal of the Hellenic Diaspora* 11, 3 (Fall, 1984), pp. 69–80; Giorgios Margarites, 'Emphylies diamaches sten katoche (1941–4): analogies kai diaphores', in Hagen Flaiser and Nikos Svoronos, eds, *Praktika tou Diethnous Istorikou Synedriou: Ellada 1936–44: Diktatoria, Katoche, Antistase* (1989), p. 510; Peltekis Archive, Benaki Museum, Athens, file 6, no. 8, R.P. McMullen, 15 Feb. 1944; Zalokostas, *Chroniko*, p. 102.

9. FO 371/37208/166, R 12331, Political Intelligence Summary, no. 6, 17 Nov. 1943.

10. Papastratis, *British Policy*, pp. 36, 74–85; Fleischer, 'The anomalies in the Greek Middle East forces, 1941–4', *Journal of the Hellenic Diaspora* 5,3 (Fall, 1978), pp. 7–9; Nikolaos Stavrou, *Allied Politics and Military Interventions* (Athens, 1974), pp. 23, 92.

11. K. Konstantaras, *Agones kai Diogmoi* (1964), p. 80; Nikolaos A. Antonakeas, *Pos Eidon ton Apelevtherotikon Agona kata ta Ete, 1941–5* (1945), pp. 297–8.

12. Hondros, *Occupation*, p. 231; Papastratis, *British Policy*, p. 208; Nars, RG 84, Athens Embassy Confidential Records, military attaché's report, 3 Aug. 1944.

13. George M. Alexander, *The Prelude to the Truman Doctrine. British Policy in Greece, 1941–7* (Oxford, 1982), pp. 22–3; Stavrou, *Allied Politics*, pp. 23, 51.

14. G.A. Leontarites, *Pioi Ethelan ta Dekemvriana?* (1986), pp. 14–15; G. Margarites, 'Politikes prooptikes kai dynatotetes kata ten apelevtherose', *Mnemon* 9 (1984), pp. 177–8.

15. Phoivos Gregoriades, *To Antartiko* 6 vols (1964), III, pp. 16–17; Hondros, *Occupation*, pp. 144–7; Myers in Marion Sarafis, ed., *Greece from Resistance to Civil War* (Nottingham, 1980), p. 109; Komnenos Pyromaglou, *E Ethnike Antistase* 2nd edn (1975), p. 329.

16. Zalokostas, *Chroniko*, p. 199.

17. P. I. Papathanasiou, ed., *Gia ton Elleniko Vorra: Makedonia, 1941–4* 2 vols (1988), I, pp. 170–1.

18. Benetatos, *Chroniko*, p. 136; Chatzes, *Nikephora*, II, pp. 178–82, 292–4, 361; FO 371/37207/240, R 11752; 371/37208/166, R 12331; 371/43689/11, R 10083.

19. N.P. Evstratiou, *To Laikon Komma. Apo tes Protes mechri tes Trites Archegias* (1948), p. 115; Papathanasiou, ed., *Elleniko Vorra*, I, p. 140.

20. FO 370/43699/131, R 21461; G. Kasimates et al., *Georgios Papandreou (1888–1968): Koryphaies Stigmes tes Neoteres mas Istorias* (1988), pp. 124–30; Papathanasiou, ed., *Elleniko Vorra*, I, pp. 105, 140, 144, 163–5; II, pp. 576–7; Pyromaglou, *Ethnike Antistase*, pp. 305–7.

21. Lars Baerentzen, ed., *British Reports on Greece* (Copenhagen, 1982), pp. 126–8, 153–4; Baltogiannes, *Ethnike Antistase*, pp. 160–2, 179; FO 371/37204/26, R 7213; Pyromaglou, *Ethnike Antistase*, pp. 312–3; Komnenos Pyromaglou, *O Georgios Kartales kai e Epoche tou* (1965), pp. 297–314.

22. Lazaros Arseniou, *E Thessalia sten Antistase* 2 vols (1977), II, pp. 209, 227; FO 371/37204/113, R 7535; Papathanasiou, ed., *Elleniko Vorra*, II, pp. 580, 616–17, 623, 653–8; Ralles, *Ralles*, pp. 146–7; Stefanos Sarafis, *ELAS: Greek Resistance Army* (1980), p. 145.

23. Papathanasiou, ed., *Elleniko Vorra*, II, pp. 608–9; Gregoriades, *Antartiko*, III, p. 290; FO 371/37205/113, R 9254; Peltekis Archive, file 6, G1.7, M. Ward, 'report on visit to Greece, 21 Oct. to 25 Dec. 1943'.

24. Nikolaos A. Anagnostopoulos, *E Euvoia sten Katochen* 3 vols (1950–73), I, p. 320; Arseniou, *Thessalia*, I, pp. 137–8; FO 286/1165, British Consul-

General, Salonika, to Leeper, 14 Apr. 1945; 286/1166, anon, 'notes on Crete, 26 March–6 April 1945'; 286/1181, British consul Patras, 29 Aug. 1946; Gregoriades, *Antartiko*, V, pp. 184–5; Evangelos Kofos, *Nationalism and Communism in Macedonia* (Salonika, 1964), p. 124; Thanases Metsopoulos, *To 30 Syntagma tou Elas* 4th edn (1987), p. 32; C.M. Woodhouse, *Apple of Discord* (1948), pp. 91–3.

25. Peltekis Archive, file 7, nos. 65–6, J. Smith-Hughes report, n.d.; Daskalakes, *Istoria*, I, pp. 235–8, 563–4; P.J. Carabott, 'A British military occupation: the case of Samos', *Journal of Modern Greek Studies* 7 (1989), pp. 287–320.

26. Margarites, 'Emphylies', in Flaiser and Svoronos, eds, *Praktika*, pp. 506–8; captured Communist correspondence, Leonidas to Ioannides, 17 Nov. 1944; Metsopoulos, *30 Syntagma*, p. 183; FO 371/43787/-, no. 19472, R 19913.

27. Anagnostopoulos, *Euvoia*, II, p. 320.

28. Baerentzen, ed., *British Reports*, p. 157.

29. Aschenbrenner, 'Civil War', in Lars Baerentzen, John O. Iatrides, Ole L. Smith, eds, *Studies in the History of the Greek Civil War, 1943–9* (Copenhagen, 1987), p. 115; Konstantaras, *Agones*, p. 97.

30. Metsopoulos, *30 Syntagma*, p. 33; Konstantaras, *Agones*, p. 71.

31. Philip Argenti, *The Occupation of Chios by the Germans and their Administration of the Island* (Cambridge, 1966), p. 65; FO 371/43695/62, R 18578; Nars, RG 226, no. 80241, early June 1944; Chrestos Tyrovouzes, *Avtodioikese kai 'Laike' Dikaiosyne* (1991), pp. 217–18.

32. Vasiles Bouras, *E Politike Epitrope Ethnikes Apelevtheroseos* (1983), pp. 50–5; Chatzes, *Nikephora*, I, p. 449.

33. Hondros, *Occupation*, p. 144; Hondros, 'The Greek resistance,1941–4: a re-evaluation', in Iatrides, ed., *Greece in the 1940s. A Nation in Crisis* (1981), p. 41; Hagen Fleischer, *Stemma kai Svastika: e Ellada tes Katoches kai tes Antistasis, 1941–4* (1988), p. 311.

34. Costas Couvaras, *OSS with the Central Committee of EAM* (San Francisco, 1982), pp. 6–17, 43–4, 53; Zoides, Kailes et al., eds., *St'Armata!*, pp. 537–9; Hondros, *Occupation*, p. 149.

35. Sarafis, *ELAS*, pp. 102–3; Mazower, *Inside Hitler's Greece*, p. 135.

36. Hondros, *Occupation*, p. 162.

37. Giannes Ioannides, *Anamneseis: Provlemata tes Politikes tou KKE sten Ethnike Antistase, 1940–5* (1979), p. 172; Daskalakes, *Istoria*, I, p. 200.

38. Gerolymatos, 'Role', p. 74; Sarafis, *ELAS*, pp. 40–6, 266.

39. Hondros, *Occupation*, p. 149; Peltekis Archive, file 6, G1; Papathanasiou, ed., *Elleniko Vorra*, II, p. 580; Tyrovouzes, *Avtodioikese*, p. 309.

40. Lars Baerentzen, 'The liberation of the Peloponnese, September 1944', Iatrides, ed., *Greece in the 1940s*, p. 133; KKE, *Keimena tes Ethnikes Antistases* 2 vols (1981), I, pp. 92–4.

41. Daskalakes, *Istoria*, I, pp. 194, 251, 266–7, 275, 281; Baerentzen, ed., *British Reports*, p. 28; Pyromaglou, *Ethnike Antistase*, p. 319; Hondros, *Occupation*, pp. 134–5; Papathanasiou, ed., *Elleniko Vorra*, II, pp. 618–19.

42. Hondros, *Occupation*, pp. 152, 160.

43. Zalokostas, *Chroniko*, pp. 156, 178–9, 180–3; Gregoriades, *Antartiko*, III, pp. 307–8, 311; V, pp. 260, 267, 282; Daskalakes, *Istoria*, I, pp. 194, 208; FO 371/37205/106; Peltekis Archive, file 6, no. 8, R.P. McMullen, 15 Dec. 1943.

44. Papathanasiou, ed., *Elleniko Vorra*, I, pp. 289, 346; II, pp. 470, 485–8, 583,

612–13, 630–1; Nicholas G.L. Hammond, *Venture into Greece. With the Guerrillas* (1983), pp. 67, 87.

45. Papastratis, *British Policy*, pp. 104–11; Gregoriades, *Antartiko*, III, p. 207; Panagiotes Kanellopoulos, *Emerologio. 31 Martiou 1942–4 Ianouariou 1945* (1977), p. 476; Chatzes, *Nikephora*, II, pp. 204–5.

46. Chatzes, *Nikephora*, II, pp. 206–9; Hondros, *Occupation*, p. 168; Richard Clogg, 'The Special Operations Executive in Greece', in Iatrides, ed., *Greece in the 1940s*, p. 117.

47. Gregoriades, *Antartiko*, IV, pp. 422–3; Hondros, *Occupation*, pp. 171–2; Chatzes, *Nikephora*, II, p. 288; Ioannides, *Anamneseis*, pp. 200–1; FO 371/37208/155, R 12299, EAM central committee statement, 19 Nov. 1943.

48. Benetatos, *Chroniko*, p. 199; Zalokostas, *Chroniko*, pp. 211–12; Nars, RG 226, entry 144, box 91, folder 976, G.R. Tampling, 30 Oct. 1943; Gregoriades, *Antartiko*, IV, pp. 413–14.

49. Hondros, *Occupation*, pp. 177–80; Papastratis, *British Policy*, pp. 158–60; Pyromaglou, *Kartales*, p. 280; FO 371/37207/229, R 11750; 371/37208/6, R 11787; 371/37206/74, R 10248.

50. Petros Rousos, *E Megale Pentaetia* 2 vols (1976–8), II, pp. 54–7; Papathanasiou, ed., *Elleniko Vorra*, I, p. 177.

51. Papastratis, *British Policy*, p. 165; Kanellopoulos, *Emerologio*, pp. 518, 534; Gregoriades, *Antartiko*, V, p.46; Kasimates et al., *Papandreou*, pp. 124–30; Alexander, *Prelude,* p. 21.

52. Ioannides, *Anamneseis*, p. 219.

53. Nars, RG 84, Athens Embassy General File, 'EAM leaders discuss Greek governmental crisis', 1 June 1944.

54. Ioannides, *Anamneseis*, p. 213; Daskalakes, *Istoria*, I, p. 188, report of a KKE meeting in Athens on 9 July 1944.

55. Alexander, *Prelude*, p. 37; Papastratis, *British Policy*, pp. 170–1.

56. John L. Hondros, ' "Too weighty a weapon": Britain and the Greek Security Battalions, 1943–4', *Journal of the Hellenic Diaspora* 15,1&2 (Spring–Summer 1988), pp. 36–7; Lars Baerentzen, 'The arrival of the Soviet military mission in July 1944 and KKE policy: a study in chronology', *ibid.* 13, 3&4 (Fall–Winter 1986), pp. 96–110; FO 371/43689/134, R 10503, Leeper to FO, 5 July 1944.

57. Angeliki Laiou-Thomadakis, 'The politics of hunger: economic aid to Greece, 1943–5', *Journal of the Hellenic Diaspora* 7, 2 (1980), pp. 28–30; John L. Hondros, 'The Greek resistance, 1941–4: a re-evaluation', in Iatrides, ed., *Greece in the 1940s*, p. 46; Sarafis, *ELAS*, p. 296.

58. Bouras, *PEEA*, p. 128; B. Kondis, 'The "Macedonian question" as a Balkan problem in the 1940s', *Balkan Studies* 28, 1 (1987), p. 154; Rousos, *Megale*, II, p. 163–4, 179, 202–3.

59. Peter J. Stavrakis, *Moscow and Greek Communism* (Ithaca, 1989), pp. 27–9; Alexander, *Prelude*, pp. 28–9, 42–3, 46; Ioannides, *Anamneseis*, p. 253; Bouras, *PEEA*, pp. 135, 142–3; M.S. Macrakis, 'Russian mission on the mountains of Greece, Summer 1944 (a view from the ranks)', *Journal of Contemporary History* 23 (1988), pp. 399–401.

60. E.g. Thanasis D. Sfikas, *The British Labour Government and the Greek Civil War* (Keele, 1994), p. 37.

61. Diary in Metsos Partsalides, *Diple Apokatastase tes Ethnikes Antistases* (1978), pp. 240–2; Rousos, *Megale*, II, pp. 205–9; Chatzes, *Nikephora*, II, pp. 483–517; Vasiles Bartziotas, *Ethnike Antistase kai Dekemvres* (1985), pp. 275–8; Ioannides,

Anamneseis, pp. 257–8. Ebert and Noske were the German Social Democrat leaders who when in power after the end of the First World War had condoned the suppression of the extreme left by the army.

62. Zalokostas, *Chroniko*, p. 261.
63. Sarafis, *ELAS*, p. 280; Takes E. Papagiannopoulos, *5/42 – Psarros: Matomenos Thrylos* (1981), pp. 73–91, 148–9; Nars, RG 226, entry 154, box 39, folder 580, J.T. Hartmeister, n.d., 'secret activities in Greece', (May–Oct. 1944); box 40, folder 620, A.M.M. Wines to P. West, 24 May 1944; Gregoriades, *Antartiko*, V, pp. 21–4.
64. Nars, RG 84, Athens Embassy General File, J. Sperling to MacVeagh, 2 July 1945; Konstantaras, *Agones*, pp. 124–5, 149, 157, 238; Papathanasiou, ed., *Elleniko Vorra*, II, pp. 613–74; Sarafis, *ELAS*, pp. 405–6.
65. FO 371/43694/201, telegram, 11 Oct. 1944; FO 371/43764/-, no. 7185, R 14557; Nars, RG 84, Athens Embassy Confidential Records, 1944, H.F. Maclean, 'report of activities and military action, area no. 1 (Western Macedonia), Greece'; *Elevtheria*, 27 Jan. 1965, p.5; Chatzes, *Nikephora*, II, p. 346; KKE, *Keimena*, I, pp. 93–4; Margarites, 'Emphylies', in Flaiser and Svoronos, eds, *Praktika*, p. 507.
66. Zalokostas, *Chroniko*, p. 292; Gregoropoulos, *Apo*, pp. 268–9; Bartziotas, *Ethnike Antistase*, p. 237; Nars, RG 226, no. 59899, Source Z, 22 Jan. 1944; RG 226, nos. 94553, 93654; FO 371/43691/192, R 13425, periodical intelligence report no. 28, to 16 Aug. 1944.
67. Mazower, *Inside Hitler's Greece*, pp. 341–9; Hondros, *Occupation*, p. 150; Bartziotas, *Ethnike Antistase*, pp. 235–7; Chatzes, *Nikephora*, II, pp. 342, 345; Stefan Troebst, 'E drasis tes Okhranas stous nomous Kastorias, Florinas kai Pellas,1943–4', in Flaiser and Svoronos, eds, *Praktika*, p. 260; KKE, *Keimena*, I, pp. 90–1, 101; FO 371/37210/14-5, R 13508; Konstantaras, *Agones*, p. 147; Giannes K. Douatzes, *E Tagmasphalites tes Euvoias: Anekdota Engrapha* (1982), pp. 87–112; Nars, RG 226, no. 75731; P.I.C. Paper no. 55, 'Greek Security Battalions'; no. 83476, pp. 12–13.
68. Arseniou, *Thessalia*, II, p. 238; Metsopoulos, *30 Syntagma*, p. 312; KKE, *Keimena*, I, p. 101; Zoides et al., eds, *St'Armata!*, p. 381.
69. Margarites, 'Emphylies', in Flaiser and Svoronos, eds, *Praktika*, p. 513; S. Aschenbrenner, 'The civil war from the perspective of a Messenian village', in Baerentzen, John O. Iatrides, Ole L. Smith, eds, *Studies*, pp. 116–17.
70. FO 371/43692/120, R 14791; 371/43691/192-3, R 13425, periodical intelligence summary no. 28, to 16 Aug. 1944; Peltekis Archive, file 6, G1, p. 7g, C.E. 'Tom' Barnes, n.d.; Chatzes, *Nikephora*, II, p. 503; Metsopoulos, *30 Syntagma*, p. 367; Mazower, *Inside Hitler's Greece*, pp. 319–20, 337.
71. Argenti, *The Occupation of Chios*, p. 109; Chatzes, *Nikephora*, II, p. 517.
72. Quoted in B. Jelavich, *History of the Balkans. Twentieth Century* 2 vols (Cambridge, 1983), II, p. 301.
73. Ioannides, *Anamneseis*, p. 290.
74. FO 371/43691/192, periodical intelligence summary no 28, to 16 Aug. 1944, R 13425; Nars, RG 226, entry 108, box 68, 7 Nov. 1944.
75. Gregoriades, *Antartiko*, V, p. 277; Ioannides, *Anamneseis*, p. 530, n. 91; Zalokostas, *Chroniko*, pp. 295, 318–19, 379; FO 371/43693/244, R 16218.
76. Alexander, *Prelude*, pp. 54–5; Sarafis, *ELAS*, pp. 379–83; Ioannides, *Anamneseis*, pp. 280, 298, 304; V. Bartziotas, *Exenta Chronia Kommounistes* (1986), p. 201; Gregoriades, *Antartiko*, V, pp. 238, 312.

77. Woodhouse, *Apple*, pp. 101–2.
78. Nars, RG 84, Athens Embassy Confidential File, box 3, from A–21, Charley, 18 Sept. 1944, Helot; Daskalakes, *Istoria*, I, pp. 195–223; Gregoriades, *Antartiko*, V, pp. 305–6; Ralles, *Ralles*, p. 144; Mazower, *Inside Hitler's Greece*, p. 358.
79. Sarafis, *ELAS*, p. 493; Daskalakes, *Istoria*, I, p. 196; FO 371/43699/122, R 21879, A.I.S. report for week ending 25 Nov. 1944; Zoides, Kailes et al., eds, *St'Armata!*, pp. 455, 463; Metsopoulos, *30 Syntagma*, pp. 391, 394, 404–7; Ioannides, *Anamneseis*, pp. 388, 395; Konstantaras, *Agones*, pp. 254–5; Richard Capell, *Simiomata, a Greek Notebook, 1944–5* (1946), p. 89.

CHAPTER FIVE

Revolution Defeated, October 1944–February 1945

GROWING COMMUNIST POWER

During the four months after the Caserta agreement of September 1944 the balance of power in Greece swung from the Communists to their opponents. There are aspects of this process that are still puzzling, even after all that has been written by participants and by historians. The greatest mysteries concern the Communists' intentions. The following analysis which is based on their actions, their correspondence, and their retrospective accounts indicates the following conclusions: that they remained determined to win national power; aimed to make their hold on power exclusive; but tried as far as possible to avoid conflict with the British. Their ambition was manifest and feared by many; but their opponents were divided by diverse backgrounds and motives, and agreed only in seeking protection by the British. The latter gave it because they were determined to bring Greece securely back within their sphere of influence, their determination being reinforced – in the minds of politicians, diplomats, and officers alike – by repugnance for the Communists' mentality and methods. Unfortunately the British did not at first have the strength to make their determination clear.

Prime Minister Papandreou, on arriving in his capital on 18 October, found the civilian population and all vital services controlled by EAM, which, like the Communist Party, had just established its headquarters in the administrative heart of the city. These organizations demonstrated their control over the civilian population during the coming weeks by organizing vast, regimented demonstrations, which even British officers confessed they found unnerving. The force at Papandreou's disposal consisted at first of little more than the 3,000-strong city police – and according to

Communist sources nearly a quarter even of them supported EAM. Outside Athens the British troops restrained themselves to the harassment of the retreating Germans and the protection where possible of Greek anti-Communists, and did not otherwise enforce Papandreou's authority. Thus Papandreou had no option but to cooperate with EAM and the Communist Party, even though he still regarded the latter as a revolutionary force obedient to Moscow.[1] His keynote speech on arrival, before a great crowd in Constitution Square, made vital concessions to EAM: it included the EAM slogan *laokratia* (people's rule); promised the prompt punishment of EAM's arch-enemies the collaborators; and most significantly of all announced that the gendarmerie – the traditional pillar of government authority – was in a state of 'moral crisis' as a result of its behaviour under Metaxas and during the occupation, and would be replaced in time by a new body. On 5 November his government formally entrusted authority throughout the mainland, outside the metropolis and EDES-controlled territory, to the EAM militia (*politophylake*). The few gendarmes in the provinces who had not disbanded, or been arrested by ELAS, were brought to the capital to remain demobilized under British protection.

Papandreou let the Communists at first hope that the government's armed forces would, when formed, be dominated by EAM's army ELAS. One of the three joint commanders of ELAS, Sarafis, recounted that during October its units were disposed 'as far as possible in the towns where they would probably be stationed after the army reorganization'. On 11 November Papandreou appointed as commander-in-chief of his projected army General Alexandros Othonaios, who although widely respected was seen by the Communists as an ally, and Othonaios appointed Sarafis, an old colleague of his, as in effect his chief of staff. Together they immediately began to plan the organization of the new army. Soon afterwards Siantos ordered provincial party organizations to ensure that members of ELAS and the EAM militia presented themselves at the recruiting stations when called up, and after recruitment retain their political organization within the new force. Local secretaries complied by recording the political views of civilians liable to be called up. ELAS members not recruited were to retain their organization under the camouflage of official veterans' associations: 'in this way we shall have a force ready to take the field at any moment', wrote another of the joint commanders of ELAS, the Communist guerrilla leader Ares Velouchiotes, on 15 November.[2]

The Communists prepared also to permeate the central administration. A directive to EAM on 23 October read: 'We have influence over many political personalities, and we have many members who are lawyers, bank employees, civil servants, etc. Thus there is no reason why we should not place some of them in official or semi-official government posts, in order to control the administration, which today is in the hands of the Fascists [i.e. the politically conservative].' Outside the main cities, the administration was generally supplanted or influenced by EAM.[3] The government began to implement some EAM policies. The non–EAM Minister of Justice collected data about the people's courts to use in reforming the code of law. The Communist Minister of Labour placed some industrial enterprises under workers' management, while his ally Svolos as Treasurer established employees' representation in major banks. For their part, the Communist leaders ordered provincial organizations to 'cultivate the friendliest relations with . . . the British'. To maintain good relations with Papandreou, they even tried (unsuccessfully) to deter trade unions in the metropolis from striking and demonstrating for wage rises in line with inflation.[4]

More light is thrown on the Communists' strategy by the character of EAM rule in the provinces. This is described in reports by British and American officers, the latter being freer to form personal opinions because they were not influenced by official bias against the Communists. The following evidence refers to areas of EAM rule during the period of cooperation between EAM and the government from September to 3 December, although it should be remembered that EAM authority continued in most places until February or March 1945. In accordance with directives from their provisional government during the occupation, the EAM authorities called themselves Committees of Local Self-Government and were based on popular election. However the freedom of those elections was almost nullified by the lack of secrecy in voting and the choice of candidates by EAM authorities. In every town or village the real authority continued to be the EAM official, the *ipevthinos*, who was appointed from above. Especially significant was EAM's refusal to tolerate rival organizations or newspapers, with it seems the sole exception of the few places where British troops sheltered them, notably Patras and Ioannina. Although popular support for EAM seems to have been quite strong everywhere, this was also true of opposition, but the latter was intimidated into quiescence. EAM officials enforced their authority through their ability to call on their armed forces. For example in one district in Thessaly, where support for EAM was relatively strong, an American observer reported that 'there is hidden opposition to EAM . . . but the fear of ELAS terrorism is very great'. In the EDES territory of Ioannina there were 'several thousand' refugees from EAM-controlled areas to the north and west who were reportedly 'very bitter'. EDES tolerated EAM organizations in its territory, although this tolerance may have been necessitated by their popular support.[5]

The EAM authorities tried to insulate the population from contact with the British or with the government. In some places, people were afraid to speak to British soldiers. Telephones and radio transmitters were monopolized by EAM, while radio receivers required EAM permits. EAM militia picketed the roads and turned back people without passes. In Salonika the military governor appointed by the national government heard of its decisions only through EAM newspapers. In all EAM-controlled areas people were gaoled in sizeable numbers on charges of treachery, charges which, as we have seen, EAM was accustomed to apply very freely: some at least of those arrested were accused of spying for Metaxas or merely of opposing EAM. In accordance with its policy during the occupation, EAM aimed to punish as fascists not only collaborators but also prominent supporters of the Metaxas regime. In Salonika a British observer reported that prisoners numbered over 5,000, being held in 'extremely bad' conditions, with 'large crowds assembled outside the two principal prisons visited, demanding the blood of traitors and brandishing the photographs of murdered sons and husbands'.[6] Communist newspapers emphasized that they expected the government to try collaborators promptly.

The Communists no longer saw any need to conceal their role in EAM; and many civilians, even within EAM, were made anxious by the increasing evidence of their control. Thus a prominent socialist representative on the EAM central committee in Salonika told an American officer that his party were now afraid because EAM there was 'entirely controlled by violent Communist elements which formerly were camouflaged under respectable names and groups'.[7] Prominent socialists in Athens like Demetrios Strates and Alexandros Svolos were alarmed by the Communists' provocative course, and were preparing early in November to assert their independence. Allied observers in different localities noted that the majority of EAM officials and supporters wanted free parliamentary elections, but that the Communists were intolerant of opposition.

The growing prominence of Communists was accompanied by increasing evidence of class bias. In many places the authorities confiscated houses or levied taxes on wealth. In Salonika they imposed a levy on black marketeers and collaborators. Because of its increased power, the Communist Party felt fewer inhibitions about frightening property owners. Not surprisingly, opposition to EAM was especially marked among the wealthy. An American observer reported that in Thessaly (where the plains were relatively prosperous) the estimated 40 per cent of the population who were not ardently pro-EAM consisted of those who were economically better off.[8] An American reported that among the Greek community in Egypt, the richer classes were especially opposed to EAM, some of them because of their 'large economic stakes in Greece . . . '[9] Much of EAM revenue, admittedly, was spent on schools, hospitals, the distribution of relief, and the repair of communications and public utilities. But much too was clearly being spent on ELAS and – according to plausible belief – on the Communist Party. As EAM taxation was especially burdensome in conditions of general hardship it was 'extremely unpopular' according to Demetrios Strates, leader of the Socialist Party of Greece (SKE) in EAM.[10]

This evidence of EAM rule shows that the call by the Communists at this time for 'normal democratic development' had a meaning quite different from what it had in Western parliamentary democracies. Like the elections organized by EAM the previous April, the parliamentary elections which EAM now anticipated were likely to have been 'democratic' only in the sense of being dominated by a party based on mass mobilization rather than on oligarchical patronage. It is impossible to agree with the claims by Heinz Richter that the Communist Party diverged ideologically from its Yugoslav counterpart in accepting Western concepts of democracy, and that 'a post-war Greece erected on these foundations would have been a liberal, democratic . . . state'. Nor can we agree with the alleged contrast, in John Hondros's account, between the peaceful intentions of the Communists and the aggressive intentions of the British. Hondros fails to recognize the dictatorial intentions of the Communists, or their continued use of force against their opponents in Macedonia whom the British could not protect.[11]

THE DEMOBILIZATION CRISIS

The Communists' hope of peacefully dominating the national army was shattered by the arrival from Italy of the Mountain Brigade, which paraded through the capital on 9 November to the applause of large crowds, lacking heavy weapons but confident and battle-hardened. It was clearly intended by Papandreou and the British to form the nucleus of the new army, and it had come with this expectation. The protests of the EAM ministers against bringing it to Greece were overridden.

EAM had good reason for alarm, although George Alexander and John Loulis have argued otherwise. Even Liberals outside EAM feared that the Mountain Brigade would support a royalist dictatorship, so re-enacting the events of 1935–6. The recent head of the British Military Mission, Colonel Woodhouse, who was arguably the best informed of British officials, saw the Brigade's presence in Greece as a needless provocation. It seemed plain to the Communists that if, after the dissolution of ELAS, the Brigade's soldiers were employed to command the new army, they would provide

131

opportunity for revenge to the Communists' numerous enemies all over the country, and so threaten the power-base of EAM.[12] A senior British officer acknowledged that this fear was 'genuine and justifiable'.[13] For these reasons the Mountain Brigade formed the chief obstacle in negotiations between Papandreou and EAM for the demobilization of ELAS.

The Mountain Brigade's arrival caused a change in Siantos's policy, shown in his immediate cable to provincial party organizations:

> Reaction aims to create conditions favourable to a coup and dictatorship. Watch. ELAS should remain at their position until presuppositions for a normal development of the situation are secured. Will disband only when the forces from Egypt [i.e. all forces returning from exile] are disarmed and a new army is formed under the command of men cherishing the confidence of the fighting people.

On 13 November, this prospect vanished when General Ronald Scobie intervened. Given authority over all Greek armed forces by the Caserta agreement, Scobie like his fellow-officers arrived in Greece without any understanding of the polarized state of the country. Less excusably, he failed to seek the advice of better-informed officers such as Woodhouse. He acted on the groundless assumption that Papandreou's government was the legitimate one; from which it followed that the Communists were sinister trouble-makers. Devoid of political antennae, he believed that he could tame the Communist and EAM leaders by reprimanding them as if they were disorderly recruits. He even convinced himself at one point that he could bring about the demobilization of ELAS by offering money for each rifle surrendered. Now, on 13 November, he effectively prevented Othonaios from starting his new duties, and arranged the transfer of control over appointment of new officers to anti-Communists including Venteres and Spiliotopoulos, who, confident of British backing, embarked on a collision course. A week later, Papandreou tried to appease mounting Communist suspicion by generous concessions, offering in effect to disband the Mountain Brigade by giving all its members leave, and removing Venteres and Spiliotopoulos. But he failed to prevent the right-wing staff at the War Ministry from appointing former Security Battalionists to the command of eight out of fourteen of the projected new battalions. The publication of these appointments on 24 November naturally caused uproar.

In various ways, Papandreou convinced confidants of his genuine desire to prevent civil war, an aim in which indeed he had a personal interest. Having few followers of his own, he was an isolated and vulnerable figure among Greek politicians. His chief claims to the top place were British patronage and ability to maintain agreement with EAM. His problem now was the British determination to thwart the Communists' wishes. Churchill in particular distinguished himself by his obvious impatience for a military showdown, describing ELAS as 'miserable Greek banditti'. The other British authorities — Eden, Maitland Wilson as Supreme Allied Commander in the Mediterranean, Leeper as ambassador in Greece, besides Scobie — agreed with Churchill in believing that the Communist Party wanted revolution, which they were determined to prevent if necessary by force. Their suspicions were strengthened by EAM's dictatorial rule in the provinces.[14]

For this reason Papandreou's offer to disperse the Mountain Brigade was vetoed by Scobie with the backing of his military and political superiors. Another of Papandreou's problems was that opinion among officers was so polarized that few appointees to the National Guard seemed trustworthy to the Communists outside the ranks of ELAS or its sympathizers. As regular army officers and cadets had until September been victims of a campaign of assassinations by EAM, they were understandably keen to turn the tables against it. Thus the Communists in the end objected to the great majority of nominations proposed by the government or by the Military Governor in Salonika. One officer appointed to the government's new army was murdered in broad daylight in the capital by ELAS on 25 November. In at least some places, the process of recruitment — when it started in Athens and several provincial towns on 24th — was obviously inspired by an anti-Communist spirit and gave heart to local rightists. An order from Communist leaders to the Macedonian organization on the 25th shows that they were alarmed that their Greek opponents were trying to prevent Communists from enlisting.[15]

The distrust and conflict of interest between the two sides caused the deterioration of relations in many places. In the metropolitan area the Communists' suspicions were aroused by the assembly under British custody of many thousands of demobilized soldiers and gendarmes charged with collaboration, some of them being allowed much freedom of movement. As others were kept in harsh conditions, it appears that the British and the government were justifiably distinguishing between degrees of collaboration. But the Communists had reasons to see them all as dangerously hostile, and potential allies of the British. One reason was that by 14 November the British authorities were restoring some Security Battalionists to active service with the Mountain Brigade.[16]

The British for their part were worried by the reported increase near the capital of sizeable ELAS forces. As we saw in the previous chapter, ELAS continued throughout November its attempts to destroy the remaining anti-Communist bands in Macedonia, in defiance of British orders. In EDES-controlled Epirus, too, on 24 November an American officer reported that 'EAM is said to be smuggling more than 1200 assorted weapons into Ioannina. Trouble is expected.' On the same day another American officer reported the political situation in Pyrgos, in the western Peloponnese, as 'extremely tense'. In nearby Patras American and British officers spoke of 'probable open hostilities'. At the same time, Ares Velouchiotes at ELAS GHQ reported the dispatch of 300 rifles and 40,000 rounds of ammunition to Elevsis near Athens. On 1 December, in the foot-hills of Hymettos, on the eastern outskirts of Athens, there were skirmishes between ELAS and the Mountain Brigade which were evidently more seri-ous than the street-fighting which had continued sporadically since the liberation. On the same day in eastern Macedonia, an ELAS force of 5,000 launched an offensive – approved by the Communist leadership – which by the 17th had killed or captured 3,200 of Anton Tsaous's followers.[17]

Meanwhile, talks in Athens about demobilization broke down on 28 November, whereupon both sides faced the prospect of violent confronta-tion. The Communist leaders had for some time expected this outcome. A politburo meeting at Ioannides's hospital bedside on 17 November accepted the need for some kind of conflict with the British if the leaders could not secure their terms. The cadres below politburo level were still more bellicose. On the same day, the 17th, Ares Velouchiotes without authorization convened fellow guerrilla-leaders (*kapetanioi*) and told them to be prepared for conflict. A meeting on the 22nd of 150–60 cadres directing metropolitan and provincial party organizations decided that a military clash was inevitable; and about this time the Athens organization under its secretary Vasiles Bartziotas began to prepare for it in cooperation with the ELAS First Corps of reservists.

Siantos continued for several more days to seek an agreement with Papandreou because he had little choice. In this and other matters some of his colleagues in their subsequent accounts failed to recognize his difficult-ies. He could not move large quantities of troops or weapons to the metropolis, as his cadres urged, without both alerting the British and alienating the non-Communist EAM ministers, who saw no need for a conflict. When negotiations over demobilization broke down, he tried to prepare for possible fighting in the capital, but was handicapped by lack of authority over ELAS, because its GHQ, located in distant Trikala, was by the Caserta agreement placed under the government. For this reason at least two ELAS commanders queried orders by Siantos to move troops towards Athens; while GHQ on 1 December asked the EAM central committee who was to command them in the event of a clash. In the event, no ELAS troops did move towards Athens before 2 December: a delay which was perhaps critical.[18] To give himself the necessary authority over ELAS Siantos revived its central committee with himself as member on 1 December, in anticipation of the imminent resignation from the government of the EAM ministers. On that day both sides brought matters to a head. Siantos, after a night of fevered arguments and requests for guidance at Communist and EAM headquarters, announced to the EAM central committee that 'two worlds are in collision: one struggles for a new future; the other for a return to the past'. In this spirit he and the Athens organization gave orders for mass demonstrations in Athens and other towns on the 3rd, to be followed by a general strike from the 4th onwards. Scobie, on behalf of Papandreou's government, used means which included a radio broadcast and leaflets dropped from aircraft to publicize an ultimatum to ELAS to disarm by the 10th.[19]

Many years later Ioannides remarked that 'we [the Communist leadership] were deliberately proceeding to create a pretext for the war to begin', words which were taken literally by George Alexander and John Loulis. In fact, as Alekos Papapanagiotou, the editor of Ioannides's memoirs, points out, the words when taken in context *describe the impression which Ioannides presumed that his party's actions made on the government.* Ioannides, still in hospital, was not consulted during those crucial and hectic days because there was no politburo meeting after 28 November and before 5 December. Other senior Communists – Thanases Chatzes, Vasiles Bartziotas, and Papapanagiotou – make it clear in their accounts that Siantos was actually trying to put pressure on the government, hoping to topple Papandreou and replace him by someone more compliant on the issue of demobilization, preferably the Liberal Georgios Kaphantares. The fact that Siantos sent no instructions to accompany his warnings to provincial organizations, on 28,29 and 30 November, of possible civil war indicates that he had little idea what to do. But it is obvious from various Communist sources – and from his lack of military preparation – that he did not expect or prepare for the large-scale fighting to come. His critical mistake was to discount the danger of effective British intervention, at least before 10 December, the terminal date in Scobie's ultimatum.

However, the Communists could see that government forces might respond violently to the demonstration and general strike, and so Bartziotas planned the response of ELAS reservists and held them in readiness in the background during the demonstration. Already the previous day Siantos's military adviser General Mantakas asked GHQ for the secret dispatch of explosives and mines, with trained personnel, 'for probable fighting in built-up areas'.[20]

Papandreou likewise expected some violence, but not large-scale military operations, as his secretary told the American military attaché on 2 December. His forces prepared accordingly: the gendarmes began on 30 November to rearm, and the chief of the city police, Evert, sent pro-EAM policemen on leave.[21]

One reason why Siantos did not expect the British forces to intervene was their weakness. The key British figures – Churchill, Maitland Wilson, and Scobie – had seen before the end of October that the prevention of a Communist coup would require far greater forces than the 6,000 they had originally allowed for. But Maitland Wilson (and Harold Alexander who succeeded him in November) had to restrict reinforcements until they could be assured of a prolonged suspension of hostilities on the Italian front. Even then they knew that the Americans on the Joint Chiefs of Staff Committee would be reluctant to authorize the transfer of troops to Greece because they were needed in northern Europe. The total number of British troops under Scobie's command in mid–November was 26,500, besides five squadrons of aircraft (amounting perhaps to 60). Reinforcements were still arriving, bringing the total number of troops to perhaps over 30,000 by the end of the month. During most of the occupation, by contrast, there were over 300,000 German, Italian, and Bulgarian troops in the country. British weakness was accentuated by the fact that most troops were dispersed in the provinces, in order to distribute relief supplies, and also in order to protect and hearten anti-Communists. This left about 2,000 British combat troops in the metropolitan area, with some armoured and artillery units and many administrative staff, at the beginning of December, with billets and depots widely scattered, so as to use whatever vacant buildings were available without inconveniencing civilians. In their weakness, British troops gave Communists a misleading impression of neutrality by not intervening in any of the clashes between ELAS and its opponents in different regions from 24 November to 3 December.[22]

Although the prospect of Soviet intervention in Greece had apparently ceased to worry Churchill – since he had met Stalin in October and concluded what became known as the Percentages Agreement partitioning the Balkans – it still seemed real to British officers in Greece. Scobie knew of a top-level agreement on spheres of influence, but could not know how binding it was. An American officer reported on 23 November that Scobie feared that, if conflict broke out, Soviet troops in Bulgaria might enter Greece on the pretext of helping to restore order. If they did they would obviously be welcomed by ELAS. When fighting did break out in Athens in December, Churchill was subjected to strong opposition in the British parliament and pressure from the New Zealand and Canadian governments, besides unfavourable coverage by the BBC and in nearly all of the British and American press. All this criticism seriously embarassed him.[23]

THE BATTLE FOR ATHENS

When on 3 December a massive column of EAM demonstrators entered Constitution Square, it approached a thin line of armed police screening their headquarters, which were close to other key government buildings. Although the crowd was unarmed, the police had cause to feel threatened, one reason being that the police chief Evert knew that a hand grenade had just exploded and a policeman been killed or wounded outside Papandreou's house nearby. At least once during the enemy occupation EAM demonstrators had occupied government buildings; and Evert later said that he believed they intended to do so now. For whatever reason, the police opened fire without prior warning, and in front of foreign journalists continued firing for some minutes on people who were trying merely to save themselves, eventually killing a probable sixteen and wounding scores of others.

Whether anticipated or not, this disaster was for the Communist Party an international propaganda coup, enabling it to retaliate with sympathy from public opinion in the Western democracies and from non-Communists in EAM. Thus the retaliation was not, as Mark Mazower wrote, spontaneous. Late that night ELAS reservists received orders to capture all police stations in the metropolitan area.[24] By nightfall of the 6th they had occupied nineteen out of twenty-four, together with the X-ites' bases, at least one prison, and the headquarters of the hated Special Security and the gendarmerie. In the process they destroyed the archives which had been used by Metaxas's police minister Maniadakes. Although not of strategic importance, these soft targets provided First Corps with enough captured weapons to increase its armed combatants from 6,000 to 12,000. In addition, regular ELAS troops from outside the metropolitan area had started to arrive before dawn on the 4th and by the 7th seem to have numbered about 10,000, with more to come. The Greek anti-Communist forces in Athens–Piraeus at this time numbered about 10,500, as 'well-placed sources' of rightist sympathies told an American officer.[25] This estimate agrees broadly with those of Communist historians, such as the ELAS commander Orestes (Andreas Mountrichas). Thus the Communist forces were numerically far stronger than their Greek opponents, and enjoyed the added advantage of controlling the civilian population through EAM. Wearing no uniform, ELAS reservists merged with civilians, who supported them through reconnaissance, transport of supplies, sheltering fighters, and in at least one instance surrounding British troops and preventing them from disarming an ELAS unit. EAM's power was also shown in the total paralysis of all economic activity and public services in the capital by the general strike.[26]

This strength explains the confidence shown by the Communist polit-buro, at its meeting on 5 December, and by its military advisers when they met the following day. Siantos now saw the opportunity to eliminate the last of his Greek opponents. Even now he did not aim openly to seize dictatorial power. As he and his colleagues showed in private talks at this time, and in a conference with other party leaders on the 26–7th, they still aimed to participate in a coalition government, but this time ensuring their dominance by controlling a re-constituted police and army.[27] This was the tactic currently being pursued by other Balkan Communist parties.

The decisions which the political and military leaders made on the 5th and 6th were to attack their main opponents on the 7th: ELAS regulars under Orestes would attack the Mountain Brigade in the Goudi barracks in the north-east suburbs. On the same day, and without Siantos's authorization, Bartziotas and First Corps attacked a strong gendarmerie force in the Makregianne barracks close to the city centre, near the Acropolis. On the 7th Siantos also took the controversial step of ordering the distant GHQ of ELAS, and most of the ELAS forces, including most of its experienced commanders and heavy weapons, to attack EDES in Epirus and Michal Agas's band in Macedonia. Certainly these enemies had to be destroyed; but all agreed that the critical spot was Athens, and the northern units of ELAS might have turned the scale there, even allowing for the several days which they needed to arrive on foot. This decision, perhaps more than any other, later earned Siantos condemnation by Zachariades for treachery. Yet no leading Communist claims to have disputed it at the time, indicating that all assumed that the ELAS forces in and near the capital were sufficient to overcome their anticipated opponents.[28] Siantos's decision makes sense only on the assumption that he still discounted the possibility of strong or timely intervention by the British. Not till the 7th did he authorize attacks on the British in the capital, and ELAS continued to concentrate its attention on its Greek opponents for another eleven days. Although in the provinces GHQ repeatedly requested permission to attack British forces, Siantos did not grant it until the 30th.[29]

In fact Scobie had already, on the 5th, received Churchill's order to 'act as if you were in a conquered city where a local rebellion is in progress' (words which became famous a week later when they appeared in the *Washington Post*). As Churchill later admitted, he thought when he gave this order that a mere 'volley from British troops' would suffice to suppress ELAS. Scobie and his staff, while rather less optimistic, seriously underestimated the strength of ELAS resistance.[30] They gradually increased the pressure. In the small hours of the 4th, British troops surrounded and peacefully disarmed a prestigious ELAS battalion as soon as it arrived in the capital. On that day and the 5th they rescued beleaguered X–ites and police in various places. On the 6th they began fighting ELAS, and on that and the following day occupied commanding heights in the city's central areas, including the Acropolis and Lycabettos. On the 7th they started to support right-wing troops with strafing by the RAF, shelling by artillery, and mortar fire. These actions should have proved to Siantos, by the time he gave his orders to ELAS GHQ, the seriousness of British intentions.

Fatally for the Communists, the offensive against the Goudi and Makregianne barracks on the 7th failed, as did repeated attacks on subsequent days. The Communist leaders improvised their strategy hastily and then disagreed about military objectives. The attack on the Goudi barracks under Orestes's leadership was poorly timed and coordinated, losing the advantage of surprise. The attack on the Makregianne barracks, like most of the fighting by ELAS in the metropolis this month, was conducted by ill-trained reservists, who broke off the attack at a critical point when they heard a false rumour that their neighbours and kinsfolk were being massacred by the Mountain Brigade. These, like ELAS attacks on other enemy bases during the December fighting, indicate that the Communist leaders had neglected key factors. One was the strength of their main Greek opponents, who unlike most of the collaborationist troops were disciplined and determined professionals, well equipped with heavy machine-guns and light arms, and often able to rely on rescue by heavy British firepower. From the 7th onwards, the British made increasing use of tanks, artillery, and aircraft, and later of warships also. ELAS by contrast had few heavy arms: a few mortars and heavy machine-guns, and only two or three field guns in the whole course of the fighting in Athens. To attack strongly defended buildings ELAS combatants had to rely on numbers, heroism, and the frequent use of dynamite, and many hundreds of them died in the process.[31]

After ELAS's failure to eliminate its Greek opponents in the first week of fighting, the issue was virtually decided by the arrival from the 12th onwards of massive British reinforcements, which eventually amounted to two entire divisions, a brigade, and several battalions. By early January the total British forces in Greece reached 75,000, most of them in the metropolitan area. From 18 December, the British continually pressed back the ELAS positions, using Greeks as auxiliaries in a revived National Guard, which numbered about 15,000 by the end of the month and 23,000 by the close of January. Many of these were gendarmes, and many others were members of nationalist resistance organizations, who pressed their services on the British at the outbreak of fighting. But the majority of the National Guard during the fighting – at least 12,000 according to the Deputy Minister for War Leonidas Spaes – were former collaborationist troops, the decision to arm whom originated with the British.[32] Thus the British authorities now took the place of the Germans as patrons of the extreme anti-Communists.

A remaining mystery is why as late as 26 December, when their ammunition and troops were becoming exhausted, the Communist leaders rejected the chance of a truce which would have let them keep ELAS intact outside the metropolitan area. They seem to have been misled, by the protests against British policy in the media of the British Commonwealth and the United States, into believing that the British government wanted to disengage. Askoutses, a socialist in EAM, told an American officer on the 15th that his political associates, after hearing the tone of BBC broadcasts, believed that a British Cabinet crisis was imminent.[33] Their belief seems to have been encouraged by Churchill's visit to Athens to attend negotiations on the 26–7th between the Communists and other political leaders. The Communists were probably encouraged too by the slow progress of British troops, who as late as the 26th occupied only one-quarter of the metropolitan area, their delay being due to their reluctance to harm the civilian population more than necessary, and the effectiveness of ELAS in urban guerrilla warfare. Elsewhere on the mainland the British were on the defensive.

The Communists' miscalculation was soon apparent. By 5 January most of ELAS had been forced to abandon the capital in disorder, 'morally and physically shattered' according to Ioannides.[34] The fighting in the metropolis alone had cost ELAS 2,000–3,000 lives (according to British calculations), as well as 7,540 combatants or supporters taken prisoner. The Greek right-wing combatants had lost in total 3,480 killed (comprising 889 police and 2,591 soldiers), and many captured: an ELAS commander referred to over 1,000 soldiers and policemen held near the Communist base at Trikala. The British had lost 210 killed, 55 permanently missing, and 1,100 captured who were found by American officers in January and reported to be 'badly in need of medicines, food, shoes, clothing, and blankets'. Outside the capital, the fatalities included 800 of EDES, at least 500 of Michal Agas's band in western Macedonia, and 300–400 of Anton Tsaous's forces in eastern Macedonia. ELAS suffered 680 casualties in its fight against EDES, and over 300 in fighting Anton Tsaous.[35]

The terrorization of civilians during the conflict in the capital is thus described by an American officer:

> Persecution within the ELAS area of all those people of Rightist tendencies was extremely intense, and conversely, no person with Leftist leanings was safe in the Government-held territory in Athens. As a result a great many people fled from their houses and went to that territory held by the Armies of their own political thinking. Thus in Lamia [over 100 miles north of Athens] we literally had thousands of people who had left Athens due to the persecution going on

there. And Athens, itself, was jam-packed with Democrats, Royalists, and anybody else who was not an out and out ardent supporter of ELAS in the Provinces and had come to the capital for safety.[36]

According to the Communist participant Pavlos Nepheloudes, tens of thousands of EAM civilians fled from the capital in the wake of defeat.

COMMUNIST SURRENDER

Everywhere on the mainland outside the capital ELAS had triumphed. Immediately after 3 December it disarmed the newly formed National Guard battalions, so acquiring another 4,000 rifles. On 19–25 December, ELAS routed the EDES forces in a two-pronged offensive into Epirus. Thousands of them deserted, and of the rest, 6,540 combatants, with 3,233 civilian hangers-on, were evacuated to Corfu by British ships. In Macedonia, the bands of Michal Agas and Anton Tsaous were also destroyed. In different regions ELAS raised many new recruits, and supplied them with arms that were captured, and arms received from Bulgaria.[37] The British Commonwealth troops in the ports of Salonika and Patras were immobilized, while those elsewhere had to escape by ship, sometimes with casualties and abandoning their stores. The British forces in the capital could not advance far outside it, for military and political reasons already indicated: such further action would be opposed by the Joint Chiefs of Staff and by the British and American public. To complete the British victory in the rest of the country would have required an indefinite commitment by far greater forces. Encouraged by these military considerations, the Communist leaders' immediate intention after the retreat from the capital was merely to seek a breathing-space. To this end they decided on 8 January to seek a truce, which was agreed to and came into effect on the 15th.[38]

They soon discovered that they lacked the means to continue the war. In their obsession with destroying their Greek opponents, they had temporarily forgotten what one of them, Iannes Zevgos, then a minister in Papandreou's government, had privately noted on 18 October: 'The question of bread takes first priority.'[39] By January the Communists' greatest weakness was their countrymen's need for foreign aid, the distribution of which was interrupted by the hostilities. British military authorities exploited the weakness by denying food to hostile areas, while supplying it to supporters or sympathizers. During the fighting the result was the appearance or intensification of hunger and destitution, which were felt immediately in the major cities. In Salonika early in December the nunist leaders were forced to let dockers return to work quickly to continue unloading food. In Athens lack of food hampered ELAS operations. Worsening destitution appeared in many other parts of the country. For example, an American officer reported on 24 December that 'most of the population of Eastern Macedonia and Thrace are desperate. Economic conditions are getting progressively worse. Medical supplies are almost entirely lacking. Shoes and clothes are needed badly. The quality of the bread has deteriorated.'[40]

In many places EAM authorities increased their taxation, particularly on the wealthy, and in at least some places, like Salonika and Florina, people were gaoled for non-payment.[41] Given the Anglophile feelings of a majority of the population, the result of these material sacrifices was increasing opposition to EAM rule. As the Communist leaders had not hitherto dared to challenge British popularity, their allies were completely unprepared for conflict against British forces. Bewilderment and demoralization arose within ELAS and intensified after the defeat in the capital, causing desertions in some places. Thus an American officer reported on 15 January 1945 that in Thessaly 'a growing number of ELAS officers and men were questioning the true aims of ELAS. Those who had not by this time absorbed the spirit of social revolution were either arrested on various pretexts or removed from influential positions.'[42] Ioannides admitted that many in the ranks of EAM were speaking behind the Communists' backs of the British as allies. ELAS had accumulated enough food to survive six months of war, but would do so at the cost of starvation for its countrymen.[43]

Even in these circumstances, the Communist Party might conceivably have continued the war if it had been helped by fraternal parties. From the end of November it sent repeated delegations to press the leaders of the Albanian, Yugoslav, and Bulgarian parties for aid. All returned quite empty-handed. The Yugoslav Communist leader Tito, who actually encouraged the Communists' intransigence in late November, buckled under British protests. He would not even agree to let ELAS forces use Yugoslav soil as a base, and tried to conceal from foreign observers the presence of at least one of the Greek delegations. The politburo member Petros Rousos tried to reach the Soviet Union from Bulgaria but was arrested in Sofia by the Soviet authorities and taken back to Greece. During the fighting in Athens the Soviet press, unlike the American, refrained from condemning the British. Strict Soviet instructions to stick to peaceful activities eventually reached the Greek Communists on 13 January via Georgi Dimitrov, the Bulgarian Communist leader. By this time the advice was no surprise: the realization of abandonment by fraternal Communist parties came in the first half of December. Their motives can be surmised without difficulty: Stalin wanted no dispute by the Western allies of his control of Poland, Romania, and Bulgaria, and the new leaders of the Bulgarian and Yugoslav Communist parties were still establishing their authority in their own countries and did not dare to differ from Stalin, or to risk possible Western reprisals or the loss of foreign economic assistance.[44]

By early February the Communist leaders also saw that they had suffered badly in domestic and international opinion by revelations of atrocities committed by their supporters during the fighting. The damage done in the eyes of the British and American peoples was especially serious, because they had heard relatively little hitherto of EAM ruthlessness. To Churchill, defending himself against domestic criticism, these reports were a godsend. Photographs of decomposed corpses of ELAS's victims, showing marks of execution and sometimes mutilation, and retrieved from mass graves and wells, became a staple element of anti-Communist propaganda from now on. The corpses were examined by critical foreign observers, such as American officers, who also questioned witnesses of executions and relatives of victims. In September 1945 the Greek government announced that 1,208 were executed, which is credible even if it refers only to Athens–Piraeus. A senior member of an EAM execution squad told an American officer that he estimated the number of *authorized* executions in the metropolitan area as 600, while not denying the occurrence of unauthorized ones. There are convincing reports of many hundreds more victims of political execution, and of mass arrests, in various provinces.[45]

American officers found indications from witnesses that Communists had taken advantage of the fighting to settle scores with various opponents: EDES-ites, gendarmes, and suspected collaborationists. Many of those responsible were former members of EAM's terrorist unit which had been dissolved in November, whereupon its members were employed in the EAM police. Those in Athens who were forced into hiding to save their lives included indisputably patriotic characters whose only fault was to have opposed EAM during the occupation, like the future politician Anastasios Pepones, Metaxas's official Evangelos Kalantzes, and the leader of the regular army's Military Hierarchy, Theodoros Gregoropoulos. The ELAS commander Konstantinos Konstantaras, then stationed in north-eastern Greece, described executions as widespread, many of them only for opposition to EAM, and some for personal revenge. 'We did not punish anyone [in our own ranks],' he admitted, 'because, amidst so many enemies, a general climate was created in which a demonstration of severity was considered a proof of faith in the cause.' Civilian hostages estimated by the American embassy – on the basis of eyewitness accounts by officers – at about 15,000 in the capital and about 3,000 in Salonika were forced to march long distances, thinly clad, wretchedly fed, and in bitter weather. Several thousand died of exposure, or execution, and the survivors returned after the truce with horrifying reports of brutality by their guards.[46]

Many of the Communists' victims were articulate and influential members of the bourgeoisie or of the traditional official establishment: civil servants, army officers, and police officers, some of the last being tortured before execution. The lasting damage which the Communists suffered is illustrated by the carefully documented accounts of these atrocities published during the dictatorship of 1967–74 by, among others, the politician Demetrios Theocharides and the professor of history Apostolos Daskalakes.[47] The Communists replied that their own suspected supporters had been arrested *en masse* and indiscriminately by the British in the early stages of the fighting in Athens; that 1,000 hostages had been taken by EDES and maltreated; that some of the alleged victims of execution by ELAS had died of other causes. But compared with the evidence for the prosecution, this defence was not very impressive.[48] Much of the population had been left with appalling memories of *eamokratia* (EAM rule).

For all these reasons, the Greek Communists had no hope of continuing the war with success. Contrary to the original intentions of the Supreme Allied Commander in the Mediterranean, the entire British forces remained in Greece during February, and two full divisions with air support remained for a long time thereafter. Thus it became clear to the Communists that unless they made peace nothing could prevent the British in time from occupying other major ports and their hinterlands. The British and their Greek supporters would be able to strangle the country economically and destroy the civilian organization of EAM in the centres of population and food-producing areas: the trade unions, cooperatives, and newspapers. ELAS could expect to be driven back into the mountains as in the occupation, but now without public support or the chance of obtaining help from fraternal Communist parties.[49] In a debate at Trikala at the beginning of February, the central committee understood more fully than ever before what its members had glimpsed the previous July: that in war against Britain the party would be isolated domestically and internationally.

So the Communists sought peace in return for guarantees of free elections and a general amnesty. In the course of negotiations in the seaside village of Varkiza near Athens, the EAM representatives, who included Siantos, were forced to abandon their hope of participation in the government and even of a comprehensive amnesty for their supporters. In the agreement reached on 15 February, after an all-night session, they agreed to demobilize ELAS and accept the exclusion from amnesty of those found guilty of common crimes. These were crippling concessions. Already a vendetta against EAM by the government's forces was raging in Athens; while Stylianos Gonatas – who had participated in organizing the collaborationist forces in the occupation – had been appointed civil governor of Macedonia. These events showed what could be expected throughout the country. In what was now a surrender, the Communist Party did what it had rejected as unthinkable the previous November: it granted a monopoly of armed force to its bitter opponents. Yet all but two members of the central committee (Zevgos and Kostas Karagiorgis) voted to accept the Varkiza agreement. The majority decision was facilitated by the fact that it was a return to the Communists' long-term strategy for winning power by political means, a strategy from which their leaders believed they had been deflected by British intransigence.[50]

The demobilization later that month proceeded without incident, and with the willing compliance of the bulk of the rank-and-file of ELAS. Many of the Communist commanders, however, were resentful, and a few including a group around Ares Velouchiotes were defiant. The demobilization followed one precaution which the commanders in apparently all regions undertook with encouragement or orders from the party leaders: the concealment of their better-quality arms. According to Ioannides, who supervised much of the process, enough were hidden to arm 30,000 people.[51]

The fact remained that Siantos and Ioannides had finally opted for a course like that of the Communist leader Palmiro Togliatti in Italy rather than that of Tito in Yugoslavia: the pursuit of power by political methods in a state dominated militarily by their opponents. To this end the leading cadres returned immediately to Athens to rebuild their civilian organizations, passing on their way through the pickets of the hostile National Guard. The prospects for peaceful political development were dim indeed.

In retrospect, the British defeat of EAM in the 'December events' appears as a turning-point in Greek history, the event which determined that after the war Greece would belong to the Western not the Soviet sphere of influence. It was also a spectacular exercise in *realpolitik*, arguably comparable in ruthlessness with the Red Army's action in allowing the Polish Home Army to be crushed by Nazis in Warsaw in August 1944, and jarring with the Declaration on Liberated Europe made by Churchill, Roosevelt, and Stalin at Yalta in February 1945, immediately before the Varkiza agreement. It provided Stalin with what must have been welcome precedents for further acts of ruthlessness soon afterwards in Poland, Romania, and Bulgaria. Thus it marked an early stage in the Cold War. Indeed it proved to be the only occasion during the Cold War in Europe when the forces of a Western democracy fought against those of a Communist party.

NOTES

1. Harold Macmillan, *War Diaries. Politics and War in the Mediterranean* (1984), p. 546; Nars, RG 226 no. 101619, C. G. Yavis to W. L. Langer, 27 Oct. 1944.
2. Nars 868–00/1–2245, enclosure to dispatch no. 427 in no. 2: Ares, at GHQ, to?, 15 Nov. 1994.
3. Giannes Ioannides, *Anamneseis. Provlemata tes Politikes tou KKE sten Ethnike Antistase, 1940–5*, ed. A. Papapanagiotou (1979), p. 235; Stefanos Sarafis, *ELAS: Greek Resistance Army* (1980), pp. 477–8; George Papandreou, *Politika Keimena* (1964), II, pp. 6–7; Nars 868.00/1–2245, enclosure to despatch no. 427, captured Communist correspondence (hereafter captured correspondence), KKE headquarters to provincial organizations, 22 Nov. 1944; to Ares 24 Nov.; to ?, n.d. (Nov. 1944).
4. C. Tyrovouzes, 'E prote prothypourgia tou G. Papandreou', in G. Anastasiades and P. Petrides, ed., *Georgios Papandreou. E krise ton Thesmon, oi Kommatikoi Schematismoi kai o Politikos Logos* (Salonika, 1990), p. 182; Christos Hadziiossif, 'Economic stabilization and political unrest: Greece 1944–7', in Lars Baerentzen, John O. Iatrides, Ole. L. Smith, eds, *Studies in the History of the Greek Civil War, 1943–9* (Copenhagen, 1987), p. 28; Ioannides, *Anamneseis*, p. 324; Vasiles Bartziotas, *Exenta Chronia Kommounistes* (1986), p. 207.
5. Geoffrey Chandler, *The Divided Land. An Anglo-Greek Tragedy* (1959), pp. 20–1; N. Antonakeas, *Phos eis to Skotos tes Katoches* (1947), p. 396; Nars, OSS papers, RG 226, box 1138, no. 105563, 19 Nov. 1944 (OSS reports are all RG 226, the date given being that on which information was received by the source); RG 226, no. 105814, 30 Nov. 1944; RG 226, entry 108, box 69, source 27 Feb. 1945; RG 226, entry 154, box 40, folder 620, A.M.M. Wines to P. West, 18 Apr. 1944; RG 226, no. 105272; captured correspondence, Macedonian office to Ioannides (before 8 Oct. 1944); RG 226, no. 105563, 19 Nov. 1944; entry 190, box 77, p. 18, S.J. Milton, 'Report of the Elephant Mission', n.d.; FO 371/43695/25, R 18137; and 65, R 18599; 371/43697/27, R 19953; 371/43700/72, R 21878; 371/43699/123, 132, R 21388, R 2146; 371/43694/232, R 17645.
6. Chandler, *Divided Land*, pp. 27–8; William H. McNeill, *The Greek Dilemma. War and Aftermath* (New York, 1947), p. 130; FO 371/43695/16, R 18066; 371/43695/109, R 2042; 371/43700/95, A.I.S. Weekly Report for week ending 25 Nov. 1944; FO 371/43697/48, Leeper to FO, 26 Nov. 1944; 371/43699/48, Leeper to FO, 26 Nov. 1944; Nars, RG 226, box 1166, no. 106679, sub-source's personal observation, 8 Dec. 1944; RG 226, box 1130, doc. 102651, report on Salonika, 26 Oct. 1944.
7. Nars, RG 226, no. 105274, 25 Nov. 1944; RG 226, box 1129, no. 102451, source 2 Nov. 1944; RG 226, no. 109058, box 1193, 22 Dec. 1944; RG 226, entry 108, box 68, 7 Nov. 1944.
8. Chandler, *Divided Land*, pp. 20–1; Thanases Chatzes, *E Nikephora Epanastase pou Chatheke* (1977–9), III, pp.191–6; FO 371/43695/13, R 17965, Leeper to FO, 6 Nov. 1944; 371/43697/27, R 20492, W.F. Reid, 'Appreciation of the situation in Greece. November 1944'; 371/43700/85, R 21879, report on Patras, 28 Nov. 1944; 371/43699/132, R 21461, A.I.S. Weekly Report, 9–16 Nov. 1944; Nars, RG 226, box 1214, doc. no. 110637, 9 Jan. 1945; RG 226, box 1138, no. 103344, 11 Nov. 1944.

9. Nars, RG 226, box 1175, doc. no. 107378, 8 Dec. 1944.
10. Nars, RG 226, entry 108, box 68, 7 Nov. 1944.
11. Heinz Richter, *British Intervention in Greece. From Varkiza to Civil War* (1986), p. x; J.L. Hondros, *Occupation and Resistance. The Greek Agony, 1941–4* (New York, 1983) , p. 234.
12. Reginald Leeper, *When Greek Meets Greek* (1950), pp. 93–4; Macmillan, *War Diaries*, p. 622; C.M. Woodhouse, *Apple of Discord. A Survey of Recent Greek Politics in their International Setting* (1948), p. 220; Christopher M. Woodhouse, *Something Ventured* (1982), pp. 94–5; George M. Alexander, *The Prelude to the Truman Doctrine. British Policy in Greece 1944–7* (Oxford, 1982), pp. 156–66; J.C. Loulis, *The Greek Communist Party 1940–4* (1982), pp. 193–4; Petros Rousos, *E Megale Pentaetia* (1976–8), II, p. 321; Nars, RG 84, Athens Embassy Confidential Records 1944, box 2, S.L. Larrabee, 13 Nov. 1944; RG 226, entry 108, box 68, doc. 47670, 19 Dec. 1944; Pericles Mission Report (by Costas Couvaras, no reference number, xerox copy in Dept of War office, US National Archives), 18 Dec. 1944, conversation with member of Mtn Bgde.
13. Alexander, *Prelude*, p. 162.
14. Leeper, *When Greek*, pp. 90–2; T.D. Sfikas, 'The people at the top can do these things which others cannot do', *Journal of Contemporary History* 26 (1991), pp. 317–21; W. Jackson and T.P. Gleave, *History of the Second World War. The Mediterranean and Middle East* (1988), VI p3 pp. 22–3; J. Ehrman, *History of the Second World War. Grand Strategy* (1956), VI, p. 61; W.S. Churchill, *History of the Second World War* (1954), VI, p. 9.
15. Captured correspondence; Alexander, *Prelude*, p. 73; Macmillan, *War Diaries*, p. 621; Nars, RG 84, Athens Embassy Confidential Records 1944, box 2, S.L. Larrabee, 28 Nov 1944; FO 371/43700/73, 85, R 21878–9; Henry Maule, *Scobie: Hero of Greece. The British Campaign, 1944–5* (1975), p. 92.
16. Nars 226, RG 226, entry 108, box 68, 14 Nov. 1944.
17. Leeper, *When Greek*, pp. 86, 92; Rousos, *Megale*, II, p. 323; Chatzes, *Nikephora*, III, p. 270; K. Konstantaras, *Agones Kai Diogmoi* (1964), pp. 306–7; Nars, RG 226, entry 120, box 30; RG 84, Athens Embassy Confidential File 1944, box 2, T.D. Spencer; captured correspondence; FO 371/43700/95, A.I.S. Report for week ending 25 Nov.
18. Vasiles Bartziotas, *Ethnike Antistase kai Dekemvres* (1979), pp. 337–8, 351; Ioannides, *Anamneseis*, p. 326; Chatzes, *Nikephora*, III, pp. 264, 271–2, 282, 352; Sarafis, *ELAS*, pp. 420, 426, 499; G. Kasimates et al., (eds), *Georgios Papandreou (1888–1968). Koryphaies Stigmes tes Neoteres mas Istorias* (1988), p. 145; captured correspondence.
19. KKE, *Keimena tes Ethnikes Antistases* (1981), I, pp. 121–3; Chatzes, *Nikephora*, III, pp. 270–4; Bartziotas, *Ethnike Antistase*, p. 352.
20. Ioannides, *Anamneseis*, pp. 343, 534; Chatzes, *Nikephora*, III, pp. 289–90, 325, 344; Bartziotas, *Exenta Chronia*, p. 212; captured correspondence.
21. Nars, RG 84, Athens Embassy Confidential File, S.L. Larrabee, 'Memorandum for the Ambassador', 2 Dec. 1944; Pericles Mission report of 2 Dec. from 'communist sources' and entry for 5 Dec. 1944.
22. McNeill, *Greek Dilemma*, p. 146; Ehrman, *History*, p. 61; Jackson and Gleave, *History*, pp. 21, 77, 80; Nars, RG 84, box 66, Athens Embassy, General Records 711–715, MacVeagh to Sec. of State, 18 Nov. 1944; Confidential Records, box 2, S. L. Larrabee, 22 Nov. 1944; C. Vrachniares, *Poreia mesa*

ste Nychta. E Thessalia stes Phloges tou Emphyliou (1990), p. 12; Maule, *Scobie*, pp. 80, 85, 102.

23. A.J. Foster, 'The politicians, public opinion and the press: the storm over British military intervention in Greece in December 1944', *Journal of Contemporary History* 19 (1984), pp. 455–8, 488–9; Rousos, *Megale*, II, p. 345; Nars, Pericles Report, sheet headed 'Greece political', 2 Dec. 1944, source 'a high Communist party official'; Pericles report, Source Z Plover, reporting remarks by 'one of the three top men of the Greek Communist Party'; RG 84, Athens Embassy Confidential File, box 2, R.E. Kent, 12 Dec. 1944, reporting discussions by a Canadian officer with members of EAM, 7–10 Dec. 1944; Maule, *Scobie*, pp. 90–1.

24. Bartziotas, *Ethnike Antistase*, pp. 355–6; Lars Baerentzen, 'The demonstration in Syntagma Square on 3rd December 1944', *Scandinavian Studies in Modern Greek* 2 (1978), pp. 28–31, 49; Metsos Partsalides, *Diple Apokatastase tes Ethnikes Antistases* (1978), pp. 246–7; C.G. Couvaras, *OSS with the Central Committee of EAM* (San Francisco, 1982), p. 105; Mark Mazower, *Inside Hitler's Greece* (New Haven, 1992), pp. 369–70.

25. Nars, RG 226, no. 110483, Source Z Raven, 1 Dec. 1944.

26. Apostolos Daskalakes, *Istoria tes Ellenikes Chorophylakes* (1973), I, pp. 362–9, 397; McNeill, *Greek Dilemma*, p. 146; Ehrman, *History*, p. 61; Jackson and Gleave, *History*, pp. 21, 77, 80; Ioannides, *Anamneseis*, pp. 291–2; Chatzes, *Nikephora*, III, pp. 336, 341; Pavlos Nepheloudes, *Stes Peges tes Kakodaimonias* (1974), p. 232; Demetres Vlantas, *Emphylios Polemos, 1945–9* (1981), pp. 328–9, 333; Jackson and Gleave, *History*, p. 77; Rousos, *Megale*, II, pp. 335–6; Nars Pericles Report for 5 and 6 Dec.; RG 226, entry 226, box 154, folder 618, R.E. Moyers, n.d.

27. Komnenos Pyromaglou, *O Georgios Kartales kai e Epoche tou* (1965), pp. 496–8; Pericles Report, 5 Dec.

28. Ioannides, *Anamneseis*, pp. 338–9, 382–3; Chatzes, *Nikephora*, III, pp. 344, 435; Bartziotas, *Ethnike Antistase*, p. 362.

29. Ioannides, *Anamneseis*, pp. 352, 358–9, 381–2; Rousos, *Megale*, II, p. 350.

30. Churchill, *History*, VI, p. 253; Alexander, *Prelude*, p. 86; Nars, RG 84, Athens Embassy Confidential File, W.H. McNeill, 'British operations in Athens 6–9 December 1944', 10 Dec. 1944; Jackson and Gleave, *History*, pp. 78–84.

31. Ioannides, *Anamneseis*, pp. 355–6, 388; Daskalakes, *Istoria*, I, p. 392; Chatzes, *Nikephora*, III, p. 364; Hondros, *Occupation*, p. 246; Bartziotas, *Ethnike Antistase*, pp. 342, 360, 365.

32. Sfikas, 'The people', p. 322; Leeper, *When Greek*, p. 137; Daskalakes, *Istoria*, I, p. 528; FO 371/43700/169, R 21981; RG 226, no. 113872, military attaché, 29 Jan. 1945.

33. Nars, RG 226, no. 105882.

34. Nars, RG 84, Athens Embassy Confidential File, W.H. McNeill, 27 Dec. 1944, 'British operations. Athens–Piraeus area 20–6 December', Ioannides, *Anamneseis*, p. 366.

35. S. Gregoriades, *Dekemvres-Emphylios 1944–9* (1984), p. 180; V.G. Valaoras, 'Some effects of famine on the population of Greece', *Milbank Memorial Fund Quarterly* 24 (1946), pp. 216–17; G.O. Blanas, *Emphylios Polemos Opos ta Ezesa* (1976), p. 25; Nars, RG 218, Dept of Army, Joint Chiefs of Staff CSS 381 Greece, Memo of Info., Jan. 1945.

36. Nars, RG 226, entry 226, box 154, folder 618, R.E. Moyers reporting on duties Dec. 1943–Mar. 1945; Nepheloudes, *Peges*, p. 58.

37. Nars, RG 226, entry 108, box 69, 23 Dec. 1944.

38. L. Spaes, *Penenta Chronia Stratiotes sten Yperesia tou Ethnous kai tes Demokratias* (1970), I, pp. 247–9; Jackson and Gleave, *History*, p. 102; Ehrman, *History*, p. 94; Chatzes, *Nikephora*, III pp. 445–7.

39. Partsalides, *Diple*, p. 240; Alexander, *Prelude*, p. 210; Pericles Report for 7 Dec.; George M. Alexander, 'British perceptions of EAM–ELAS rule in Thessaloniki', *Balkan Studies* 21 (1980), p. 210; Nars, RG 226, box 69, source 1 Jan. 1945, re. Evros; box 1193, doc. no. 109058, source 22 Dec. 1944.

40. Hondros, *Occupation*, p. 246; Nars, RG 226, entry 108, box 69; A. Laiou-Thomadakis, 'The politics of hunger: economic aid to Greece, 1943–5', *Journal of the Hellenic Diaspora* 7, 2 (1980), pp. 37–40.

41. Alexander, *Prelude*, p. 213; Nars, RG 226, box 1214, doc. 110637, 9 Jan. 1945; entry 108, box 69, Source Z, Sapsucker, 19 Jan.; entry 108, box 68, Source Z Duck, 12 Dec. 1944; ibid. Source Z, 24 Dec. 1944.

42. Nars, RG 226, entry 108, box 68.

43. McNeill, *Greek Dilemma*, p. 161; R. Capell, *Simiomata, a Greek Note Book 1944–5* (1946), p. 185; Ioannides, *Anamneseis*, pp. 367–8; Nars, RG 226, entry 108, box 69, 9–10 Jan. 1945.

44. Kenneth Matthews, *Memories of a Mountain War* (1972), pp. 88–9; Chatzes, *Nikephora*, III, p. 280; Ioannides, *Anamneseis*, pp. 345, 377, 534, 536; Peter J. Stavrakis, *Moscow and Greek Communism, 1944–9* (Ithaca, 1989), p. 52; Ivo Banac, *With Stalin against Tito* (Ithaca, 1988), p. 33; Lawrence Wittner, *American Intervention in Greece, 1943–9* (New York, 1982), p. 28.

45. Leeper, *When Greek*, p. 139; Foster, 'The politicians', p. 486; Rousos Koundouros, *E Asphaleia tou Kathestotos* (1978), p. 146, n. 10; Daskalakes, *Istoria*, I, p. 519; Documents Regarding the Situation in Greece, January 1945, Great Britain, Parliamentary Accounts and Papers, Command 6592, vol. 10, p. 8; Nars, RG 226, entry 108, box 69, Source Z Sapsucker, 19 Jan. 1945; box 69, Source Z, 7–8 Dec. 1944; Pericles Report, 3 Mar. 1945.

46. A. Pepones, *Prosopike Martyria* (1970), pp. 136–7; T. Gregoropoulos, *Apo ten Koryphe tou Lophou* (1966), p. 303; Konstantaras, *Agones*, pp. 249–50, 326; Hondros, *Occupation*, p. 250; Nars, 868.00/1–1245, 1–2045, MacVeagh to Secretary of State; RG 226, no. 119833, 15 Mar. 1945.

47. D.T. Theocharides, *E Makedonia stes Phloges* (1968), passim; Daskalakes, *Istoria*, I, pp. 507, 513–46.

48. Sarafis, *ELAS*, p. 510; Nars, 868.00/3–1645, enclosure 3 to despatch 76; RG 226, entry 108, box 69, Source Z, 19 Jan. 1945.

49. Ehrman, *History*, VI, p. 64; Ioannides, *Anamneseis*, p. 370.

50. Chatzes, *Nikephora*, III, pp. 460–4; Leeper, *When Greek*, pp. 145–8; Ioannides, *Anamneseis*, p. 371; Nars, Pericles Report, source Z Plover, 6 Feb. 1945.

51. Nars, RG 226, entry 108, box 69, Source Z, 25–6 Feb. 1945; RG 84, Athens Embassy Confidential File, box 8, C. F. Edson to MacVeagh, 20 Feb. 1945; Blanas, Emphylios, pp. 23–6, 35–6; Ioannides, *Anamneseis*, pp. 176, 292, 371–2.

CHAPTER SIX

The White Terror, February 1945–March 1946

RIGHT-WING VENDETTA

During the December fighting there was a realignment of political forces, which was accomplished by the British government in cooperation with Greek politicians. The result was to terminate the cooperation by the Greek government with EAM, and to restore its alignment with the traditional state and social hierarchy. An early sign of this realignment was the hasty rehabilitation and rearmament by Papandreou of the gendarmerie just before the fighting broke out.

There was no further question of admitting EAM to government, or of accommodating its wishes in appointments to the armed forces and the machinery of state. The leadership of the new government was basically settled in the consultations between British representatives and Greek politicians on 26 December in war-torn Athens, leading to successful pressure by Churchill and his Foreign Minister Sir Anthony Eden on the Greek king in London to accept as regent the head of the Greek church, Archbishop Damaskinos, until the question of the monarchy could be settled by plebiscite. The king also agreed to accept as new prime minister in place of Papandreou the Venizelist hero and former general Nikolaos Plastiras – the veteran of the 1922 revolution and the 1933 coup – who it was hoped would win back the Asia Minor refugees and republican army officers from EAM/ELAS, and restrain the anti-Communism of the mainly monarchist army, police, and National Guard.

Prime ministers continued until the general election of March 1946 to be virtually appointed by British diplomats, as they had been since the German invasion in April 1941. Thus the British ambassador in 1945, as one diplomat remarked later, held a position resembling that of a colonial governor.[1] But after the Varkiza agreement British troops refrained from further conflict. Henceforth they trained Greek soldiers to do their own fighting, and held themselves in reserve as guarantors of the government. Although designed primarily to protect the government against possible Communist revolt, their presence may well have served to deter any attempts at a coup by anti-Communist officers during the two years or so after the Varkiza agreement.

Plastiras appointed several old colleagues and friends to prominent posts in the army, the administration, and the police, one of them being General Giorgios Dromazos as chief of the general staff. Thus he diluted the Metaxist composition of the security forces. But Plastiras and his appointees could not combat the *ethnikophrosene* – the fiercely anti-Communist and now monarchist spirit – which prevailed in the army and police. As we have seen, some veteran Venizelists such as the politicians Napoleon Zervas and Stylianos Gonatas, and the army officers Konstantinos Venteres and Solon Gikas, were now prominent in the *ethnikophron* ranks. The Venizelist officers brought back into active service by Plastiras had been in retirement since 1933–5, had rusted professionally, and lost touch with the lower ranks and with each other. Thus they held posts as staff officers, area commanders, and provincial governors, rather than as commanders of troops. They like Plastiras had moreover been too frightened by EAM in the December fighting to resist effectively the witch-hunt against leftists being conducted by their *ethnikophron* colleagues.

The *ethnikophron* officers, by contrast, possessed self-confidence arising from cohesion, a strong sense of purpose, and in most cases relatively recent experience of active service. They were monarchists, either because of their Metaxist background or because they now considered the monarchy to be a necessary bulwark against Communism. Even under Plastiras as prime minister (January–April) five out of eight members of the general staff, and ten out of thirteen military governors, had held prominent posts under Metaxas. In June, under Plastiras's successor Admiral Petros Voulgares, out of 56 colonels in active status (a colonel being the highest rank in direct command of troops), only seven were democrats, i.e. Liberals or left-wing republicans.[2]

The freedom of the Liberal government led by Themistocles Sophoules, from November 1945 to April 1946, to appoint partisan supporters in the armed forces and the police was strictly limited by British training missions, one for the army which started work in February, and one for the police which started in July. The missions combined instinctive anti-Communism with a determination to ban political interference in the organizations which they supervised. So in practice they opposed attempts by governments to appoint any officers whose opinions were not ardently *ethnikophron*. They had much professional justification for this attitude, in that many of the *ethnikophron* officers had fought alongside the British in the Aegean, the Middle East, and Italy, and so were better qualified than the democratic officers.

An early beneficiary of this policy was Venteres, who returned from abroad to be appointed deputy-chief of general staff in January, and directed an organized effort by like-minded officers to screen left-wingers and liberal Venizelists from active service. He directed the Association of Young Officers (SAN) and cooperated with the Sacred Union of Greek Officers (IDEA); the latter originated in the exiled army and wielded great influence until the late 1960s. Confining its membership to junior officers on the assumption that they were less influenced by politicians and easier to discipline, IDEA acquired a strength of 2,000 in 1945. Its members believed in the 'national idea of Greece' and its 'just territorial expansion', and aimed to purge the officer corps of those 'of doubtful national feelings'. It aimed specifically to reinstate capable Security Battalionists.[3] It was these organizations which ensured, by posting agents in all units down to company level, that most democrats, and nearly all former members of ELAS, were excluded or relegated to 'List B', the list of retired officers created under Plastiras's government. Former collaborationists became prominent and numerous in the army officer corps, as in the whole range of right-wing forces, being valued for their experience and motivation. They included for example 107 of the 300 entrants in 1945 to the college for military cadets, and 228 of those who became officers in active status during 1945–6. The reinstatement of collaborationists was especially threatening to EAM because their personal safety required its destruction. Much of the officer corps in 1945 expressed admiration for the Metaxas dictatorship, which was of course repugnant to politicians. Reports by foreign observers about officers' attitudes leave no doubt that most of them during the next five years favoured a dictatorship, on the grounds that civilian governments were too feeble and corrupt to resist Communism. During 1945 there were frequent rumours that a military coup was imminent. The barrier to it was the known opposition of the army's British and later its American patrons, who controlled its finance and equipment. While restraining its political ambitions, this foreign patronage gave the officer corps a privileged and independent status, which was reflected in its relatively high pay at a time of general economic hardship.[4]

It was chiefly through their leadership of the National Guard battalions that army officers influenced the political situation early in 1945. Before the Varkiza agreement the National Guards established government authority in the metropolis and Salonika; after it they spread into the provinces following British troops, and some months later reached a strength of about 60,000. They were recruited by the conscription of army reservists but usually in such a way – in cooperation with gendarmes relying on local information – as to exclude left-wingers and to include ardent anti-Communists including, as we have seen, collaborationists. The 'Athens battalions' initiated the process of recruitment in many places, then moved on leaving new battalions to operate in their home areas. These units spear-headed local counter-revolutions which were usually violent, and led in many places to killings. So in the three months or so after the Varkiza agree-ment, the National Guards were largely responsible for the white terror whereby the agreement was extensively violated. They arrested people in great numbers and delivered them to nearby gaols and lock-ups to be beaten up and detained in foul conditions. It seems that all those who had taken an active part in ELAS or its civil guard were targeted for retribution, possibly excepting those with influential protectors such as senior Communists and army officers. The National Guards also wrecked EAM offices and printing presses. They cooperated with predatory gangs to which they channelled weapons in large numbers (a total of 15,000 by September 1946 according to a British Intelligence estimate), a major source of supply being those sur-rendered or hidden by ELAS.

The National Guards fulfilled an important role by breaking down the fear of EAM/ELAS which British troops at first found to be general among civilians. Thus they replaced EAM local administrations with bodies loyal to the government, and these consisted often of the old Metaxist appoint-ees. The National Guards also made it possible for government officials of all kinds, including gendarmes, public prosecutors, and tax collectors, to resume their functions.[5] But they were obviously storing up future trouble for the government by driving left-wingers into the mountains and further antagonizing the Slav-speakers in Macedonia. For these reasons the government transferred authority as soon as it could to the gendarmerie, and incorporated much of the National Guard into the growing army.

The riotous and provocative behaviour of the National Guards was however continued by unofficial gangs, which appeared immediately after the demobilization of ELAS, and operated thereafter in most parts of the country, but were especially numerous in the southern Peloponnese, Epirus, and southern Thessaly. In the towns various vigilante organizations – many of them, like National Action or X, surviving from before libera-tion – cooperated with the police in patrolling the streets and seeking suspects by methods which collaborationists had used in the occupation, such as random checks of identity cards, and *blokas* (encirclement of neigh-bourhoods followed by a search for suspects).[6] In larger towns, however, left-wingers found a certain safety in numbers, and enjoyed easier access to relief supplies.

In the countryside, right-wing gangs were usually fairly small, dependent on particular villages and towns, and identified with some leader, who in many if not all cases had led an anti-Communist group during the occupation. They presumably recruited many of their members from the gaoled collaborators who were released by the National Guards as soon as they arrived in a provincial town. The front page of the Communist organ *Rizospastes*, on 13 July 1945 showed a map of Greece covered by the territories of these bands, under the headline '150 BANDIT-GANGS WITH 18,000 ARMED MONARCHISTS. THEY ARE THE REAL STATE!'.

The existence of these gangs over much of the countryside was, as John Koliopoulos has pointed out in an unpublished paper (see note 6), a feature of the conditions of economic and administrative collapse after the liberation, when the only commodity in abundant supply in many rural areas was weapons. The same phenomenon had appeared early in the German occupation. The bands parasitized neighbouring communities at a time when legitimate sources of livelihood were scarce. Left-wingers were forced into outlawry by persecution and denial of relief supplies; right-wing bands then pointed to them as justification for their own activities.

The prevalent ethos of the gendarmerie and city police was so fiercely anti-Communist that it seems that hardly anyone who dissented from it could remain on active service. Those police who had exposed themselves to suspicion by participating in the organized resistance were relegated after Varkiza to the retired list. Some Security Battalionists now held prominent positions, such as the deputy-director of the training college for gendarmerie officers. In early May a Greek colonel of Liberal views was reported to have asked the new prime minister Voulgares whether the projected expansion of the gendarmerie would contribute to law and order 'inasmuch as those being added to this service, as well as those already in it, were mostly from the Metaxas dictatorship'. Voulgares replied, with only a little exaggeration, 'That's all that is available.'[7]

In the case of the gendarmerie, this bias was combined with a generally low level of professional training. The gendarmerie had been badly disrupted during the occupation and December fighting. Having been dissolved outside the metropolis, and having suffered heavy casualties in the fighting, it was reduced to a small demoralized rump. Many officers had been killed or had joined the resistance; while many under-qualified officers had been appointed by the quisling governments, or by Plastiras's administration, which reinstated Venizelists purged in 1933–5. The training college for officers had not functioned since 1940, and now had much work to do.[8] Much time was needed therefore to build up the gendarmerie's numbers, so as to make it an efficient and disciplined force capable of enforcing impartial respect for the law.

Unfortunately time was unavailable. The government urgently needed to reimpose its authority in the countryside, while the British wanted to withdraw their own troops at the earliest opportunity, and therefore needed conditions orderly enough for parliamentary elections to take place which could produce a government with independent authority. In their haste to build up the police, the British mission let training programmes be avoided or skimped. Officers did not take the retraining courses which they needed, and the lowest ranks received little training or none, many consisting of military conscripts without police experience. The city police were expanded to a strength of about 6,500 within a year of the Varkiza agreement, and the gendarmerie to a strength of over 23,000 – both figures much higher than in Metaxas's time. From the beginning of 1945 the police began to take over responsibility for order in the main cities; and by September had at least nominally assumed this duty in most regions.[9]

The police had an overriding sense of purpose which the British mission barely comprehended: to repeat their achievement under Metaxas of destroying the Communists' organization. One essential preliminary step, which they seem to have started immediately after the Varkiza agreement, was to reconstruct the comprehensive archive of party members which had been largely destroyed by Communists since 1941. The police energetically collected files with biographical information, so as to enable themselves, when they were ordered by a future government, to arrest party members *en masse*. In the more ideologically charged climate of the post-war years it was apparently difficult to plant agents within the party, as Metaxas's police minister Maniadakes had done with such success.[10] But the police enjoyed another asset not available to Maniadakes, which was keen assistance from the great and varied mass of people in all regions who wanted revenge against the left. These unofficial helpers, working through political organizations or gangs of thugs, eagerly sought out known activists, and delivered them to the police for brutal interrogation.

In nearly all rural regions and market towns during 1945 the police, working with the National Guard and vigilante groups, seriously restricted the legal organization of the KKE and EAM by arresting its members, wrecking offices and printing presses, and preventing the circulation of newspapers. The limitations on prosecution in the Varkiza agreement were widely subverted or ignored. The government reported in December that over 80,000 people were being prosecuted, and the British mission calculated that about 19,000 of these were then in gaol. We know from various sources that the great majority of these people were victims of right-wing persecution. Many people sought refuge in the main cities which by mid-1946 seem to have been almost the only places where the organizations of the Communist Party and EAM still operated openly.[11] According to EAM, between the Varkiza agreement and the general election of March

155

1946, 1,289 of its members were killed (953 by bandits, 250 by the National Guard, 82 by police, 4 by the British), 6,681 were wounded, and 677 EAM offices and the property of 18,767 individuals were wrecked.[12] These figures are made plausible by the observations of British and American officials in many parts of the country.

Thus the white terror was conducted by an informal alliance of army officers, National Guards, police, armed thugs, and political organizations, supported by the vast numbers of people who had grudges against EAM. All were now determined to destroy the Communist and EAM organization. The great majority were, in addition, determined to prepare the ground for a rigged plebiscite and election which would lead to the return of the king. There were myriad personal links between the organizations: many of the militia and police were recruited from anti-Communist bands, and some of the most famous guerrilla leaders like Anton Tsaous were former army officers or NCOs. In Epirus National Guards and irregular gangs were recruited from former members of EDES, the forces of which after fleeing to Corfu in December had been reorganized by officers of the Greek army, before returning to the mainland to give Zervas authority over Epirus.[13] This anti-Communist network became known by its opponents as the 'shadow state' (*parakratos*). This and its successors during the next twenty years or so wielded considerable power behind a facade of parliamentary democracy. During 1945 attempts were made, at regional and national level, to coordinate its persecution of the Communists. Thus there was regional coordination between gang leaders in Thessaly, and among EDES groups in Epirus. Later in 1945 a cabal of senior officers under Venteres was generally considered to be acting as the executive of the right-wing organizations. Many of the gangs were instigated by politicians or officers of the army or gendarmerie, who could thus avoid direct responsibility for their actions. Much of the liaison at the grassroots was conducted by George Grivas's X – the organization which had feuded with EAM in Athens during the occupation – which from May 1945 sent agents into the provinces to recruit members, and within a few months accepted affiliation by many local monarchist and patriotic organizations in the Peloponnese, Sterea Ellada, and Macedonia; while in Epirus its work was done by EDES.

It is possible that these coordinating committees gave a comprehensive and systematic character to the white terror. The local right-wing organizations rigged the process of electoral registration and compiled lists of people to be arrested in the event of a coup. However, the immense membership which X claimed by the end of 1945 seems to have been nominal. It could not mobilize its supporters all over the country as EAM could; and the arms which it claimed to possess were, according to American intelligence, held by the gendarmerie and army. As the general election approached early in 1946, its role diminished, and its most effective fund-raisers transferred their support to monarchist politicians. Sophoules's government closed X's national offices in January, and its Populist successor did not let them reopen. The gendarmerie, army, and politicians seemed by 1946 to regard X as a superfluous competitor, which was an embarrassment because it discredited the government in international eyes. What is significant is that these groups were prepared to associate themselves briefly with this conspiratorial organization, presumably so as to be prepared to support a coup if necessary.[14]

The outcome of these efforts by the second half of 1945 was a network of committees covering much of the country and trying to fulfil many of the functions of EAM in 1944: repression of opposition, propaganda, allocation of relief supplies, control of local administration. Locally there appeared political organizations with florid titles, which were usually based in market towns and sent speakers, organizers, and armed gangs into outlying villages. This network blanketed the regions of Epirus, the Peloponnese, the Ionian Islands, Sterea Ellada, and Attica. It was more fragmented in the area of greatest EAM strength in Thessaly, the slavophone stronghold of western Macedonia, and areas of Venizelist strength in the north-east and Crete. In some communities where EAM enjoyed overwhelming support, such as Kavala in eastern Macedonia and the island of Lesbos, and in others where Venizelists dominated, such as Herakleion in Crete, the National Guard and gendarmerie encountered strong resistance.[15]

The power of the right was based primarily on its monopoly of armed force, and secondly on its control over the allocation of United Nations relief supplies, which seem to have been distributed throughout the country but – in rural areas at least – usually in a partisan way. Newspapers and professional speakers were financed by certain wealthy businessmen, some in Egypt who wanted a safe haven for their funds in Greece, and some in Greece who had done well out of the occupation or suffered from a measure of Papandreou's government giving itself the right to refuse payment of dues in devalued drachmas. Another financial backer was the wealthy landowner and prominent Populist politician, Petros Mavromichalis, who was important in fund-raising. The eagerness of local groups of right-wingers to affiliate with X in mid-1945 was evidently due to their hope of subsidies from its headquarters, a hope which was disappointed when X was overshadowed by other organizations.[16] The American diplomat and future historian, W.H. McNeill, concluded that 'the rightist organizations never succeeded in mobilizing the same enthusiastic energy as had the Left, nor did they ever come to dominate the daily life of the population with speeches, demonstrations, lectures, etc . . . '. For example a meeting supported by the right-wing organizations of Salonika in June 1945 was attended only by 5,000–6,000 people, and displayed little enthusiasm, even though it had been intensively advertized beforehand. A rally in Athens the following January, addressed by the political leaders of the right, attracted under half the numbers which had attended an EAM meeting shortly beforehand. It was because of their organizational weakness that the rightist organizations failed to suppress rival political activity to the same extent as EAM had done.[17]

Government ministers took a direct part in the vendetta against the left. In accordance with a Metaxist law giving the right of dismissal to a minister, but in violation of the Varkiza agreement, many hundreds of public servants were sacked, transferred or suspended for alleged participation in EAM. Plastiras's government arbitrarily replaced the EAM-ite executives of the General Confederation of Greek Workers and agricultural cooperatives with those who had held their posts under the occupation governments or Metaxas. Thus began a process, completed three years later, whereby the trade unions and cooperatives were brought once more under government control, enforced through police intervention in their elections.[18]

The cooperation between the forces of the shadow state, and the relations between them and the government, are illustrated by the Kalamata incident of January 1946, which provoked an uproar in the national press, and prompted Sophoules's government to take exceptional measures to restore order. As shown in an earlier chapter, the area of the port of Kalamata in the southern Peloponnese saw especially savage conflict during 1944. Civil strife was fuelled by the partial amnesty decreed by Sophoules's government in December 1945, which led to the release of 3,000 prisoners in Greece and 82 in Kalamata alone. Most or all of those released were alleged to have attacked rightists before the Varkiza agreement; and therefore many became targets of right-wing revenge, while many others retaliated against the right. Among these acts of retaliation was the murder of an X chief and his six year old daughter near Sparta on 16 January, following soon after the much-publicized murder by leftists of the mayor of Naoussa in western Macedonia. Apparently in revenge, on the night of 18 January in Kalamata, someone fired a machine-gun into a café frequented by leftists, killing two of those inside. The following day the local leftists protested with a general strike and a mass funeral assembly attended by at least 4,000 people. Leftist crowds rough-handled many opponents and delivered some to the police as suspects. Allegedly in order to prevent this retaliation from going further, armed X-ites from surrounding villages began assembling that afternoon outside the town and killed three leftists, one of whom was distributing the Communist newspaper *Rizospastes*. The next day, the 20th, about 1,000 X-ites under the leadership of a famous bandit Manganas, a close member of whose family had been killed by ELAS, entered the town. They overpowered the police guarding one prison and released 32–5 right-wing prisoners; terrorized the town during the night, killing six people; and retreated on the following day with 76 hostages. After 900 soldiers and a destroyer arrived to enforce martial law, the commander of this force, Colonel Nikolaos Papadopoulos, a former member of the Mountain Brigade, sent an ultimatum to Manganas to return the hostages, which he duly did, minus six who had been executed.[19]

Papadopoulos took little interest in further action. When an EAM delegation gave Papadopoulos the names of 1,700 armed rightists from 106 villages in the area, demanding that he disarm them, he replied that he was not Hercules. When he and the gendarmerie subsequently acted against the right, it was under pressure from the Liberal government and the British police mission. Eventually, on Papadopoulos's recommendation, 72 out of 98 of the gendarmes in Kalamata were transferred to other locations as a penalty for their collusion with the X-ites. Manganas remained free long enough to break into a gaol in the nearby port of Pylos in May and kill three prisoners. In June he was caught when an officer of the British police mission, seconded from Scotland Yard, happened to recognize him standing by a country road near Kalamata. Evidently he was later allowed to escape, because by 1948 he had resumed his career of banditry near Olympia.

Manganas was just one of those in many parts of the country who seem to have started their career of violence during the occupation, and lived by extortion and intimidation during these years, with the tolerance of the gendarmerie and the army, and the protection of some politicians. They did much to fuel civil war by forcing left-wingers to band together in retaliation; yet did little to combat these left-wing bands.[20] The Kalamata incident itself supported the verdict of the British ambassador Leeper, in his parting report on 22 February 1946, that 'too much blood has been shed and there is too much hatred for the two sides to live together peacefully or for anybody to mediate between them'.[21]

The white terror had some rational ends, which were the converse of those which had inspired the EAM persecution of its rivals in 1944. One was to deprive the Soviet bloc of potential clients. Fear of Communism in Greece was fed by the march to power of Communist parties in all other Balkan countries. In Albania and Yugoslavia, the Communist Parties had during the Axis occupation built up front organizations still more powerful than EAM was in Greece. By February 1945, governments in all Balkan countries outside Greece were in the hands of front organizations dominated by Communists, who were persecuting opponents and harassing, or dissolving, rival parties. The government in Bulgaria admitted by this time to having executed 2,138 opponents, many of them eminent politicians (the real total being much higher), and this was after flagrantly rigged trials which terrorized the population. The Communist forces in Yugoslavia massacred tens of thousands of Croatian, or Ustashe, nationalists, and tens of thousands more Serb, or Cetnik, nationalists, so bringing to conclusion the struggle which it had waged during the German occupation. The Cetnik Draza Mihailovic, Tito's most famous opponent, was finally hunted down, tried, and executed in 1946. There were large-scale executions in Albania, and widespread intimidation of opponents in Romania. As in Greece, accusations of collaboration with the Germans served Communists as a pretext for disposing of opponents.

All these Communist parties were still loyal without question to the Soviet Union and to the Stalinist model of socialism. While the regimes in Yugoslavia and Albania were based on their own armed forces, those in Bulgaria and Romania were backed by the reserve power of the Soviet army, much as the Greek government was backed by the British forces. The Romanian Communist Party, which had been very small when the Soviet armies invaded in August 1944, consolidated its power with a fraudulent general election in November 1946, but did not establish a complete monopoly of power until 1948. The other Communist parties had built up their own power by the time the Soviet forces arrived, and so were able to consolidate it earlier, with rigged elections in the last two months of 1945. By this time they had moved towards socialism by confiscation and redistribution of businesses, land, and houses, and persecuting religion. As the Yugoslav, Albanian, and Bulgarian parties had organized guerrilla warfare before the arrival of the Soviet forces, former guerrilla fighters held honoured positions in their post-war regimes. Although Zachariades drew parallels between the Greek Communist Party and those of France and Italy, its more obvious affinities were with those of the three Balkan countries immediately to the north, which shared similar experiences of pre-war persecution and war time resistance. It was natural therefore for his opponents to assume that the Greek Communist Party would behave like its Balkan counterparts if it came to power.

Non-Communists in Greece, aware of the overwhelming military superiority of the Soviet satellites in the Balkans, were anxious also about Greek security. In retaliation for Anglo-American criticism of its repression in eastern Europe, the Soviet Union began to attack the 'fascism' of the Greek government, and champion the interests of the Greek left. From June 1945 the Soviet media called for a base in the Straits of Constantinople and for territory in eastern Turkey. In February 1946 the

Soviet Union invited the Greek government to promise a base in the Dodecanese islands in return for aid, and tried to use its influence in Albania to give itself access to Adriatic ports. In January 1946 it complained to the UN Security Council about the British military presence in Greece, in obvious retaliation for Western complaints about Soviet troops in Iran. The ensuing controversy in the UN polarized Greek opinion still further between the Greek Communists who opposed the British presence and the bourgeois parties which reaffirmed support for it.

Meanwhile the situation on Greece's northern frontier became tense. During 1945, the Albanians persecuted their large Greek minority, causing many of them to flee to Greece. The Yugoslav federal government, and the republican government of Yugoslav Macedonia, championed the interests of the Greek slavophones in Greek or what they called Aegean Macedonia. The Bulgarians maintained their claim on the Greek territory which they had occupied in 1941–4.[22] On the Greek side of the frontier, government forces in March–May 1945 inflamed tensions by savage persecution of the Albanian-speaking Muslims, the Chams, in Epirus, and of the slavophones in western Macedonia. EDES gangs massacred 200–300 of the Cham population, who during the occupation totalled about 19,000, and forced all the rest to flee to Albania. In western Macedonia, where there was widespread resentment of former collaboration with the enemy by the slavophones, the National Guards forced about 25,000 of them to flee to Yugoslavia and Bulgaria, after raids on their villages which were eventually condemned by the Greek gendarmerie and by the Governor-General of Macedonia. As a result of all this violence, tensions became severe on the borders, with occasional exchanges of fire between troops and some raids by outlaws. In July several groups of guerrilla fighters from Yugoslavia, totalling a few hundred, raided western Macedonia, killing a few civilians and a British soldier, and spreading the message among the slavophone population that they would be liberated.

Right-wing politicians and newspapers appealed both to public fears, and to the conviction among the overwhelming majority of the population that they were entitled as victors in the Second World War to territorial gains, specifically at the expense of Albania and Bulgaria. The Communists were forced to bow to such feeling, and tried ineffectually to counter it with claims against Turkey in eastern Thrace and against Britain in Cyprus.[23] Although the Greek claims against Bulgaria and Albania were rejected at the Paris peace conference in July–October 1946, Greek governments continued to make them. The result was to give added incentive to the three northern neighbours to support Communist guerrillas, and to force Greek governments still further into dependence on Britain and America.[24] By 1946, then, Greece had become a western capitalist foothold in the Balkan peninsula, and an increasingly precarious one as it was apparent that Britain lacked the resources to maintain its economic and military patronage.

In these circumstances backing by Britain and the United States was a propaganda asset to the right. Another component of right-wing propaganda was the old accusation that Communists menaced traditional values: the family (meaning of course the patriarchal family), private property, traditional morality, religion, and individual liberties. These accusations were now supported by alleged examples drawn from recent EAM rule, as well as from the Communist dictatorships which were appearing in the rest of the Balkans. Instances of the persecution of religion by Greek Communists were still scarce, but could be drawn from other Balkan countries; and there was also EAM's announced intention in its programme published in July 1945 to expropriate monastic lands, apparently with little or no compensation. Presumably for these reasons, Archbishop Damaskinos and probably the majority of the bishops feared the Communist Party, and later let themselves be drawn onto the government's side in the civil war against it.[25]

The conflict between socialism and free enterprise formed part of the propaganda war. The conflict was not as clearly defined in Greece as in most of western Europe, because of the powerful role traditionally played in the economy by the state, and by the banks and public utilities which were state-owned or closely associated with it. However there were many businessmen, large and small, who had reason to fear expropriation by a Communist government as a penalty for collaboration or for profiteering during the occupation. There were even more people who had reason to fear direct taxation, which EAM had imposed in many localities, on exorbitant profits from selling scarce commodities in the occupation. Successive governments after the Varkiza agreement also tried to impose direct taxation on businessmen; but these attempts were not as threatening, and were successfully resisted. It was presumably for these reasons that right-wing parties and newspapers benefited greatly from the support of wealthy businessmen.[26]

Monarchism was from 1945 the rallying point for the right, but not through any enthusiasm for the aloof, weak, and self-seeking character of George II. Nor does there seem to have been very much enthusiasm left in Greece even for the hereditary principle, except perhaps in the Peloponnese where monarchism was identified with regional feeling. The main reason for the popularity of monarchism was that it seemed the only safe alternative to a Communist dictatorship, given the Communists' proven and formidable powers of mass mobilization.

THE BRITISH ROLE

The white terror was made possible only by British backing; and this leads one to ask what the British motives and intentions were. These were enigmatic to contemporary observers, and remain difficult even for historians to understand. Recognizing that the country was deeply divided after the German occupation, the politicians and diplomats responsible for British policy were initially determined not to instal in power a vindictive faction which would provoke another civil war. 'I told Scobie to tell Papandreou that we were <u>not</u> (repeat <u>not</u>) prepared to become the tool of a right-wing reaction,' noted Harold Macmillan, Churchill's representative in the Mediterranean, in the middle of the fighting of December 1944. Churchill repeated this intention in the conference of Greek political leaders on 26 December, and it remained a consistent though weakening thread of British policy.[27] It was for this reason that British representatives pressed the regent during 1945 to appoint prime ministers who were either not politicians, like Admiral Petros Voulgares (April–September), or drawn from the political centre, like Plastiras and Sophoules. When the right-wing reaction nonetheless took place, British policy-makers were remarkably prescient about its effects. They all saw that the wave of right-wing feeling in 1945 might be only a temporary reaction to the December fighting. Leeper, in response to the possibility of a right-wing coup, told the American ambassador about October 1945, 'If the right begins it, the left will win it.' The British Minister of State for Foreign Affairs, Hector McNeil, wrote on 1 March 1946: 'I've been wondering what we do about the emerging [right-wing] government between the period when they take over and when the banked-up civil war overtakes them.'[28]

The British undoubtedly did want elections to be held in fair and orderly conditions, for the sake of political stability, and to satisfy their own critics, domestic and international. A token of this wish was the transport of Zachariades from Germany to Greece in a British military aircraft in May 1945. Yet genuinely fair conditions would have raised the possibility of a Communist victory, which the British would certainly have considered contrary to their own interests, because it would have turned Greece into a Soviet satellite. Moreover their desire to prevent Communist victory grew at the expense of their concern with fair elections. In March 1946, the Foreign Secretary Ernest Bevin warned his colleagues that 'without our physical presence in the Mediterranean' all the states on its northern rim might 'fall, like Eastern Europe, under the totalitarian yoke. We should also lose our position in the Middle East.'[29]

In theory the British had the power to make their Greek clients respect the law. For over two years after the Varkiza agreement the Greek army and police were financed, equipped, and trained by the British. The Greek government during 1945 and for some time thereafter depended on British financial support, and derived its revenue from selling United Nations Relief and Rehabilitation Administration (UNRRA) goods which were financed largely by the United States, and could not at first be distributed without the British military presence.[30] For about three months after the Varkiza agreement, British troops supervised the takeover of power at the local level by National Guardsmen, and for some months thereafter helped them to search for hidden weapons. Thereafter they remained a guarantee of government authority and of the country's territorial integrity against possible incursions from the Communist countries to the north. For these purposes there were still 31,000 British troops in the country in September 1946,[31] and the last of their successors did not leave until the 1950s. Why then did the British not use their power to prevent the white terror?

One answer is that the British failed to investigate and perceive the full extent of right-wing provocation because they themselves were blinded by disgust with the Communists. There were few British representatives after 1944 who spoke to Communist leaders and left-wing guerrillas or tried to understand their point of view. For example, soon after his profession of good intentions, Macmillan heard without sympathy two Communist leaders who complained legitimately about violations of the Varkiza agreement.[32] British representatives paid no heed to Zachariades's emphatic declarations, immediately after his return from Germany, that he accepted Britain's special interest in Greece. The members of the military and police missions understood little or nothing about political divisions in the country, and believed in a simple-minded way that right-wing officers were sound people and that Communists were a bad lot. For example, in a letter quoted approvingly by a British official in January 1946, a member of the police mission reported that: 'The Communists here are a bad crowd, they seem to be all criminals and murderers, unkempt, lousy and brutal.' An army officer in Macedonia, after investigating complaints about attacks on EAM meetings, reported on 20 September 1945 that 'some pelting with apples, earth, and possibly stones took place, but seems to have been well asked for'.[33]

Another part of the answer is that British soldiers and police were far too few to restrain the white terror. Most seemed ready to stop flagrant physical violence when they saw it. In western Macedonia for example British officers secured the withdrawal of one particularly lawless battalion of National Guards, and punished another by confining it to barracks. But right-wing forces ensured without difficulty that their crimes were rarely seen. For example the police mission by May 1946 had prevented the city police from carrying rifles when engaged in crowd control. It also believed that it had almost stamped out the 'Balkan' practice of beating up prisoners; yet admitted a year later that it had caught fifteen policemen red-handed, and that a disciplinary council had just imposed 'hopelessly inadequate' sentences on them. Nor could it stop the police from arresting Communists for lawful activities such as singing political songs and circulating leaflets. If the mission could not even restrain the police in the metropolis, it could hardly influence the behaviour of the gendarmerie in the countryside.[34]

Even when British officials did detect terroristic practices, they had remarkably few sanctions available to them. They could not take command of Greek troops because they could not speak Greek, and the purpose of their presence in Greece was to train the Greek forces to be self-sufficient. They could not discipline the Greek government, as United States representatives later did, with conditions attached to a long-term aid programme, because their aid was too limited and their officials had too few powers to supervise its use. They could refuse extra funds in November 1946 for the arming of civilians;[35] but could not plausibly threaten to purge the officer corps and the police forces because they would be difficult to replace. The right-wing forces and politicians derived confidence from their recognition that they were serving British interests by resisting Communism, a fact of which they repeatedly reminded British officials. As Woodhouse said after touring the Peloponnese in August 1945, 'the Right take our approval for granted'.[36]

The case of Woodhouse illustrated another problem: that those who knew most about Greek conditions were low in the official hierarchy, while those who were furthest removed from Greek conditions had great power over policy. For example Ernest Bevin, the British Foreign Minister, and James Byrnes, the US Secretary of State, insisted against the advice of their ambassadors that a general election be held on 31 March 1946 in conditions of nation-wide intimidation by the right.[37] Indeed to postpone the election would be an admission that their policy had failed.

The basic weaknesses of the British were their own lack of resources and the disorganization of their Greek clients. As a result, British influence in Greece seemed precarious.

COMMUNIST REVIVAL

After the Varkiza agreement the Communists tried to insist on the fulfilment of its promise of democracy and civil liberties, and to compete peacefully with other parties. When Zachariades returned to Greece in

May, still full of vigour after nearly eight years of imprisonment, he began purposefully to implement this strategy, aware that it was essentially the same as that of the Communist parties in France and Italy. It was the only realistic course in a country regarded by the Soviet Union as within the Western sphere of influence.

Zachariades gave the party a sense of purpose which it sorely needed. Before his return it was, naturally enough, demoralized by uncertainty and mutual recriminations. According to the party's figures about a quarter of the remarkably high total of 420,000 members deserted after Varkiza, while 20,000–25,000 were purged.[38] The eminent socialists in EAM – Svolos, Askoutses, Strates, Tsirimokos – were permanently alienated by the December fighting, and in April announced their desertion from EAM to form a separate party, the Socialist Party-Union of Popular Democracy, (SK-ELD). EAM was now, more obviously than ever, a front, which enabled people to work with the Communist Party without joining it.

Despite these setbacks, the leading Communists began immediately after the January truce to rebuild their organization. Even before the end of January numerous cadres were sent back to Athens for this purpose. By March there was an obvious revival of trade union activity, party meetings, and the circulation of party newspapers in many parts of the country. Illustrating the party leaders' determination to adopt a strategy for political expansion and economic reconstruction was a circular to grassroots organizations in the southern Peloponnese – presumably similar to those distributed all over the country – instructing them to conduct a thorough socio-economic analysis of local communities and discover among many other things 'what work can be undertaken now or in the future to increase [economic] production, e.g. irrigation of dry fields, cultivation of trees and drainage of swamps . . . '.[39]

From June reorganization and purges of the party were supervised by Zachariades, who restored it to something like its pre-war form. He presumably took advice from Soviet representatives who travelled around the country during 1945. Zachariades immediately announced his intention of returning to orthodox party practices by improving the ideological level of cadres and reducing the proportion of peasant members. The latter was eventually achieved by the crude device of ordering peasant members to join the satellite body, the United Agrarian Party (AKE), which however cadres did relatively little to organize. According to US intelligence in August 1945, the number of full-time professional organizers in the Communist Party was about 500. According to a report to the Soviet party in September 1946 there were then about 7,000–8,000 experienced cadres and a total of 45,000 members. These figures excluded many tens of thousands in the EAM youth organization.[40] The party members were more disciplined than during the occupation years, because Zachariades reimposed his old, absolute authority. Thus the habit of debating policy, and tendency towards collective leadership, which characterized the occupation period, were replaced by strict Stalinist discipline.[41]

Few cadres defied the course of legality, one being Ares Velouchiotes who with his characteristic courage and political folly tried to revive guerrilla warfare. He was consequently expelled from the party, and savagely denounced by Zachariades in June as a former *delosias* (renegade under Metaxas) and an adventurer serving the ends of the reactionaries. Immediately afterwards, lacking information from the party network, he was caught with 80 followers in an ambush by government forces in the central Pindus ranges and, in anguish because of his disgrace, committed suicide while under hot pursuit. His severed head was exhibited in Trikala. It seems that Ares had been maligned by Zachariades and had actually made his recantation on party orders. In the late 1970s and early 1980s, when the cult of the resistance was at its height, he was seen as a symbol of guerrilla heroism. But in the few months following the Varkiza agreement he was obviously a menace to the party.[42]

While thus proving his determination to bury the party's guerrilla past, Zachariades reaffirmed that the party's goal was the establishment of popular democracy, and he now gave this formula an unambiguously parliamentary interpretation, claiming that it implied peaceful competition with other parties, as in Italy and France. Although Zachariades claimed at the twelfth plenum of the central committee in June that this policy was consistent with that adopted at the sixth plenum in January 1934, it was in fact quite different in spirit. The phase of bourgeois-democratic transformation, which was to precede socialism, was now to be supervised by a parliamentary government, not as in 1934 by a soviet dictatorship of workers and peasants.[43]

But this policy was combined with an attempt to destabilize successive governments by taking advantage of the economic chaos bequeathed by the occupation. Greece differed from Italy and France in its still more doubtful prospects of economic recovery, so providing the Soviet Union with a chance to weaken Western influence.[44] In 1945 agricultural and industrial production were under half the pre-war level. Among the reasons were the lack of raw materials and basic essentials like diesel oil; the disappearance of markets for Greek exports; the sinking of three-quarters of the merchant fleet and four-fifths of coastal shipping; and the devastation of roads, railways, harbours, and bridges. A British parliamentary delegation reported in August 1946 that the majority of highways were still impassable, as were the Corinth Canal and the Athens–Salonika railway. To add to these misfortunes, an extraordinary drought wrecked the grain harvest of 1945.[45]

The whole population depended on a vast influx of foreign aid, which from April 1945 until June 1947 was the responsibility of UNRRA. During the year or so after the Varkiza agreement the import of over one pound of food per head daily averted mass starvation, but left a third of the urban population and a half of the rural population, according to government and UNRRA estimates, unable to buy enough basic necessities.[46] Various factors blunted the contribution of foreign aid to economic recovery. It depended for distribution on several thousand Greek officials many of whom were biased and corrupt. The government depended on revenue from its sale, and set prices which many people could not afford, so that they sold their ration coupons to wealthy businessmen, who in this way cornered the market for many commodities and made monopolistic profits. Raw materials, credits, and licences to import goods or operate various enterprises were channelled by ministers to relatively few favoured businessmen. Thus UNRRA aid reached the population only through unscrupulous businessmen in the towns and right-wing extremists in the countryside. The big profits thus made by a few people were invested in gold or other inflation-proof items rather than in industry or commerce, because of the widespread fear of a Communist coup.[47]

The destruction of the administration and government by successive invaders left the country politically as well as economically pauperized. Governments were debilitated by the feeling that only foreign aid could solve their problems. The civil service was made vulnerable to corruption by low pay at a time of rapid inflation, and made more inefficient by several years of politically motivated appointments under weak governments. For these reasons the central administration failed to accomplish crucial tasks: the imposition of higher direct taxation, especially on war profits; the equitable distribution of basic necessities; and the control of prices. It was not until November 1945 that it could even report on the extent of war damage to housing and communications. Thus the government in 1945 could raise only about half the money which it spent, and like the occupation governments paid for a bloated civil service by printing money.[48] The resulting inflation provoked discontent among those who depended on wages or salaries, and further impeded productive investment.

In these circumstances traditional distortions in the economy were accentuated. The powers of economic control (for example through import licences and exchange restrictions) that were necessarily vested in the government accentuated the traditional problem of administrative centralization, at a time when the defects of the civil service were unusually serious. The results were illustrated by an American expert who commented in November 1948 that 'the export trade of Patras is dead because of the problem of getting permits from Athens'.[49] Local officials had to waste much time in Athens trying to wrest decisions from government departments.[50] Wealth and with it political influence were concentrated more than ever before in the hands of relatively few businessmen and bankers. As the Communists pointed out in September 1945, half the ministers were employed by the Bank of Greece or the National Bank, and had close personal relations with a handful of wealthy industrialists.[51] It is calculated plausibly that between 1939 and 1951 the real incomes of merchants and industrialists doubled, while their contribution to government revenues fell by half, and the real incomes of the mass of consumers and wage-earners remained static or fell.[52]

The criticisms levelled at these abuses by Communists were echoed by expert observers, like Paul Porter, the head of the US Economic Mission, and Kyriakos Varvaressos, professor of economics and Governor of the Bank of Greece. The scale of inequality was displayed in the capital by the co-existence of conspicuous luxury in wealthy quarters like Kolonaki with mass poverty in the nearby quarters inhabited by Asia Minor refugees.[53] The lack of public spirit among wealthy businessmen and 'good families' seriously discredited the post-war political system, and alienated, among others, many of the most ardently *ethnikophron* army officers, whose professional ideals and often humble origins led them to despise the high living which they witnessed in Athens.[54]

Varvaressos, in his capacity as deputy prime minister and Minister of Supply from June to September 1945, was the one minister who really tried to reform taxes and control prices. He was defeated mainly by wealthy businessmen (who retaliated by withholding supplies from the market), but also by the inertia of the bureaucracy and obstruction by the Communists. The Communist Party was determined to prevent any economic recovery by a government which did not include itself, and so used its influence on civil servants in the taxation department to obstruct the tax reforms. It also fomented strikes against increased prices, and denounced the hardship which the new taxes allegedly threatened to small businessmen. This campaign was part of a longer-term attempt to use strike action to obstruct economic recovery and destabilize governments which excluded EAM, apparently in order to weaken Britain's manifestly shaky control over its satellite. Pretexts for strikes were found in the constant increase in prices and the reduced sense of responsibility of employers who no longer felt obliged, as they had during the occupation – through patriotic solidarity and fear of EAM – to keep redundant employees on their payrolls or to pay wages in kind. Because of the blatantly destructive nature of the Communists' industrial activity, the attempts by the city police in Athens to break strikes sometimes earned widespread public sympathy.[55]

The failings of successive governments nevertheless enabled the

Communists and EAM to start winning back supporters and recovering morale soon after the Varkiza agreement. The conditions of 1945 gave fresh relevance to the traditional Communist criticisms of the Greek state as authoritarian and associated with an economic oligarchy which represented the interests of the imperialist powers. The Communist advocacy of state planning and state control was arguably a sensible response to the anarchy of private enterprise, particularly as a means of regulating the high price of basic necessities. In all the provinces, especially those that were more remote, the Communist Party benefited from resentment of neglect by an over-centralized and inefficient state machine. Throughout the country, also, there was growing resentment of the terrorism by the shadow state, and of corruption by right-wing businessmen. The nationalism of the right could be countered by the patriotic record of the left in the resistance, and by accusations of leniency towards collaborators, and dependence on foreign patronage.[56]

The Communists could conceal their lack of a remedy for Greece's current problems by blaming the government. They also drew public attention to their long-term programme, which was based on the achievements and policies of EAM. In June the Communist central committee published an updated but in essence identical version of the programme for popular democracy of April 1943; and this was published by EAM in July, being soon afterwards accompanied by an abbreviated illustrated booklet. This programme included the most popular aspects of EAM's system of government during the occupation. Thus the electorate was presented with a vision of the future opposed to the bankrupt traditional order defended by the bourgeois parties.[57]

The Greek Communists' programme included proposals for economic development compiled with the help of academic economists, and designed to sustain a welfare state and make the country more independent.[58] The proposals derived from the long-standing preoccupation of Marxist–Leninist parties with economic development, which at this time – when capitalism was still discredited by the Great Depression – contributed much to the international appeal of Communism. With the wisdom of hindsight, we can see that this programme was marred by a characteristically Soviet bias towards heavy industry: for example in the illustrated version of the EAM programme there is a quite irrelevant smoke stack in the background of some pictures. But at the time the programme expressed an interest, lacking among other parties, in the need to provide productive jobs for the surplus rural population.

Three American observers, when interviewing EAM and KKE leaders early in 1947, commented on their belief in their own social mission. They talked of Greek economic problems as men who had spent months and years studying them – a notable contrast to the vagueness and evasion of typical royalist politicians [then in power] when the same subjects were broached to them. In many respects, the programs of EAM leaders for Greek industrial and agricultural advance closely paralleled those of the Food and Agriculture Organization of the United Nations (FAO) mission.

C.M. Woodhouse at about the same time condemned successive post-war governments for 'living mentally in a dead past' and noted that the Communist Party, by contrast with them, 'does profess a social programme . . . and it is not unaware of the existence and grievances of the semi-civilised world beyond Athens'. The programmes presented by the bourgeois political parties, shortly before the general election of 31 March 1946, were pathetically vague.[59]

The persistence of public support for the left became apparent soon after the Varkiza agreement. This report from one medium-sized town, as early as May 1945, epitomized the change in public opinion that seems to have been taking place in much of the country:

> In Florina . . . the extreme Right has undoubtedly lost considerable ground. Their attacks on a variety of respected moderates have led some persons to conclude that the extreme Right is less interested in a just cause than in matters of personal interest. The terrific inflation and hiding of merchandise have also damaged the rightists, for it is generally accepted that the (rightist) shop-keepers are primarily to blame, particularly for hoarding supplies. Further, a Red Cross scandal directly involving two leading Metaxists . . . as well as a number of other less important rightists, has done the Right a great deal of harm . . . It is beyond doubt that there have been more murders, beatings and terroristic arrests since the arrival of the National Guard than during the Civil War [of December 1944].[60]

The contrast between the long-term programmes of EAM and the bourgeois parties makes understandable the strong support for the left by the educated. American officers immediately after the Varkiza agreement were surprised to find a 'vigorous support of the left among certain youthful elements of Athens who come from wealthy educated families', some for democratic reasons and some for revolutionary socialist reasons. The American ambassador Lincoln MacVeagh reported early in 1947 that 'the fellow-travellers have probably increased quite a bit in the professional classes and the universities. The intelligentsia rather falls for the kind of propaganda put out by the Communists.'[61] The available evidence, and the data available to American intelligence services, indicate that in the latter half of the 1940s professional people – especially schoolteachers, lawyers, students, and journalists – formed a majority of Communist cadres, despite the party's preference for blue-collar workers who consequently dominated its highest levels. For example there were 429 women detained on the peninsula of Trikeri in 1951, well after the end of the civil war, who were presumably cadres or dedicated members of the party, because they had refused the opportunity to gain release by recanting Communism: two-thirds were professionals, teachers, nurses, clerks, students or graduates of high school.[62]

The composition of committed left-wing supporters (not merely cadres or hard-core Communist party members) seems to have been similar to that of EAM during the occupation. The authorities analysed 912 people arrested as leftists in July 1947 in the city of Salonika, the medium-sized town of Drama, and the small town of Polygyros in Macedonia: 15 per cent were professionals of all kinds, 5 per cent were employers, business-men, or property-owners, 7 per cent were white-collar employees, 11 per cent were retailers or café owners, 30 per cent were artisans, industrial workers, or tobacco workers, 23 per cent were unskilled or menial workers, 5 per cent were farmers or fishermen, and 3 per cent were house-wives.[63]

After Varkiza EAM supporters were driven by persecution into closer association with the Communists. A gendarme admitted that the result of indiscriminate mass imprisonment was that 'prisoners go in as ordinary people and come out as Communists', a tribute to the Communists' custo-mary organization and propaganda among prisoners. As the former ELAS commander, Sarafis, warned Woodhouse in a private talk in June 1945, the white terror was forcing into the Communist Party 'tens of thousands' of professional people and clerical workers who otherwise might not have remained interested in politics. These groups were valuable to the party for their organizational ability and intellectual skills. Workers and peasants were being forced into collaboration with the Communists in the same way. The socialists who had seceded from EAM in 1945 continued to cooperate closely with it, if only because they had no choice.[64]

The total adult strength of EAM after Varkiza was estimated by British and American intelligence at 700,000, of whom 200,000 were active, rep-resenting a fall of 30 per cent since the liberation. Proof of this residual strength appeared during 1945 in the overwhelming victories which the left won in most trade unions, covering a wide variety of occupations and comprising on Communist estimates about 250,000 organized members. In June the left won similar victories in elections in the agricultural coopera-tives. By June it seemed that EAM and its youth organization had recovered something like their former strength in the working-class suburbs of Athens and Salonika. Nearly all the frequent strikes which occurred among blue-collar workers during the year after Varkiza seem to have been directed by Communists.[65] From August and for seven months thereafter EAM demonstrated its power to mobilize in mass-meetings the inhabitants not just of the main cities but also of the larger provincial towns where they were generally exposed to physical attacks by thugs: in for example Arta, Ioannina, Larissa, Volos, and Patras. These rallies were addressed by leading figures in EAM who thus made themselves publicly known as they never had been before: at least one of them was wounded, another physically attacked, and one later assassinated.[66] The peak of this activity was an assembly on 20 January 1946, under the auspices of the Union of Democratic Associations of Athens, attendance at which was estimated by a British official as 150,000. Considering this 'really impressive – as an example of organizational discipline if not of spontaneous enthusiasm', the American diplomat Karl Rankin, who was strongly anti-Communist, added that 'EAM is a unified, dynamic movement that knows what it wants and how it proposes to get it. In contrast, the right and center present a picture of leaderless disunity and befuddled incompetence.'[67]

ELECTION VICTORY FOR THE RIGHT

The Varkiza agreement provided for a plebiscite on the constitution as soon as possible, to be followed by an election to a constituent assembly. This provision complied with the Declaration on Liberated Europe which the three Allied powers had just made at Yalta.[68] The British and Americans felt themselves under pressure thereafter to rebut Soviet accusations that they were subjecting Greece to a disguised occupation. Indeed they invited the Soviet Union to help supervise the polling, but the Soviet Union refused, evidently so as not to provide a precedent for Western intervention in other parts of eastern Europe. It soon became apparent that a fair election was a vain prospect given the terrorism by the shadow state, which was rigging the electoral registration and intimidating voters. Electoral registration proved difficult, partly because the existing electoral lists were ten years old, and the law required people to vote in the constituency where they had resided at the time of the previous census of 1940, since when there had been large population movements. The customary process of registration was complex and in the hands of gendarmes and local authorities who were strongly biased towards the right.[69]

Consequently the British, the regent, and successive Greek governments were forced during the year to retreat from the Varkiza objectives. They decided that a plebiscite would sharpen the polarization of the country, because it would be rigged by the right in order to restore the monarchy, and so they agreed to postpone it until after an election. In November the British and American representatives persuaded the regent to accept the appointment of the 84 year old Sophoules, former lieutenant of Elevtherios Venizelos, as head of a government composed entirely of members of the political centre – which consisted mainly of the Liberal Party, the core of the Venizelist camp – in the hope that it would create conditions for a fair election. The date of the election was deferred to 31 March to allow time for a second revision of the register and for the establishment of more peaceful conditions. An Allied Mission for Observing the Greek Elections (AMFOGE) consisting of over 1,200 British, American, and French representatives arrived in force in February in order to check the accuracy of the registration lists and the fairness of voting procedures.

For various reasons the British hope of preventing the distortion of the electoral results was vain. The members of AMFOGE were influenced by the British and committed to their governments' desire that elections be held soon. Their ignorance of Greek conditions made them figures of ridicule, and they could do nothing to eliminate the effect on voters of the coercion that preceded their arrival and was expected to follow their departure.[70] The attempts by Sophoules to restrain the army and gendarmerie were hindered by the British training missions, in their opposition to what they saw as partisan intervention in those forces. One of Sophoules's few successes was to transfer the irrepressible anti-Communist intriguer Venteres from his key position in the general staff to a regional command. Yet the damage done by the British missions is exaggerated by George Mavrogordatos, in his influential chapter on the election.[71] Even if they had cooperated with Sophoules, it is unlikely that he could have created conditions for a fair election, because the security forces (i.e. army officers, National Guard, gendarmerie, city police) consisted overwhelmingly of right-wingers, and were in any case outnumbered by the right-wing gangs. Sophoules's weakness is shown by his fruitless proposal to the British government that he create a force of 3,000 gendarmes, consisting of Venizelists recalled from retirement, to restore order in Macedonia and the southern Peloponnese.[72] Presumably the personnel did not exist to do any more, and the result of this proposal would have been two rival police forces.

By February, then, it was becoming apparent to informed observers foreign and Greek that conditions would still be far from suitable for a fair election by the new deadline. The shadow state determined to give the election a plebiscitary character, and the government despaired of restraining it. Reports from *nomarchs* (prefects) indicated that lawlessness was rife in most parts of the country. Politicians of the political centre found that right-wing gangs prevented them from campaigning outside the cities, and at least some who attempted to do so were shot at.[73] Sophoules protested accurately on 18 March that 'throughout Greece free movement of voters and freedom to express opinions are enjoyed only by monarchists'. Showing more self-respect than he did, one of his ministers accepted dismissal and eleven others resigned rather than take responsibility for the electoral farce. One of these, the Minister of Public Order, Stamates Merkoures, complained in the press that the police had become accomplices of right-wing gangsters, and had consistently defied his efforts to make them enforce the law.[74]

Liberals were in any case divided and demoralized by fear of the left. At least as early as the autumn of 1944 a strong movement of Liberal supporters towards the monarchical fold was perceptible even in their former strongholds like Thrace and Crete. During 1945 certain prominent Venizelists declared their support for the monarchy: they included Gonatas, Apostolos Alexandres, and the maverick Zervas who now displayed limitless ambitions and established the National Party of Greece, based on the wholesale intimidation practised by EDES in Epirus. Sophocles Venizelos (son of Elevtherios) and George Papandreou eventually joined with Panagiotes Kanellopoulos in the National Political Union, which declared itself ready to accept the results of a plebiscite on the monarchy. EAM and prominent figures on the centre, including former members of Sophoules's government such as Tsouderos, Kaphantares, Kartales, and Sophianopoulos, refused to participate in the election; while a mass of voters who sympathized with them abstained.

The election was held by proportional representation and gave the Populist Party 156 seats and its monarchist allies another 80, out of a total of 354. Of the remaining 118, the National Political Union received 68 seats, and the Liberals, the only staunch republicans, received a mere 48. Thus an overwhelming majority of votes and seats went to parties determined to pursue a vindictive policy against the left. Studies by Mavrogordatos and Elias Nikolakopoulos have shown that the election results were a grotesque distortion of public opinion. The Allied mission of election observers estimated 29 per cent of the votes on the register to be invalid or disputable, and so recommended a new census and revision of the electoral lists before a plebiscite. The mission also considered that much of the unusually high abstention rate of 40 per cent was attributable to political motives. Nikolakopoulos has shown, by comparing the abstention rate with those in previous and subsequent elections, that the rate of deliberate abstention was 25 per cent. He has also estimated that the monarchist parties would without the abstentions have received 48 or 49 per cent of the votes, which is close to the 54 per cent which the right-wing organizers themselves predicted in February when they expected EAM to participate.[75] Only left-wing analysts predicted a majority of votes for EAM if it participated, but all agreed that the EAM vote was much larger than that for the centre. What we can also be sure of is that the votes for the right were greatly swollen by falsification of the register and intimidation. In rural areas it was dangerous to abstain, or even to vote for parties other than the right, because voting returns were broken down into small districts; and in small communities it was not difficult for the police to find out who gave dissident votes. Nikolakopoulos gave a striking example of the importance of intimidation from the case of Epirus where Zervas's party won twice the vote in 1946 than in the more orderly election of 1950.[76] Thus the right-wing parties, which probably represented well under half the population, received an overwhelming majority of seats, while the left, which certainly represented a large minority, received none. The estimated 370,000 voters who abstained in protest were exposed for many years afterwards to police discrimination because they were betrayed by their unstamped election booklets. Thus the election sharpened and made irreversible the polarization of the country.

COMMUNISTS ON THE BRINK

Among the leftists driven into the mountains by persecution after Varkiza, there seem to have been several thousand ELAS veterans who retained or acquired arms. In addition there were several thousand slavophone Macedonians who were also veterans of wartime guerrilla bands and inhabited both sides of the border with Yugoslavia.[77] A British officer reported in August, presumably on the basis of reports from the gendarmerie and army officers, that there were about 1,000 Communists with access to arms in the Peloponnese. An American officer in June considered that there were 500 'well armed' EAM supporters solely in Chalkidike, the peninsula of central Macedonia. Another officer wrote thus at the end of May about an area where slavophones were especially numerous: 'the mountainous area from Kastoria north to the [Yugoslav] border is apparently under complete ELAS control . . . even in the plain[s] region, members of ELAS seem to come and go pretty much as they choose . . . '.

Bands of such refugees seem to have existed in most regions, among the exceptions being those eastern Aegean islands like Lesbos and Samos where the white terror was restrained by the growth of support for EAM early in 1946 with the return of those members of the army in exile who had been imprisoned by the British in the Middle East. Bands of outlaws had to be small so as not to strain the resources of the local communities from which they drew supplies. They were helped with warnings of hostile raids by information from EAM supporters in local towns: thus in the Peloponnese an important asset was the sympathy of telephone operators who like other white-collar workers had been efficiently organized by EAM.[79]

For about eight months after the Varkiza agreement, these groups were almost everywhere preoccupied with self-defence and survival. The few cases of left-wing aggression occurred almost entirely in the areas dominated by slavophones, where as early as 4 April 1945 the British Consul-General in Salonika reported constant raids by Macedonian autonomists from Yugoslavia to recruit members or rob nationalist villages. Elsewhere scattered clashes were caused by the attempts of gendarmes to disarm outlaws.[80] These refugees were from the end of 1945 recruited by former commanders of ELAS into gangs that were increasingly aggressive. Their participation in EAM/ELAS left them with strong, simple ideals: an independent, democratic, and just society. Examples of their motives appear in letters to the tabloid newspaper *Elevtherotypia*, stimulated by the publication in serial form in 1978–86 of excerpts from the archives of the Communist Democratic Army that had recently been discovered in the ruins of a house at Myrovleto near the Albanian border. One woman outlaw wrote: 'I never wanted to go to the mountains in the years 1946–1949. I went because my life was in danger and we knew how hard is the life of an *andarte* especially in those conditions . . . We held out because the ideals in which we believed aimed at a society that would be just for all.'[81] Confirmation that her attitude was typical is found in the interviews conducted in 1947 by the American investigators Frank Smothers and William and Elizabeth McNeill, and also by a Greek soldier in the national army, George Kousoulas.[82]

From October onwards there was, according to the British police mission, 'an increasingly steep rise' in the number of violent incidents reported to it, with a national total of 45 murders and 32 woundings in October, and 110 murders and 112 woundings in May 1946. The increase occurred in most regions, and about four-fifths of these incidents were judged to be politically motivated. In Athens in December, according to William H. McNeill, 'gunfire can be heard almost nightly' as a result of fighting between 'small groups of young toughs'. Right-wing aggression was reported as prevalent in the Peloponnese, Sterea Ellada, and southern Thessaly. From the end of 1945, left-wing aggression prevailed in the north. From December there was an increasing number of left-wing attacks in the north on government officials in remoter areas, and by January 1946 over 30 village presidents had fled for protection to the nearest detachment of British troops. Gendarmes were however the prime targets, and in

January–May 1946, 28 were killed and 28 wounded, mainly in northern Thessaly and Macedonia. Thus state officials, who had only just restored their authority in the geographical peripheries of the country, were forced to retreat.[83]

The main reason for the revival of left-wing aggression seems to have been exasperation with the white terror. Communists began to feel that non-resistance was getting them nowhere, and, because of their increasing numbers, outlaws were better able to resist gendarmes. Apparently the first case of left-wing aggression in the Peloponnese was the successful resistance to a squad of gendarmes, who were trying to arrest an ELAS–ite, by the entire village of Agios Vasileos led by its priest on the massif of Parnon.[84]

From his return to Greece in May, Zachariades gave increasingly strong warnings that the party might be forced to retaliate. At the twelfth plenum of the central committee in June he announced the formation of self-defence committees. These were carefully organized, and although not authorized to use firearms until twelve months later, did use strikes, demonstrations, and probably some violence. They were allegedly effective in providing party members with some protection in their organizational work.[85] At Salonika on 24 August 1945 Zachariades warned that the Communists might be forced to revive ELAS, and from September the party newspaper *Rizospastes* began to refer to the existence of armed supporters in the mountains, while leaving it to be inferred that their resort to arms was on their own initiative. At the seventh party congress in October, Zachariades emphasized again that the Communists might have to resort to force. The self-defence committees were now referred to as 'popular' in character, implying that they were large-scale organizations. The congress also set up a Panhellenic Military Committee of the central committee under Zachariades's chairmanship. At this time the party organization in the armed forces, the Communist Organization of the Army and Security Forces (KOSSA), apparently assumed a more important role and, according to American intelligence, controlled 15 per cent of the personnel of the army. British intelligence learnt that at the end of December Zachariades discussed with regional cadres in Salonika the reorganization of the party's armed forces. Apparent examples in January 1946 of 'popular self-defence' were the Kalamata disturbances already described, and in Volos a demonstration which defied the gendarmerie, and was fired on with the loss of four civilian lives, whereupon the gendarmerie had to be rescued by British police. Thus the party's response to the white terror became gradually more militant.[86]

By this time the white terror, and the British insistence on a general election in conditions of systematic intimidation, gave the Communist Party the impression that the British and the Greek right intended to suppress it by all means available. The Communist leaders must have foreseen that the probable outcome of an election would be a government which would back the extremists who dominated the army and police, and repeat Metaxas's feat of destroying their party organization. Tangible evidence that this fate was approaching was the steady progress that the police were making with the collection of files on party members. As early as June 1945 the politburo warned its members that this was happening. A leading Communist, Bartziotas, later wrote that by February 1946 the politburo should have decided on an immediate coup, because it was predictable that party members would eventually be swept up in mass arrests.[87]

Zachariades was wrongly criticized by later historians for ignoring this danger. In fact he was aware of difficulties ignored by his critics. When the question of armed revolt arose at the second plenum of the central committee, on 12–15 February 1946, Zachariades prevailed on those present to refer it to the Panhellenic Military Committee which met concurrently. Zachariades proposed to this committee an armed revolt in the towns, but immediately withdrew this proposal when it was pointed out that the party could not challenge the government's armed forces. The only alternative was to strengthen guerrilla forces in the mountains, in which Zachariades showed little interest at this stage. The committee merely heard reports on the party's military strength in some provinces and decided to leave military preparations to the discretion of provincial party organizations. The policy which Zachariades therefore announced to the second plenum was that the guerrilla struggle would be increased gradually to defend the party and to press the government to reach a political compromise. Thus the military effort would be merely an adjunct to the political struggle in the towns.[88]

The effect of this decision was that guerrilla activities were for the first time authorized by the party. In some areas such as western Thessaly armed supporters were organized on a territorial basis from March onwards. In Sterea Ellada they began to be organized from May onwards. Leading officials of the party organizations in Epirus and Macedonia, who attended the meeting of the Panhellenic Military Committee, came away with the belief that it had decided on a national revolt, and imparted this belief to their regional organizations; so that the Epirus organization proceeded far with preparations for a coup, in cooperation with some regular army officers. In at least one case, soon after the second plenum, Zachariades authorized an attack on a sizeable and particularly troublesome government band. At Litochoro, under the peaks of Mount Olympus, on the night of 30 March, 33 leftists attacked a government force of gendarmes and National Guards and killed twelve of them, burning buildings and seizing weapons. This was the strongest act of military defiance by the left since the Varkiza agreement; and some of the attackers who were captured said that they understood that similar events were occurring throughout the country. Thus the second plenum of the Communist Party managed to create on both sides a widespread expectation of civil war. In fact the timing of the Litochoro attack, on the eve of the election, was probably a coincidence; and the significance which the incident later acquired as the opening battle of the civil war was mythical and due to the fact that it suited both the right to portray the Communists as the aggressor and the Communists to claim that they had been acting according to a revolutionary plan.[89]

One reason for Zachariades's lack of interest in guerrilla war at this stage may have been a dogmatic preference for the traditional Leninist view that revolutions should ideally be led by the working class in the cities. It was indeed in the towns that the party's centre of gravity overwhelmingly lay by early 1946, as a result of both the white terror and Zachariades's neglect of peasant members. But in 1946 there was another reason for his attitude which has been strangely overlooked by his later critics in the party, and by its recent historians.[90] It was the lack of supplies of any sort for a revived ELAS. This insuperable obstacle was pointed out by John Koliopoulos in a still unpublished article: a desperate shortage of basic necessities existed in most mountain regions.[91] It was not until the latter half of 1946 that a good wheat harvest, and the cumulative effect of the import of relief supplies since the liberation, made it possible for guerrilla bands to build up minimal stocks of food. Their supplies of arms and ammunition were limited because the national forces had been discovering the ELAS caches. As early as July 1945 the American Major Jerome Sperling reported that the number of weapons already discovered was over 10,000 and might have been over 20,000, 'invariably of good quality'.[92] The process continued thereafter; so that the Communist Party had lost much of its arsenal by early 1946.

The wartime construction of ELAS was a feat that could not easily be repeated. During the occupation it had been a slow process made possible by universal hatred of the foreign conqueror, and the consequent impotence of the quisling governments. The Communists' attempt from 1946 to maintain that the country was again under foreign occupation must have struck the majority of the population as fictitious. Whereas the Germans and their allies had sucked massive resources from the country, the British and Americans were pouring massive resources in – directly, in the case of the British, and indirectly, in the case of the Americans, through the relief agency Military Liaison, which was administered by British and American officers, and then by the UNRRA, supervised by British and American officials. The contrast between the two 'occupations' was revealed in mortality statistics. The death rate per thousand inhabitants in 1950 (the first post-war year which was reasonably peaceful) was 7.4, compared with 12.8 in 1940, while during the Axis occupation it had been higher still. (The figure for Bulgaria, Romania, and Yugoslavia, taken together, was by contrast 13.9 in 1948)[93]. This change must have been due in large part to the provision of food, medical supplies such as antibiotics, sulphonamides, and vaccines, and insecticide for combating malaria. Moreover the countries which, with the beginning of the Cold War in 1946, were coming to constitute the Western bloc included Greece's main pre-war trading partners, sources of investment, recipients of emigrants, and customers for shipping. Symptomatic of the United States's image as a rich uncle was the fact that its consulate was besieged in 1946 with applicants for immigration. Thus post-war governments differed from quisling governments in benefiting from foreign economic patronage. Moreover most of their officials, unlike those during the occupation, were loyal to them, and cooperated zealously with their political masters in combating Communism.

In these circumstances an armed revolt led by the Communists could not hope to gain the support of the majority of the public. Although Zachariades seems to have suffered from the delusion that it might, he saw that he would have to gain strong support from the Communist countries. Without such support it would be suicidal to strengthen the guerrilla forces in any conspicuous way, because such a move would send valuable supporters into the mountains to starve, and provoke the British and the Greek government to suppress the party's mass organization in the towns and plains.

Zachariades tried hard from as early as January 1946 to win the backing which he needed. On 17 January, according to his own account, a leading Communist, Metsos Partsalides, put it to representatives of the Soviet Communist Party in Moscow that 'in view of the continuing slaughter of our National Resistance fighters, it seemed very difficult to avoid armed conflict. We hoped that there no longer existed the wartime obstacles to the full development of support for our people.'[94] He received the advice, which is known to have originated in the Soviet Minister Vyacheslav Molotov, to participate in the forthcoming elections, and retain the option of armed action later if it seemed appropriate. When Partsalides reported this advice to a politburo meeting in Greece, Zachariades shouted him down, insisting instead that the party should abstain from the election. Zachariades's display of independence from Moscow is especially striking when we bear in mind that most of the central committee, at its recent plenary session, had supported participation in the election, and had been persuaded by Zachariades to leave a decision to the politburo after it heard the Soviet advice.[95]

On 20 March, eleven days before the election, Zachariades left Greece for a series of talks with other Communist leaders, in which he sought support for military action. He apparently won a promise of military support from the Bulgarian Communist leader Georgi Dimitrov and from the Czech Communist Party, and was certainly promised immediate support by Tito, who had a strong motive, in the hope of acquiring a satellite and perhaps the territory of 'Aegean Macedonia'. The latter was certainly an important motive to the Macedonian branch of the Yugoslav Communist Party; and Zachariades may have encouraged this hope by promising favourable consideration to Macedonian autonomy. Tito's backing was especially valuable because Albania was then a Yugoslav satellite. Zachariades claimed later that Tito promised to arm 20,000 members of ELAS; but events showed that Tito regarded this promise, if he did give it, as vague and long-term. Zachariades managed also to obtain a hearing from Stalin, Molotov, and their colleague Zhdanov in Moscow, followed by another meeting with Stalin in the Crimea. He was strongly criticized by Molotov for EAM's abstention from the election, but received cautious approval of his dual strategy from Stalin, who advised him to build up gradually the guerrilla struggle in the villages, so as to avoid provoking the British and to put pressure on the government to compromise. Then he would be in a position to attack the towns when the British withdrew from Greece. Stalin evidently did not envisage strong military action in the near future, and gave no promise of military support.[96]

When he returned to Greece in April, Zachariades pursued the dual strategy which he had just advocated at the second plenum. This was obviously his only option until other Communist states provided adequate supplies; and it was also an implementation of the orthodox Leninist principle that legal methods of political action should be utilized as long as they were available. However this policy made puzzling the party's abstention from the election on 31 March 1946. Abstention made it possible for the monarchists to win a parliamentary majority; excluded the left from parliament; and exposed its supporters to intensified persecution.

Why then did Zachariades insist on this step, against such strong opposition? The explanations which he himself gave seem plausible. He defended himself to Molotov by saying that he could not legitimize a fraudulent election. This was in the circumstances a reasonable view which as we have seen was shared by a wide spectrum of Communist, socialist, and Liberal opinion in Greece. By March, moreover, the Communist Party had been insisting so strongly on fair conditions for an election that it must have seemed difficult to back down. It seems though that Zachariades's motive was not to secure the full implementation of civil liberties. In a work written in 1952, he placed his decision plausibly in the context of a revolutionary strategy. He had, he wrote, decided by the time of the second plenum of February that a legal course of action was no longer feasible, and his statement is supported by the arguments for military action which Partsalides made to the Soviet authorities the month before. Zachariades said that his decision was caused not only by the white terror, but also by the accession of Communist parties to power in the rest of the Balkans. He might also have added the indications that Britain intended soon to withdraw from Greece. It was this apparently favourable turn of international events which made a revolutionary policy seem possible. Zachariades spoke also of a socialist revolution, as if he had decided that it would now be possible to leap over the bourgeois democratic phase which he had hitherto claimed to be necessary. Here again, he was presumably influenced by the proximity of other Communist states, and intended to move in line with them.

A likely interpretation then of Zachariades' decision on abstention was that he wanted to prepare Communist supporters mentally for revolution by moving towards confrontation with the Greek state. The Italian Communist historian, Antonio Solaro, who was well informed from Greek Communist sources, stated plausibly that Zachariades wanted also to put pressure on other Communist parties to supply him with military aid by showing them that participation in parliamentary politics was no longer feasible.[97] Zachariades must have realized the risk he was running. An increase in guerrilla attacks, combined with abstention from the election, exposed the party to the danger of massive retaliation from a right-wing government. Everything now depended on the prompt arrival of military aid.

The major political actors early in 1946 seemed trapped in a situation which precluded the exercise of statesmanship, or even of realism, if realism be defined simply as a recognition of one's interests. Thus Zachariades had committed his party to military action of an undetermined nature without assurance of the foreign aid or the domestic support needed to make it feasible. The monarchist politicians, and their allies in the army and gendarmerie, had driven the Communist Party to the brink of military revolt, without any apparent thought of the consequences, or any assurance of the foreign aid which they needed to maintain their authority. The British government, and its diplomatic and military representatives in Greece, had allowed their Greek clients to take this course even though the diplomats could foresee its likely consequence: a war which would embroil them still longer in Greek affairs. Among the major actors, those who eventually came nearest to achieving their wishes were the Greek army and police officers who gambled with success that the Western powers would have to back them in a war. But the civil war which resulted from their gamble would cost them and their fellow countrymen dearly in casualties and suffering. As for the monarchist politicians, the majority of them ensured their eventual political demise, because they got the blame for starting the war, while the army secured the credit for winning it.

NOTES

1. Thanasis D. Sfikas, *The British Labour Government and the Greek Civil War* (Keele, 1994), p. 90.
2. Nars, RG 226, entry 108, box 69, Source Z, date of information 7 Apr. 1945: RG 84, Athens, Embassy Confidential File, W.H. McNeil, 'Military leagues in the Greek army', 20 Oct. 1945; RG 226 entry 108, box 70, 22 June 1945. See above, p. 91.
3. Nikolaos Stavrou, *Allied Politics and Military Interventions* (Athens, 1974), pp. 51, 98, 115.
4. Nars, RG 84, Athens Embassy Confidential Records, C.F. Edson, weekly report no. 17, 4 July; RG 226, entry 108, box 70 Source Z, 22 June 1945; RG 84, Athens Embassy General Records, A. Mylonas to H. McNeill, 15 Nov. 1945; David H.Close and Thanos Veremis, 'The military struggle', in David H. Close, ed. *The Greek Civil War, 1943–50. Studies of Polarization* (1993), p. 165.
5. FO 286/1165, British Consul-General, Salonika, to Leeper, 16 Mar. 1945, 14 Apr. 1945; Georgios Vontitsos–Gousias, *Oi Aities gia tes Ettes* 2 vols (1977), I, p. 144; Close, 'Reconstruction', in Close, ed., *The Greek Civil War*, p. 13.
6. Nikos Karkanes, 'Apo te Varkiza ston Emphylio', *Rizospastes*, 9 Feb. 1986; John S. Koliopoulos, 'Uneasy truce: band activity in post-Varkiza Greece, 1945–6', paper presented to the Lehrman Institute conference on the Greek Civil War at Vilvorde, Copenhagen 3–5 June 1987; Nars, Dept of Army, Pericles Report, 2 July 1945; *Journal of the Hellenic Diaspora* 12, 1 (Spring 1985), p. 42, report by military attaché's office, enclosed with MacVeagh to Secretary of State, 26 Oct. 1945.
7. Nars, RG 226, entry 108, box 70, Source Z, 10 May 1945.
8. Apostolos Daskalakes, *Istoria tes Ellenikes Chorophylakes* 2 vols (1973), I, p. 539.
9. Close, 'Reconstruction', in Close ed., *The Greek Civil War*, p. 161.
10. *Kathemerine*, 24 May 1945, p. 2; M. Partsalides, *Diple Apokatastase tes Ethnikes Antistases* (1978), p. 192; Demokratikos Stratos tes Ellados, *Etsi Archise o Emphylios* (1987), p. 10.
11. Stratos, *Etsi Archise*, p. 10; Heinz Richter, 'The Varkiza agreement and the origins of the civil war', in John O. Iatrides, ed., *Greece in the 1940s. A Nation in Crisis* (1982), p. 170.
12. Close, 'Reconstruction', in Close ed., *The Greek Civil War*, p. 164.
13. Nars, RG 226, entry 108, box 69, Source Z, 8 Jan. 1945, 5 Apr. 1945.
14. *Journal of the Hellenic Diaspora* 12 (1985), pp. 42–3, report by military attaché's office; Nars, RG 226, XL 41498, W.H. McNeill, 2 Feb. 1946; RG 226, box 1490, no. 132570, report, 30 May 1945; RG 226, entry 108, box 69, 26 Mar. 1945; Nars, Dept of Army office, Pericles Report, 2–3 July 1945; C.M. Woodhouse, *Apple of Discord. A Survey of Recent Greek Politics in their International Setting* (1948), pp. 266–7.

15. Nars, RG 226, entry 108, box 70, report, 6 June 1945; K. Konstantaras, *Agones kai Diogmoi* (1964), p. 332.
16. Nars RG 226, XL 28714, Caracalla, 15 Oct. 1945; XL 41498, W.H. McNeill, 2 Feb. 1946.
17. W.H. McNeill, *The Greek Dilemma. War and Aftermath* (New York, 1947), p. 165; A. Pepones, *Prosopike Martyria* (1970), pp. 155–6; Nars, RG 226, entry 108, box 70, Source Z, 3 June 1945.
18. Nars, Dept of Army, Pericles Report, Source Z Peacock, 2 Apr. 1945; Adamantia Pollis, 'US intervention in Greek trade unions 1947–50', in Iatrides, ed., *Greece in the 1940s*, pp. 264–6.
19. FO 286/1175, Wickham's report, 22 Jan. 1946; Nars, 868.00/2-746, Rankin to Secretary of State, enclosing OSS report 'What happened at Kalamata'.
20. Karkanes, 'Varkiza', *Rizospastes*, 9 Feb. 1986, p. 6; Nars, 868.00/6-1846, Rankin to Secretary of State; FO 371/78416/-, R 4111, Chancery to FO, 14 Apr. 1949; 371/87771/-, RG 1642, police mission report for Mar. 1950; 286/1175, P.S.O. Noble's report, 27 Aug. 1946; *Elevtheron Vema*, 20 Mar. 1946, p. 1; Leften S. Stavrianos, *Greece – American Dilemma and Opportunity* (Chicago, 1952), p. 178.
21. Quoted in Haris Vlavianos, *Greece 1941–9: From Resistance to Civil War* (1992), p. 162.
22. Vlavianos, *Greece*, pp. 157–9; B. Kondis, 'The "Macedonian question" as a Balkan problem in the 1940s', *Balkan Studies* 28, 1 (1987), pp. 155, 157; McNeill, *Greek Dilemma*, p. 213.
23. Nars, RG 226, entry 108, box 69, report, 28 Mar. 1945; box 70, report 30 June 1945; Evangelos Kofos, *Nationalism and Communism in Macedonia* (Salonika, 1964), pp. 148–9; McNeill, *Greek Dilemma*, pp. 206–9, 219–20.
24. *Foreign Relations of the United States, 1947* (henceforth *USFR*), 5.482; George M. Alexander, *The Prelude to the Truman Doctrine. British Policy in Greece 1944–7* (Oxford, 1982), pp. 202, 250–1.
25. Close, 'Reconstruction', in Close, ed., *The Greek Civil War*, p. 158.
26. Nars, RG 226, XL 11220, XL 41498, L 55168; Christos Hadziiossif, 'Economic stabilization and political unrest: Greece, 1944–7', in Lars Baerentzen, John O. Iatrides and Ole L. Smith, eds., *Studies in the History of the Greek Civil War, 1945–9* (Copenhagen, 1987), pp. 32–3.
27. Harold Macmillan, *War Diaries* (1948), pp. 610, 618.
28. Robert Frazier, *Anglo-American Relations with Greece. The Coming of the Cold War, 1942–7* (New York, 1991), pp. 90, 94; *Journal of Hellenic Diaspora* 12, 1 (Spring 1985), p. 38, report by military attaché's office in US embassy, enclosed by MacVeagh to Secretary of State, 26 Oct. 1945.
29. Sfikas, *British Labour Government*, p. 79.
30. Ibid., p. 102; R. Leeper, *When Greek Meets Greek* (1950), p. 174.
31. Alexander, *Prelude*, p. 214.
32. Macmillan, *War Diaries*, p. 716.
33. FO 371/58753/-, quoted by A.G. Ralph, 14 Jan. 1946 (written as 1936); 286/1165, 5th Indian Infantry Brigade's Progress Report, 25 Aug. 1945, 15 Oct. 1945.
34. British police mission reports: FO 371/58758/51, May 1946, pp. 10–11; 371/67131/4, May 1947, p. 3; Stavrianos, *Greece*, pp. 155–6; Geoffrey Chandler, *The Divided Land. An Anglo-Greek Tragedy* (1959), p. 85.
35. Woodhouse, *Apple*, p. 274; Frazier, *Anglo-American Relations*, p. 174.

36. FO 286/1169, 11 Aug. 1945; John O. Iatrides, ed., *Ambassador MacVeagh Reports: Greece, 1933–47* (Princeton, 1980), p. 704.
37. Frazier, *Anglo-American Relations*, pp. 87–8.
38. Ioannides's report of 12 Sept. 1946, *Avge*, 6 Dec. 1979, p. 3; comment in Heinz Richter, *British Intervention in Greece. From Varkiza to Civil War* (1985), p. 270.
39. Nars, RG 226, entry 108, box 70, March 1945; RG 84, Athens Embassy Confidential File, 1945, memorandum by naval attaché's office, 22 Mar. 1945; Vasiles Bartziotas, *Exenta Chronia Kommounistes* (1986), p. 231.
40. Peter J. Stavrakis, *Moscow and Greek Communism, 1944–9* (Ithaca, 1989), pp. 116–19; Nars, RG 84, Athens Embassy Confidential File, report by W.H. McNeill, enclosed in L. MacVeagh to Secretary of State, 8 Aug. 1945; *ibid.*, memorandum for ambassador by naval attaché's office, with excerpts from Combined Weekly Intelligence Review, 12–19 Mar. 1945; Bartziotas, *Exenta Chronia*, pp. 231–2.
41. Richter, *British Intervention*, p. 240.
42. Christophe Chiclet, *Les Communistes Grecs dans la Guerre* (Paris, 1987), pp. 143–6; C. Vrachniares, *Poreia mesa ste Nychta* (1990), pp. 30, 39; Sfikas, *British Labour Government*, p. 66.
43. Vlavianos, *Greece*, pp. 199–204.
44. Sfikas, *British Labour Government*, p. 77.
45. *USFR, 1945*, VIII, p. 285; *Report of the British Parliamentary Delegation to Greece, August 1946*, HMSO, p. 10.
46. Hadziiossif, 'Economic stabilization', in Baerentzen et al., eds, *Studies*, p. 29.
47. KKE, *Deka Chronia Agones* (1977), p. 329; McNeill, *Greek Dilemma*, pp. 445–7; K. Vergopoulos, 'The emergence of the new bourgeoisie, 1944–52', in Iatrides, ed., *Greece*, pp. 303–13, 422; *Elevtheron Vema*, 8 Jan. 1946, p. 2.
48. Nars, RG 84, Athens Embassy Confidential File, 1945, H.A. Hill, memo 21 Apr. 1945, enclosed with MacVeagh to Secretary of State, 23 Apr. 1945; *Kathemerine*, 7 Mar. 1946, p. 2; *Elevtheron Vema*, 12 Feb. 1946, p 1; L.S. Wittner, *American Intervention in Greece, 1943–9* (New York, 1982), pp. 47–8; Nars, RG 84, American Embassy Confidential File 1947, table from Greek Government, Economic Counsellor's Office, 16 Apr. 1947.
49. *USFR*, 1948, IV, p. 199.
50. FO 286/1169, C.M. Woodhouse, 11 Aug. 1945.
51. S. Sarafis, *Meta te Varkiza* (Athens, 1979)', pp. 47–8.
52. Wittner, *American Intervention*, p 175; B. Sweet-Escott, *Greece. A Political and Economic Survey, 1945–53* (1954), pp. 131–2.
53. Wittner, *American Intervention*, pp. 168–70.
54. Biographical notes on General Solon Gikas (formerly prominent in IDEA) in Nars, RG 319, P & O, 091.713 (1949), Section 1, Case 4, 1949–50 files.
55. Haziiossif in Baerentzen et al., eds, *Studies*, pp. 31–7; Stavrakis, *Moscow*, pp. 49, 74, 96; *Elevtheron Vema*, 10 Jan. 1946, p. 1.
56. FO 286/1168, report by A.G. Guillard, 5 Feb. 1945; Nars, RG 84, Athens Embassy General File, semi-weekly political situation report, 20 Dec. 1945.
57. KKE, *Episema Keimena*, V (1981), pp. 136–45, Jan.–Apr. 1943; VI (1987), pp 23–9, 17 June 1945; pp. 388–95, 23 July 1945.
58. Bartziotas, *Exenta Chronia*, p. 235.

59. Frank Smothers, W.H. and E.D. McNeill, *Report on the Greeks. Findings of a Twentieth Century Fund Team which Surveyed Conditions in Greece in 1947* (New York, 1948), p. 206; Woodhouse, *Apple*, pp. 15, 281; election speeches by right-wing politicians in *Kathemerine*, 19 Mar. 1946, p. 2; 5 Mar. 1946, p. 2; 17 Mar., p. 4.

60. Nars, RG 226, entry 108, box 70, Source Z, report dated 17 June 1945; Petros Rousos, *E Megale Pentaetia* 2 vols (1978), II, p. 392.

61. Nars, RG 226, no. 119202, 5 Mar. 1945; Wittner, *American Intervention*, p. 154.

62. Nars, RG 84, American Embassy Confidential File, 1945, W.H. McNeill's report enclosed with L. MacVeagh to Secretary of State, 8 Aug. 1945; FO 371/95129/-, E.J. Morgan to police mission, 16 Oct. 1951.

63. Close, 'Introduction', in Close, ed., *The Greek Civil War*, pp. 18–19.

64. Sarafis, *Meta*, pp. 33–4; Athens Embassy General File, semi-weekly political situation report, 20 Dec. 1945; Chandler, *Divided Land*, p. 98.

65. Nars, RG 226, entry 108, box 70, early June 1945; *ibid.*, report of 17 May 1945; Bartziotas, *Exenta Chronia*, p. 238; Chiclet, *Communistes Grecs*, p. 150; *Avge*, 6 Dec. 1979, p. 3.

66. Sarafis, *Meta*, pp. 60–72; Chandler, *Divided Land*, pp. 103–6.

67. Nars, RG 84, Athens Embassy Confidential File, 1945, box 10, to Secretary of State, 14 Feb. 1946.

68. George T. Mavrogordatos, 'The 1946 election and plebiscite: prelude to civil war', in Iatrides, ed., *Greece in the 1940s*, p. 182.

69. Stavrianos, *Greece*, pp. 163–4.

70. McNeill, *Greek Dilemma*, pp. 189–93; Stavrianos, *Greece*, pp. 169–71; FO 371/58928//11, R 11963, D. Lascelles, notes on journey to Crete (June–July 1946).

71. Mavrogordatos '1946 election', in Iatrides, ed., *Greece in the 1940s*, pp. 192–3, 374.

72. Alexander, *Prelude*, p. 177; FO 371/58753/185–7, R 2318.

73. Panagiotes Kanellopoulos, *E Zoe Mou* (1986), p. 93; Karkanes, 'Varkiza', *Rizospastes*, 6 Apr. 1986, p. 7.

74. *Elevtheron Vema*, 19 Mar. 1946, p. 3; 20 Mar. 1946, p. 1; Mavrogordatos, '1946 election', in Iatrides, ed., *Greece in the 1940s*, pp. 190–1, 377.

75. 868.00/2-1446, Rankin to Secretary of State; Elias Nikolakopoulos, *Kommata kai Voulevtikes Ekloges sten Ellada, 1946–64* (1985) pp. 140–1.

76. Chandler, *Divided Land*, p. 134; Stavrianos, *Greece*, pp. 169–70; Tasos Vournas, *Istoria tes Syngchrones Ellados. O Emphylios* (1981), pp. 22–5; Nikolakopoulos, *Kommata*, p. 136, n. 13.

77. J.O. Iatrides, 'Civil war, 1945–9', in Iatrides, ed., *Greece in the 1940s*, pp. 199–200, 386–7.

78. FO 286/1169, Brig. Arkwright to Caccia, 11 Aug. 1945; Nars, RG 226, entry 108, box 70, Source Z, 31 May 1945, 5 June 1945.

79. FO 286/1169, C.M. Woodhouse, 11 Aug. 1945; FO 371/58754/27, police mission report for Jan. 1946; Koliopoulos, 'Uneasy truce'.

80. Daskalakes, *Istoria*, I, pp. 554–8; FO 286/1165.

81. *Elevtherotypia*, 2 Apr. 1986, p. 18, Eugenia Amoiridou.

82. Smothers, McNeill and McNeill, *Report*, pp. 153–5, 167–70, 182–3; D. George Kousoulas, *Revolution and Defeat* (1965), p. 252.

83. Nars, RG 84, Athens Embassy General File, McNeill 'Annual estimate of

instability of government in Greece', 22 Dec. 1945; FO 371/58755/15; 371/58758/55–7; 371/58754/26; Alexander, *Prelude*, p. 170.

84. Daskalakes, *Istoria*, I, p. 562; Chandler, *Divided Land*, pp. 109–10.

85. Ole L. Smith, 'Self-defence and Communist policy, 1945–1947', in L Baerentzen et al., *Studies*, pp. 162–3; Richter, *British Intervention*, p. 529.

86. Stavrakis, *Moscow*, pp. 68, 85, 88, 114; FO 286/1175, M. Bayley, 11 May 1946; FO 286/1173, Linacre, report, 15 Jan., 1946.

87. Bartziotas, *Exenta Chronia*, p. 241.

88. Vlavianos, *Greece*, pp. 182–7; O.L. Smith, 'The Greek Communist Party 1945–9', in Close, ed., *The Greek Civil War*, p. 137; Smith, 'Self-defence', in Baerentzen et al., eds, *Studies*, p. 167; Stavrakis, *Moscow*, pp. 105, 108.

89. Vlavianos, *Greece*, pp. 171–5; Close and Veremis, 'The military struggle', in Close, ed., *The Greek Civil War*, p. 100; Markos Vapheiades, *Apomnemonevmata* 4 vols (1985), III, p. 138; Richter, *British Intervention*, p. 495; G. Blanas, *Emphylios Polemos. Opos ta Ezesa* (1976), pp. 51, 62; G. Vontitsos-Gousias, *Aities*, I, p. 144; *USFR, 1946*, VII, p. 130: this dispatch refers to the attack as 'near Katerine'.

90. Smith, 'Self-defence', in Baerentzen, Smith and Iatrides, eds, Studies, p. 166 (citing the Communist critics); Richter, *British Intervention*, p. 491, 495; Vlavianos, *Greece*, pp. 179, 188.

91. Soon to be published in J.O. Iatrides and L. Wrigley, eds, *Greece at the Crossroads* (Philadelphia).

92. Nars, RG 84, Athens Embassy Confidential File, 1945, to MacVeagh, 2 July 1945.

93. National Statistical Service of Greece, *Statistical Summary of Greece*, 1954 (1955), pp. 19, 26–7; L.P. Morris, *Eastern Europe since 1945* (1984), p. 122.

94. Partsalides, *Diple*, p. 199; Stavrakis, *Moscow*, pp. 90–1; Vlavianos, *Greece*, p. 192.

95. Vlavianos, *Greece*, pp. 190–3.

96. Stavrakis, *Moscow*, pp. 109, 138; N. Marake, 'Ti ekrypse e avtoktonia tou Zachariade', *Vema*, 9 Dec. 1990, p. A 10; Chiclet, *Communistes Grecs*, p. 205; Smith, 'The Greek Communist Party, 1945–9', in Close, ed., *The Greek Civil War*, p. 147.

97. A. Solaro, *Istoria tou KKE* (1975), p. 183; see also Stavrakis, *Moscow*, pp. 109–10.

CHAPTER SEVEN

Descent to Civil War, April 1946–March 1947

THE MONARCHIST REGIME

The government formed after the election was solidly monarchist, and drawn mainly from the Populist Party, of which Konstantinos Tsaldares – nephew of the pre-war party leader, and faithful to the king during the occupation – was elected leader. The spirit of the new regime was vindictive and partisan. It was responsive to the monarchist majority of deputies, who insisted on tough measures to check what they saw as a slide towards anarchy, yet shouted down those who called for measures against right-wing terrorism. At least three of the deputies had commanded collaborationist troops during the enemy occupation, and at least one minister had been closely associated with collaborators. The extremist deputies led by Zervas were ready to repudiate the government if it responded to British counsels of restraint.[1]

In accordance with convention, the government appointed partisan supporters to all places in the official establishment, and secured the consent of the British missions to replace those Venizelists in senior positions in the army and gendarmerie who had not joined the monarchist camp. Their first choice as chief of general staff was the former governor of Athens on the eve of liberation, Spiliotopoulos, later to be succeeded by Venteres, whose appointees sympathized with the promptings of the conspiratorial Sacred Union of Greek Officers (IDEA) in appointments and promotions. Most nomarchs (or prefects) were replaced, even in strongly Venizelist regions, and these in turn replaced many members of local councils and committees of UNRRA. Those public employees whose anti-Communist credentials were doubted – amounting to 13 per cent of the public service and teaching profession – were purged in April 1947. Among those who lost their posts were the three professors who had participated in EAM's provisional government.

The apex of the new regime was the monarchy, which was restored with partisan celebrations in September 1946, after a plebiscite which was rigged and coerced still more flagrantly than the general election had been. Many leftist and republican voters were prevented from voting by being gaoled without charge. It appears that a majority of the rural electorate was intimidated by the gendarmes or bandits; and certainly the secrecy of the ballot was widely violated. Multiple votes are estimated by Nikolakopoulos to have amounted to 9 per cent of the registered electorate. The government presented the issue of the plebiscite as one of national interests versus Slav communism.[2]

The parliament included few of the younger figures who had been active in the resistance, because these were found mainly on the left and centre of the political spectrum, and these groups had either abstained from or done poorly in the election. Thus the deputies could not understand the aspirations and needs which EAM represented, and half of them had been deputies in 1936 or earlier. Nearly all the new deputies who later achieved distinction belonged to the small centre groups. The Populist Party which dominated the government was the most sterile and obscurantist sector of the political world. Before the war the anti-Venizelists, of whom they had been the core, were in George Mavrogordatos's words 'an essentially negative and reactive, if not reactionary, force';[3] and they seemed to have learnt nothing since then. Tsaldares was a small-minded mediocrity, who earned the contempt of the British and American administrations by his neglect of economic problems and inept advocacy of territorial claims. His prominence, like that of Sophocles Venizelos in the Liberal Party, exemplified the major role of family connections in Greek politics. Neither Tsaldares, nor his colleagues in the 1946 ministry except Stephanos Stephanopoulos, held any ministerial portfolio after the return of peaceful conditions in 1950. Some of his ministers reduced foreign officials to despair by their attempts through partisan motives to frustrate relief efforts. For example a Minister of Health (a former collaborator) was described by an UNRRA official as 'a fool and a rogue' claiming that he would prefer malaria to continue rather than leave one Communist in public employment. The Minister of Supply was described by the head of the British economic mission as 'a clogging influence'.[4] Thus the government obstructed the attempts by foreign agencies to restore prosperity, which was a prerequisite for the restoration of public order.

A more direct contribution by the government to the advent of civil war was its endorsement of the white terror. Tsaldares and his energetic Minister for Public Order, Spyros Theotokes, emphasized their solicitude for the interests of the police and their appreciation of its work, and it was partly in its interests that the government enacted draconian security legislation. In May it reintroduced the Security Commissions now composed of a nomarch, judge, and public prosecutor, to order the deportation, often without evidence, of those considered by the police to be dangerous. The procedure was applied on an unprecedented scale: by the end of the year 4,876 people were deported and 1,227 awaiting the results of their appeals; and by the end of the civil war probably over 30,000 had been deported. This penalty was often imposed in arbitrary ways, but applied especially against supporters, friends, or families of left-wing outlaws. In one case the gendarmerie chief on the Adriatic island of Zakynthos was ordered by his regional commander to find fifteen people to deport regardless of their guilt or innocence.[5] In June the so-called Resolution Three gave the police unprecedented powers: to search houses without warrant, suppress strikes which they considered to be for non-economic reasons, and arrest on charges punishable by death those deemed guilty of acts against state security or even their moral instigation. To try offences under it, special courts martial were established in numerous towns in Thessaly, Epirus, Macedonia, and Thrace. The initial exemption of the old lands further south revealed the bias of the monarchist majority in parliament.

The courts martial soon started to impose ferocious sentences for offences such as criticizing the authorities or helping leftist guerrillas, sentences which elicited private comments like 'outrageous' and 'idiotic' from British diplomats. By the end of the year 116 people had been executed after sentence by court martial, and there followed another 688 in 1947. Such persecution seems by the end of 1946 to have suppressed most public criticism of the government outside Athens. Possibly all provincial offices of the Communist Party and EAM had by then been closed except perhaps in the Venizelist stronghold of Crete, where the white terror was slower to gather pace. Emergency legislation was also used in September to arrest numerous left-wing labour leaders, and so confirm the government's newly won control over the executives of the General Confederation of Greek Workers (GSEE), trade union federations, and the Workers' Centres. By this time the Communist Party had little power to use the trade unions for disguised economic sabotage, and the unions had diminishing power to defend workers' interests.[6]

Oppressive acts by the police were now not watched helplessly, as before the general election, but actively instigated by political superiors such as nomarchs or politicians. The American authors of *Report on the Greeks* found early in 1947 that the gendarmes were dreaded in many mountain villages for their brutal and arbitrary actions. British officials were reduced to protesting ineffectively to the government that it was encouraging the gendarmerie to behave in a lawless way, noting that indiscriminate persecution was creating the dangers that it was supposed to be combating.[7] For example it was driving Liberals to demand measures of appeasement at a time when the government needed the widest public support for its war effort. Still worse, as the British ambassador observed in June of the new security measures, 'the main result has been merely to increase the number of outlaws who are taking to the mountains in greater numbers than ever', because naturally they did not 'wait quietly in their villages for their inevitable summons before a Security Committee or Court Martial'.[8] In at least one area in northern Evrytania (in western Sterea Ellada), the authorities distributed arms to monarchist citizens merely to intimidate republican opponents before the plebiscite, and so forced leftist villagers to take to the mountains and form a guerrilla band where none had hitherto existed.

Gendarmes commonly reacted to the presence of left-wing outlaws by terrorizing or deporting their families. In October, for example, American observers by Lake Doirane on the Yugoslav frontier saw 50 or 60 women in a barbed wire enclosure with small children clinging to their skirts, later to be taken away in trucks commandeered from UNRRA. At Stephanina, also in central Macedonia, in December, a gendarme fired with a submachine gun into a crowd of women and killed five, an action for which he was later tried and acquitted.[9] The effect of such actions was especially damaging to the government in areas where the majority of the population was sympathetic to the left. In Florina, further west, for example, a town with a population of about 12,000 and the centre of a largely Slav-speaking prefecture, there were in November 1946 about 600 people, mainly Slav, in gaol in 'very bad' conditions, charged with wartime collaboration or helping guerrillas.[10]

Another force driving refugees to the mountains was right-wing banditry, which also benefited from official support and became very extensive in some areas. In Laconia and Arcadia in the Peloponnese, where the majority of the population were sympathetic, the bandit Katsareas led a band reported to be 150–350 strong, recruited partly by conscription, and with his lieutenants intimidated a large region. In Vamvacou in October, in reprisal for the killing of nine rightists, he ordered the execution of 37 leftists, most of them civilian hostages. He and other such figures were believed to be supported by the Populist Minister of the Army Petros Mavromichalis, whom Katsareas had served as bodyguard. Largely for this reason Mavromichalis was forced by British pressure to resign in November. Katsareas himself was ambushed and killed in March 1947.[11]

In the Volos region, on the east coast, the majority of the population was left-wing; but some villages wanted protection against leftist attacks, and bandit leaders for these reasons enjoyed support from the military authorities. Early in November, several travelled to Athens and back, presumably for talks with politicians. Just afterwards one of them, Kalabalikes, although under sentence of life imprisonment for collaboration, called together the presidents of many communes (village councils) in the Pelion area and told them that he had been instructed by the government to raise an armed force of 300, for which he required the vast sum of 60,000,000 drachmas ($12,000) each month from them, refusal of which would be severely punished. We do not know how many paid.[12] Because the bandits caused international scandal, the government was pressed by the British to suppress them, and in time responded by giving them official status as village militias under the army's auspices. These militias eventually reached an armed strength of 41,000, distributed through the whole country.

REVIVAL OF GUERRILLA WARFARE

The new regime stimulated increased banditry also by the left. Consequently there was a marked increase in political violence from late April onwards in many parts of the country including Athens. There were increasingly frequent attacks by left-wing bands on gendarmerie posts and patrols in Thessaly and western Macedonia, and by right-wing bands on left-wing communities in the Peloponnese. Attacks which were unusually large included one in mid-May on the town of Megalopolis, in the Peloponnese, by about 100 armed rightists, who took hostages, and one on 26 June by a left-wing band of about 150 on a village near Litochoro.[13] The left-wing guerrillas took advantage of the existence of rugged mountains in most regions, particularly the whole 600 miles (as the crow flies) of the northern frontiers. In the north mountains were extensively wooded, and their alignment near Albania and Yugoslavia was mainly across the frontiers, making them harder to defend.

The intensified persecution made the Communist leaders decide, by late June, to increase the scale of the guerrilla warfare and to direct that self-defence in towns be armed. In July a politburo member and former ELAS *kapetanios*, Markos Vapheiades, was appointed by Zachariades to direct guerrilla warfare. Another politburo member Bartziotas organized support for it in Larisa the capital of Thessaly, and then in Salonika the capital of Macedonia. In both places he impressed on cadres that this work now took priority. Urban cadres in country towns in several other regions, such as north-west Peloponnese, western Sterea Ellada, and western Macedonia, also organized supplies to guerrilla leaders, who in turn formed regional headquarters and combined scattered groups into larger ones of 100 or more.[14] Thus the party took advantage of the growing flood of political refugees to the mountains from villages and small towns. With this sort of impetus, guerrilla attacks became larger-scale and bolder. On 6 July occurred what was still an exceptionally bold attack on an army company of about 100 at Pontokerasea in Macedonia, killing or injuring six soldiers, and capturing or recruiting the rest. At least 27 soldiers were killed in this month in different attacks.[15]

From April onwards left-wing guerrillas were reinforced by a return movement of ELAS veterans, many of them former commanders, from camps at Bulkes north of Belgrade and at Skopje capital of Yugoslav Macedonia, bringing with them the names of Communist contacts in various regions of Greece. The Greek General Staff estimated that 2,000–3,000 had returned to Greece by 1 September, and that up to 5,000 more returned thereafter. From May onwards the Greek-speaking bands began to cooperate with the bands of the slavophones' Macedonian Popular Liberation Front (SNOF) in western Macedonia.[16] The returning ELAS veterans were supplied by the Yugoslav and Albanian authorities with light weapons, food, and medicines, and could withdraw for refuge across the frontiers. Their freedom to do so was a vital asset, because it enabled them to escape, if pursued or wounded, to territory which was forbidden to their enemies by the British and later the American governments, for fear of provoking an international crisis.

In the contiguous regions of northern Thessaly and western Macedonia the guerrillas soon afterwards repeated the feat of ELAS by 'liberating' large areas, and harassing or obstructing the government's lines of communication to Epirus, the western Macedonian towns, and Salonika, while keeping open their own supply lines to Yugoslavia and Albania. In western Macedonia the majority of their supporters were Slav-speakers, who were sustained by fellow Slavs in Yugoslav Macedonia. It seems that most of the population of Thessaly was sympathetic to the left guerrillas because it had been won over by EAM in the occupation, and in the north of the province was accessible to the supply routes from Yugoslavia.

In these regions, Communist supporters once more organized their own system of local government, and accumulated sizeable stocks of provisions. From about September they could assemble bands which for particular operations numbered several hundreds. Their bands captured arms and ammunition from gendarmerie posts and from village militias, as well as food from UNRRA stocks and from right-wing villagers. A new high water mark was the capture for three days, by about 1,500 leftists, of the fortified village of Deskati in northern Thessaly on 21 September, which was defended by 45 gendarmes and a company of National Guards, 47 of the defenders being killed. For some time afterwards this area formed the nerve-centre of the left-wing guerrillas. On 30 September and 2 October there were attacks on the small industrial town of Naoussa (with a peace-time population of 12,000), and on 12 October on another small town, Siatista, both in western Macedonia. On 13 November a band of about 1,000, perhaps Slav autonomists, captured an outpost garrisoned by an army company at Skra in central Macedonia after an eight-hour battle. Eighteen soldiers and 55 inhabitants were massacred, before the attackers evaded counter-attack by crossing the nearby Yugoslav border.[17]

Late in September Markos assumed command of the main left-wing forces from a headquarters in northern Thessaly. On 28 October, the anniversary of the Italian invasion of Greece, he formally established a GHQ at a conference of *kapetanioi*, all ELAS veterans, and appointed regional commanders, who began to organize their followers into military units and impose military discipline on them. In December they adopted the title Democratic Army of Greece (DSE).[18]

In October Tito gave orders that the Slav Macedonian Popular Liberation Front should in Greece come under Communist command, and its members be merged with its guerrilla units. During the German occupa-tion the organized Slav Macedonians, or ethnically conscious slavophones, owed primary allegiance to the Macedonian Communist Party. Now the Greek Communists gained the advantage of the great reserves of man-power, and the extensive networks of supply and information, which they had built up in western Macedonia. Henceforth Slav Macedonians consti-tuted a large part of the Democratic Army. But this support was gained at a heavy cost. The Slav Macedonians secured the opportunity to cultivate nationalist feeling among compatriots through their own newspapers, schools, and local administration. The Greek Communists thus exposed themselves to the constant accusation by the Greek government that they were encouraging Slav secessionism.

The DSE grew fast as it absorbed the returning exiles and the refugees from the white terror. Unlike the destitute groups of outlaws in 1945, the army maintained its activity throughout the winter, raiding villages over wide areas of the north to seize food supplies and acquire recruits, forced and voluntary. From a number of armed combatants reported by the Communist authorities to be about 4,000 in September it grew to some-thing approaching 10,000 by the end of December, and was still growing steadily. After September it sent detachments of cadres in different direc-tions to expand the small groups in various parts of Sterea Ellada, establish significant forces in eastern Macedonia, and found groups in northern Epirus. A large group entered Greece from Bulgaria to begin activities in Thrace. Late in the year there seem to have been several hundred guerrillas of local origin operating in the Peloponnese; and soon afterwards there were some active also in Boeotia, Euboea and Crete.[19] The spread of the revolt to southern areas diverted the over-stretched government forces and dispelled the myth that it depended on support by the Slav countries.

According to Ioannides, in a report which he wrote for the Soviet authorities in September 1946, most of Markos's followers were barefoot and poorly clothed. We have it from the memoirs of some of them, and from the surviving archives of the DSE, that they were lightly armed, with meagre supplies of ammunition. Many of those near the frontier possessed German weapons supplied by the Yugoslavs, while those further south made do with what they captured or the remnants of ELAS caches. In October 1946 government forces still controlled the relatively few places on the mountainous frontier where heavy weapons could be brought in; and the first such weapons to be reported were anti-aircraft guns in May 1947. In September 1946, according to Ioannides, the Communist Party was still bearing much of the cost of these armed forces, paying for its deficit of about \$20,000–\$30,000 monthly from its reserves accumulated during the occupation. The following year it seems that the party relied mainly on the Yugoslavs for supplies, and received some funds from the Soviet Union. The prominent role taken by the Yugoslavs and their Albanian clients in the Greek enterprise discouraged the Bulgarian authorities from supplying more than small-scale aid, because they had no wish to help Yugoslavia expand its territory and influence.[20]

At this stage these barefoot soldiers had assets of other kinds. Their commanders showed great skill – acquired during the occupation – in classic guerrilla tactics: surprise achieved by fast movement across rugged terrain or at night; concentration to achieve local superiority in attack followed immediately by escape; the ability to filter secretly through enemy lines and re-assemble beyond them; simultaneous or successive attacks in widely separated places. They retained a clandestine network in villages and towns which gave them an advantage in information over their foes. According to various witnesses, Greek and foreign, their morale and discipline were high, welded by 'monarcho-fascist' persecution backed by British (soon to become Anglo-American) 'imperialism'.[21] Probably all their commanders, and a sizeable minority of the rank-and-file, were Communists, which facilitated unity among the Greek-speakers, although there was, admittedly, friction between them and the large minority of Slav Macedonians.[22] The official aims of the DSE, as stated in the oath of allegiance administered to recruits, were simply national liberation and the restoration of democracy – the aims of ELAS.[23]

The revival of guerrilla warfare was greeted with great enthusiasm by many Communists, for understandable reasons. After the security measures of May–June 1946 began to be enforced, there was not much that the party could do in many places except 'go to the mountains': to stay in provincial towns was to await persecution and imprisonment. Yet at all levels of the party there was ambiguity and disagreement about the guerrilla struggle. From April 1946 onwards various leading Communists including Markos actually discouraged would-be volunteers, and in at least one reported case sent some back to their villages, to be arrested later by the police. On being appointed to lead the guerrilla struggle, Markos was given the unrealistic advice by Zachariades not to attack regular army units and keep in mind that the party's main objective was reconciliation with the government. From about August, according to Bartziotas, the party leadership in Salonika 'resisted firmly the desire, in the face of terrorism and difficulties, to abandon the towns entirely and go to the mountains'. The *kapetanios* Kikitsas wrote later that in September he was prevented from recruiting certain people in Bulkes camp by the local party authorities who told him that they had not finished screening them politically. As the inmates of Bulkes had been there for at least twelve months, this example illustrates forcibly the priority which the party leaders gave to political orthodoxy over military needs. In October the politburo warned members publicly that 'many suspect elements' in Athens, who were alleged to be enemy agents, were claiming falsely that they had orders to recruit them for guerrilla warfare. Apparently in order to divide its enemies and reassure its allies, the party continued until June 1947 if not later to claim that its aim was 'reconciliation'. This policy led to the Communist Party's participation in the plebiscite of September 1946 and its attempt to cooperate with the Liberals in opposing the monarchy.[24]

The party leaders must have realized the danger that by delaying the expansion of guerrilla war they were giving the government time to react. However the delay was imposed on them by the shortage of supplies from Yugoslavia, and continued discouragement from the Soviet Union. After the election, Zachariades and his colleagues persistently pressed Stalin, Tito, and other Communist leaders for military aid. From September, key members of the politburo spent an increasing part of their time in Belgrade and there negotiated for aid.[25] In September, Ioannides in Belgrade, presumably in accordance with Yugoslav instructions, told Markos to limit the extent of recruitment to 4,000–5,000 combatants, and then appealed for supplies to the Soviet authorities, who in November merely repeated their previous advice 'to limit the extent of the guerrilla struggle'. In April 1947 Zachariades eventually overcame the opposition of the Soviet authorities by once more presenting them with a *fait accompli*, gambling on the assumption that they could not abandon him. This time he told Stalin that the Communist politburo had decided to give priority to the military struggle, and so needed military supplies.[26]

At its meeting on 11–12 September 1947, when deciding at last to commit itself to war, the central committee reversed its line of 1946 and blamed prominent party members, and many of the rank-and-file, for having evaded orders to go to the mountains. In later years, party leaders blamed each other for delaying the guerrilla effort. These accusations were an obvious attempt to find scapegoats for what was really a collective policy. One leading cadre in Athens implicated in the accusations of September, Stergios Anastasiades, immediately replied that no one had given the necessary orders, or made the necessary preparations, to send party members to join the DSE.[27]

However the resistance to guerrilla war at various levels of the party in the large cities seems to have been due to more than one factor. It must have been very difficult for the national leadership to accept the liquidation of their massive urban organization. There was in any case an obvious need to maintain an urban organization to support and cooperate with the guerrilla struggle. It seems that during 1946 Zachariades was reluctant to give up hope of an uprising in the towns, to be achieved apparently by a combination of strikes and militant demonstrations combined with a military coup. This intention is indicated by the accumulation of arms in at least some towns, and by the instructions which, according to enemy intelligence services, were given to urban organizations to prepare for action such as sabotage and assassinations.

It is also clear that cadres in the capital were more reluctant than their comrades in the rest of the country to contemplate war. The Communists' allies were still more reluctant. Thus the EAM central committee opposed the decision to make war, and no non-Communist joined the provisional government which the Communist Party established in December. Left-wingers in the main cities were less vulnerable than their colleagues in the provinces to persecution by the shadow state, and readier to appreciate the value of dealings with other political parties. Because of their access to information, they were better able to recognize the government's superiority in resources, especially after American aid began to arrive, and they could see that most of the public opposed full-scale military revolt.[28]

In the event, the maintenance of the urban organizations did not achieve its object because the British did not withdraw militarily, and whatever preparations were made for armed action in the larger towns were checked by police vigilance.[29] By the end of 1946 left-wing terrorism in Salonika and Athens–Piraeus was becoming infrequent, and among the few examples of importance were the assassination of a gendarmerie officer in Salonika in October 1946, and of a Minister of Justice in Athens in May 1948. So effective was police control over the cities that from December 1947 the party leaders did not even try to make members evade military service.[30] For all these reasons, the mass of city Communists did not join the DSE, leaving its rank-and-file to be recruited overwhelmingly from mountain villagers.

When supplies did arrive from the Soviet Union, after mid-1947, they encouraged the party leaders to proceed with plans to build up a regular army, but were much too limited for this purpose, and seemed intended merely to prevent the party from falling too far under Yugoslav influence. According to the Yugoslavs these supplies included 30 anti-aircraft guns. The Yugoslavs claim that, mainly after mid-1947, they themselves sent 35,000 rifles, 3,500 machine-guns, 2,000 heavy machine-guns and 7,000 anti-tank guns, besides 10,000 land mines, and much food and clothing.[31] This was perhaps as much as they could afford. Even these supplies were difficult to distribute far south of the border, because within Greece they had to be transported by mule along circuitous routes across rugged terrain, bypassing the government's garrisons and patrols. Because of the government's naval strength and control of coastal waters, deliveries by sea were few and hazardous, using wooden fishing boats. Guerrilla forces far south of the frontier were forced, by their need for constant mobility and their shortage of supply depots, to travel light.[32]

There were obvious reasons why Yugoslavia and the Soviet Union did not supply Zachariades with what he requested from April 1947 onwards: enough equipment and heavy arms for a regular army of 50,000–60,000 that could liberate much of northern Greece including Salonika and establish a rebel government. Such aid would be a vast and risky commitment for an indefinite period, from which it would be hard to withdraw in the event of failure. There would be a danger of provoking an international crisis unless Britain and the United States showed that they had lost interest in Greece, which was peripheral to Soviet interests. On the other hand, limited aid could be disclaimed, and it allowed the option of retreat to neutrality.

THE NATIONAL ARMY INTERVENES

During 1945 pursuit and arrest of left-wing outlaws were tasks attempted by small units of the National Guard and gendarmerie. From late in the year the gendarmerie quite frequently sent out patrols in many regions, and these were increasingly well armed with submachine-guns and grenades. From March 1946 they were helped increasingly often by army units. For the rest of the year, the gendarmerie, already far above its pre-war strength, continued to be expanded so that it could sustain its military role. In the last months of 1946, the gendarmerie in the northern provinces was reported to be suffering casualties twice or three times as heavy as those of the army, and at least some units were becoming exhausted by the demands placed on them.[33]

The strain was worsened by the atrocities which Communists inflicted on them. Gendarmes, unlike soldiers, were normally executed after capture; and their families were exposed to danger of reprisals. In one case near Agoriane in the Peloponnese on 20 April 1947, when a gendarmerie company was ambushed, it was reported to the British police mission that 38 were captured and executed in a church, and the worst was feared for 38 others. In Macedonia and Thrace, from December 1946 to May 1947, 136 gendarmes were killed. The gendarmes responded with a savagery to captives and their families which on at least one occasion provoked condemnation by army officers.[34]

The reliance on the gendarmerie resulted from the inadequacies of the regular army, which in the words of General Keith Crawford, the head of the British Military Mission, on 4 October 1946, was 'for all practical purposes an entirely new army which must necessarily suffer growing pains'.[35] It had been increased from a strength of 8,800 at the time of Varkiza to 98,200 in December 1946. The British mission, which supervised the process of training and organization, proceeded slowly at first for lack of equipment or of a sense of urgency.[36] Then from March 1946 it was hindered by the growing diversion of men to anti-guerrilla duties, which took officers from their work as instructors, and deprived recruits of group training. The most serious shortage seems to have been a lack of suitably trained officers, sergeants, and corporals. The many thousands of officers bequeathed by the Venizelist regime of 1922–35 had been trained for a bygone era of warfare, and had rusted in retirement. The survivors of the Albanian war of 1940–1 were in many cases discredited by collaboration, or like Papagos relegated for political reasons to the retired list. Thus the officer-training college, when it resumed work in 1946 after an interruption of five years, had to fill large vacancies. Even then it did not start to provide training in counter-guerrilla warfare until late 1947.[37] The British mission had not foreseen the need to provide either the training or equipment for such warfare. Thus the army in late 1946 possessed few pack animals and no light artillery. The pilots of the small Greek airforce did not until 1947 start to support ground operations, and the Spitfires which they then flew were not really suitable for the purpose.[38]

So when in July 1946 the army formally assumed responsibility for counter-guerrilla operations in the north, it lacked almost everything it needed. Perhaps its most serious defect was psychological: civil war was a prospect viewed with revulsion by all except a small minority of fanatics on each side. But there is ample evidence from observers on both sides that morale and discipline were generally superior in the DSE, despite its hardships and shortages of supplies. Its members had their backs to the wall, and were disgusted with the corrupt and partisan character of the monarchist regime, besides its servility to the British and later the Americans. Moreover they had ideals – those of EAM/ELAS – which to many seemed worth fighting for, and were embodied in the resistance record of their leaders. The officers and propagandists of the government army had little success at first in providing their followers with comparable motivation. Their reliance on the bogy of Slav-Communism was unable to erase the bad impression made on soldiers' minds by the white terror and by the presence of former collaborators among officers. American observers reported after conversations in the Peloponnese and in Epirus that the majority of soldiers felt some respect for their opponents and had little faith in the government's cause.[39] Because the British had forbidden discrimination in recruitment, a significant proportion of the army's total numbers – 15 per cent in October 1946 according to the British mission – belonged to or supported the Communist Party, which directed their activities through a special branch. This infiltration was considered by the army to be responsible for some of the cases of desertion, evasion of orders, or easy surrenders, which were widespread in 1946 and early 1947. In July 1946 a plot was discovered in three brigades stationed near Kozane which led to the arrest of 300 participants. The General Staff was alarmed by this danger, and was forced for at least the next two years to make great efforts to identify and segregate Communists among recruits.[40]

Another serious cause of demoralization was the fact that a large proportion of the army consisted of older reservists, who had already done one or even two terms of military service, and probably in most cases had families, for whom the government made inadequate provision. Their resentment at having to serve another term was strengthened by well-known cases of evasion of military service by the rich and politically influential. The British and Americans relied heavily on these veterans until 1949 for reasons of economy: being experienced they needed less training than new recruits. Officers at first were demoralized by the unfamiliar and apparently unwinnable nature of the war. How could they overcome an enemy who usually knew their movements in advance; retreated into rugged terrain to avoid fighting; and in the last resort could escape across frontiers which they themselves were not allowed to cross? The problem continued to baffle the majority of officers for the next two years; and at first possibly a majority of officers and certainly a majority of privates felt little desire to confront it. All these causes of low morale became generally known in April 1947 when a confidential account of them by a corps commander was revealed by the Communists in *Rizospastes*.[41]

To add to the army's problems, it was prevented by political pressure from acquiring the experience which it needed in pursuit of guerrillas. Parliamentary deputies, nomarchs, and others clamoured constantly for protection of their civilian clients; and army commanders resisted this pressure at their peril because political influence was generally necessary for professional survival. Many officers anyway saw a need to strengthen the morale of right-wing civilians and prevent them from buckling to threats by left-wing guerrillas. Thus the troops available for counter-guerrilla operations were for the most part, by autumn 1946, scattered in what the British mission called 'penny packets all over the country', so that they could not learn how to attack the guerrillas. To help sympathetic villagers defend themselves, army officers distributed rifles in vast numbers to them. These village militias provided a rich source of arms to the guerrillas, who could achieve local superiority and attack them by surprise. Nearly two-thirds of the army's nominal strength was not available even for defending villages, because it was engaged in other roles and duties normal in a conventional army: defence of the frontiers, guarding installations and communications, administrative and support services, training or being trained.[42]

Because of all these difficulties, the army rarely made contact with the guerrillas in its operations against them from July to November 1946. The operations extended from the Agrapha mountains in south-western Thessaly to the northern Pindus ranges and eastwards to Thrace.[43] Thus the expansion of the DSE met with little obstruction from the government army and not much from the under-manned and over-worked gendarmerie. Nor were the government forces adequate for their other roles of frontier defence or garrisoning of the cities. For example if the Communists had been able to organize a revolt in Athens in December 1946 they would have been opposed by little more than the 3,000-strong city police.[44] The government relied heavily therefore on the guarantee provided by the small British garrison.

Greece was one of several countries where guerrilla forces opposed the dominant regime for some years after the Second World War. In Spain, left-wing guerrillas representing the republican exiles fought against Franco's gendarmerie. In Poland, the Ukraine, and the three Baltic states nationalists fought against the local Communist regime. These can be seen as rearguard actions by sections of the population which found themselves stranded on the wrong side of the Iron Curtain. Only in Greece did these guerrillas organize an army which fought sustained operations with some chance of success. For this there are several reasons: the immense public support acquired by the Communist-led resistance during the occupation;

Greece's mountainous terrain and proximity to countries with Communist regimes; and the inability of Britain – an exhausted and over-extended imperial power – to commit enough troops or money to sustain its client government.

THE TRUMAN DOCTRINE

From the time of liberation, the British government intended to withdraw its support and its troops as soon as it had established a self-sufficient government. From 1945 it began to warn the Greek government of an imminent termination of financial support; and on 3 June 1946 the British Cabinet set the terminal date for 31 March 1947. Mounting guerrilla activity caused some British officials to have reservations about the advisability of withdrawal. We have already noticed Ernest Bevin's advocacy in March 1946 of a 'physical presence' in Greece. The British ambassador Sir Clifford Norton likewise believed by September 1946 or earlier that guerrilla activity was designed by the Soviet Union, working through its Balkan satellites, to overthrow the government, which would probably succumb without British support. Greece would, he feared, then become a Soviet satellite, and Turkey would in turn be threatened. Thus a guerrilla victory would have a domino effect in the region. Thereafter, however, as the Greek government showed no sign of progress towards financial or military self-sufficiency, British authorities showed increasing despair and exasperation. Hector McNeil, Minister of State for Foreign Affairs, wrote on 29 November that 'today the economic situation is almost as bad as it ever has been'. The Chief of Imperial General Staff Lord Montgomery, after a visit in early December, concluded that if the Greek army failed to defeat the guerrillas in the spring (which no one in Greece thought likely), 'then that will be the end of Greece'. The Prime Minister Clement Attlee queried whether Greece was strategically vital after all. Underlying such remarks was probably a sense of Britain's financial exhaustion, which on 24 February 1947 caused the British government to warn the Americans that it would have to stick to its deadline of 31 March. This step, as it turned out, foreshadowed the end of nearly 150 years of British influence.[45]

The reason why the Americans responded so promptly was that they were already approaching the decision to commit large resources to the defence of Greece from the red peril. In November 1945 a senior official of the British Foreign Office complained that the usual reply from the US State Department to any request for help was: 'Greece is *your* headache.' In fact, this attitude of detachment was steadily changing. The major cause of change was the tightening during 1945 of the Soviet grip over Poland, Romania, and Bulgaria. This process destroyed the mirage, prolonged by the Yalta Declaration on Liberated Europe of February 1945, of an eastern Europe composed of independent, democratic states from which the great powers could withdraw. By as early as October 1945 the US administration was reacting with anxiety to reports of political anarchy and British weakness in Greece. Early the following year the US administration awoke fully to the spectre of an expansionist Soviet Union. In January 1946, President Truman wrote privately, 'I'm tired of babying the Soviets.' In March he agreed privately with Churchill's famous declaration that 'an iron curtain has descended across the Continent' of Europe, and that military strength was needed to check the 'expansive and proselytizing tendencies' of the Soviet Union.[46] More specifically, from 1944, US policy-makers, aware of the fast-growing importance of Middle East oil, were coming to appreciate Britain's traditional view that Greece, Turkey, and Iran formed a 'northern tier' of defence against Russian expansionism. Early in April 1946, the visit of the battleship *Missouri* to Athens was intended as a gesture to anti-Communist Greeks of military support against the Soviet Union, and as such was warmly welcomed.[47]

Later that month the Secretary of State James Byrnes agreed with Bevin that the Soviet Union should be pressed to withdraw its armies from Romania and Bulgaria, and that 'it was essential that the Communists should not get into power in Greece. This must be avoided at all costs.' In the following months the State Department and the US ambassador MacVeagh came to agree with Norton's view of Greece as a wobbling domino, and to conclude that the United States must spend money and effort to prop her up. An ideological justification for this course was at hand in resistance to Communist totalitarianism. MacVeagh, while condemning the authoritarianism of Tsaldares's government, repeated in October his long-held view that 'no "terrorism" can possibly exist in a country under Anglo-Saxon hegemony which can be equated with that which accompanies Russian-supported Communism wherever it goes'.[48] By the following February the State Department had decided that Greece was a vital American interest. Thus the British appeal was the catalyst for the decision to commit massive aid, which was extended also to Turkey. In a publicity campaign lasting three weeks the US administration managed to win the support of a majority in Congress for this shift in overseas policy from traditional isolationism to massive and sustained interventionism. The campaign culminated in a speech by President Harry Truman on 12 March to both Houses of Congress in joint session, which expressed what became known as the Truman Doctrine. The president proposed that $300 million be allocated in aid to Greece, and $100 million to Turkey, which although politically more stable than Greece, was seen as strategically still more important to the United States, and had been subjected to greater Soviet pressure for territorial concessions. Truman referred to 'the terrorist activities of several thousand armed men, led by Communists' in Greece and the danger that if Greece succumbed to them, 'confusion and disorder might well spread throughout the entire Middle East'. Truman presented the global context of this crisis as a confrontation between 'alternative ways of life', the 'free' and the 'totalitarian', and made special reference to the evils of totalitarianism which had been forced on the peoples of other countries, referring to Bulgaria, Romania, and Poland. The response of the United States must be 'to support free peoples who are resisting attempted subjugation by armed minorities or by outside pressures'. As Robert Frazier wrote, the anti-Communist theme secured the rapid passage through Congress of a bill authorizing extensive aid to Greece, and marked the start of a worldwide ideological crusade.[49]

NOTES

1. George M. Alexander, *The Prelude to the Truman Doctrine. British Policy in Greece 1944–7.* (Oxford, 1982), pp. 207–8; Demokratikos Stratos tes Elladas, *Etsi Archise o Emphylios* (1987), pp. 21–3; FO 286/1174, D. Balfour, 5 Nov. 1946.

2. David H. Close, 'The reconstruction of a right-wing state', in David H. Close, ed., *The Greek Civil War, 1943–50. Studies of Polarization* (1993), pp. 166–7; David H. Close, 'The changing structure of the Greek right, 1945–50', unpublished paper delivered to the Lehrman Institute conference at Vilvorde, June 1987; Haris Vlavianos, *Greece, 1941–9. From Resistance to Civil War* (1992), p. 232; Nars, 868.00/9-646, *reports by L.B. Morris and R.T. Windle, 7 Sept. 1946*; Elias Nikolakopoulos, *Kommata kai Voulevtikes Ekloges sten Ellada, 1946–64* (1985), p. 150.

3. George Mavrogordatos, *Stillborn Republic. Social Coalitions and Party Strategies in Greece, 1922–36* (Berkeley, 1983), p. 323.

4. FO 286/1174, N.M. Goodman to J.W. Nicholls, 19 Sept. 1946; Alexander, *Prelude*, pp. 195, 220, 229, 235,240.

5. Close, 'Reconstruction', in Close, ed., *The Greek Civil War*, p. 168; P. Delaporta, *Semeiomatario enos Pilatou* (1977), pp. 241, 243, 248; Nicos Alivizatos, *Les Institutions Politiques de la Grèce à travers les Crises* (Paris, 1979), p. 369; FO 371/67049/68-9, R 1551.

6. FO 371/67143/-, Reilly to Bevin, 28 Aug. 1947; 371/58916/102-4, R 18513; C.M. Woodhouse, *Apple of Discord. A Survey of Recent Greek Politics in their International Setting* (1948), p. 269; Adamantia Pollis, 'U.S. intervention in Greek trade unions', in John O. Iatrides, ed., *Greece in the 1940s. A Nation in Crisis* (1981), pp. 268, 272.

7. Frank Smothers, W.H. and E.G. McNeill, *Report on the Greeks* (New York,

1948), p. 169; Iatrides, ed., *Greece*, p. 186; FO 371/58757/-, 286/1175, Wickham to Theotokis, 24 Apr. 1946; 24 June 1946.

8. FO 286/1175, Norton to Foreign Office, 27 June 1946; L.S. Stavrianos, *Greece – American Dilemma and Opportunity* (Chicago, 1952), p. 178.
9. Nars, 868.00/10-1746; FO 371/67078/100, R 12727.
10. Nars, RG 84, American Embassy Confidential File, 1946, G.M. Widney, 6 Nov. 1946.
11. F0 286/1181, British Consul, Patras, to Norton, 17 Nov. 1946; 371/67131/-, British police mission report, p. 7.
12. FO 286/1173, C.N. Gonatas to W.L.C. Knight, 23 Nov. 1946.
13. FO 286/1175, M. Bayley, 'The deterioration of public order in Greece, April–May 1946'; 286/1175, Norton to FO, 27 June 1946; Nars, 868.00/5-2046, Athens Embassy to Secretary of State.
14. G. Mavros, 'Ta archeia tou Demokratikou Stratou', *Elevtherotypia*, 11 Dec. 1978, pp. 8–9; Vasiles Bartziotas, *Exenta Chronia Kommounistes* (1986), pp. 247–8, 258; FO 286/1181, British Consul Patras, 29 Aug. 1946; 3 Sept. 1946, p. 1; 21 Sept. 1946.
15. FO 371/58759/8, police mission report for July 1946.
16. Nars, 868.00/1-847, DRN information note no. 34; *USFR, 1946*, VII, p. 247; Evangelos Kofos, 'The impact of the Macedonian question on the Greek civil war', unpublished paper delivered to Lehrman Institute conference at Vilvorde, 3–5 June 1987.
17. FO 286/1175, Norton to Attlee, 12 Nov. 1946; FO 381/58759/-, police mission report for October 1946; Phoivos Gregoriades, *Istoria tou Emphyliou Polemou. To Devtero Antartiko* (n.d.), III, pp. 734, 745; D. Zapheiropoulos, *O Antisymmoriakos Agon, 1945–9* 2 vols (1956), I, p. 181.
18. Christophe Chiclet, *Les Communistes Grecs dans la Guerre* (Paris, 1987), pp. 183–5.
19. Demetres Blanas, *O Emphylios Polemos, 1946–9* (1976), pp. 123–4; Georgios Vontitsos-Gousias, *Oi Aities gia tes Ettes* 2 vols (1977), I, pp. 145, 149; Zapheiropoulos, *Antisymmoriakos* I, p. 198; FO 371/72327/-, R 2811; Nars, 868.00/3-447, Athens Embassy to Secretary of State.
20. Chiclet, *Communistes Grecs*, pp. 179–82, citing translated text in Avge, 6 Dec. 1979, p. 3; Ivo Banac, *With Stalin Against Tito. Cominformist Splits in Yugoslav Communism* (Ithaca and London, 1988), p. 35; Nars, 868.00/10-246, Athens Embassy to Secretary of State; Smothers, McNeill and McNeill, *Report*, p. 158.
21. Nars, 868.00/2-2147, enclosure to despatch 371.
22. Evangelos Kofos considers that they constituted a little over one-third of the DSE at all stages: 'The impact of the Macedonian question on the Greek civil war', unpublished paper presented to the Lehrman Institute conference at Vilvorde, 3–5 June 1987.
23. Gregoriades, *Istoria,* III, pp. 738–9.
24. Blanas, *Emphylios*, pp. 87–8, 94; Vontitsos-Gousias, *Aities*, I, p. 214; Vlavianos, *Greece*, pp. 229, 235; Bartziotas, *Exenta Chronia*, p. 265; Heinz Richter, *British Intervention in Greece* (1985), pp. 494–5, 513; letter by Kikitsas (Sarandis Protopapas), *Elevtherotypia*, 12 Mar. 1986, p. 15; KKE, *Episema Keimena* (1987), VI, p. 225.
25. Peter J. Stavrakis, *Moscow and Greek Communism* (Ithaca, 1989), pp. 140–6.
26. Stavrakis, *Moscow*, pp. 147–50.

27. *Avge*, 3 Jan. 1980, p. 3; 5 Jan. 1980, p. 3; 11 Jan. 1980, p. 3; Vontitsos-Gousias, *Aities*, I, pp. 143, 240.
28. D.H. Close and T. Veremis, 'The military struggle, 1945–9', in Close, ed., *The Greek Civil War*, p. 104; *Elevtherotypia*, 12 Mar. 1986, p. 17. A poll of the population of Athens–Piraeus in Jan. 1986 (*Elevtherotypia*, 11 Mar. 1986, pp. 12–13) showed that a majority of the oldest age-group thought that Greece would have been worse off if the left had won the civil war.
29. Richter, *British Intervention*, pp. 529–30; Nars, RG 84, Athens Embassy Confidential File, 1947, 'Organization of Communist Terrorist Organization: "Collective People's Self-Defence"', 26 Dec. 1947; *ibid.*, B.P. Gordon to U.S. Ambassador, 27 May 1947; Zapheiropoulos, *Antisymmoriakos*, I, p. 198.
30. Nars, RG 84, Athens Embassy Confidential File 1948, 'Activities and developments concerning the Communist Party of Greece (KKE) during December 1947', K.L. Rankin to Secretary of State, 29 Jan. 1948.
31. Banac, *With Stalin,* p. 35; Stavrakis, *Moscow*, pp. 149–53; Vlavianos, *Greece*, pp. 240, 317; Howard Jones, *'A New Kind of War'. America's Global Strategy and the Truman Doctrine in Greece* (Oxford, 1989), p. 253.
32. Close and Veremis, 'Military struggle', in Close, ed., *The Greek Civil War*, p. 102.
33. FO 371/58852/9, K.N. Crawford, 4 Oct. 1946; FO 371/58759/9,16,186, police mission reports in 1946; 286/1175, Norton to Attlee, 12 Nov. 1946.
34. FO 371/67131/-, police mission report for April 1947; 371/67052/118, R 7516; Nars, RG 319, US Consul in Salonika, 24 May 1947.
35. FO 371/58852/8; Thrasyvoulos Tsakalotos, *Saranta Chronia Stratiotes tes Ellados* 2 vols (1960), II, p. 26.
36. FO 371/67028/9.
37. Close and Veremis, 'Military struggle, in Close, ed., *The Greek Civil War,* pp. 104–5; FO 371/101818/-, 'The work and achievements of the British Military Mission, 1945–52'; 371/67028/116; Theodoros Gregoropoulos, *Apo ten Koryphe tou Lophou* (1966), pp. 320–1.
38. Zapheiropoulos, *Antisymmoriakos*, I, pp. 119–23.
39. Gregoriades, *Istoria*, III, pp. 755–6, 912; IV, p. 1162; Zapheiropoulos, *Antisymmoriakos,* II, pp. 414, 417; Blanas, *Emphylios*, pp. 133–4; Nars, RG 84, Athens Embassy General Files, 1948, C.A. Graessner's evidence, transmitted by H. Grady, 23 Dec. 1948; 868.00/8-14447, memo of conversation with C. Schermerhorn; 868.00/8-1347, Fred Ayer Junior to Chief of Mission.
40. Stavrianos, *Greece*, p. 179; FO 371/58851/38,115, R 11888, R 13981; 371/78393/-, R 713; Nars, RG 319, Army Staff Greece, 1947–8, assessment of army strength in April 1947; Zapheiropoulos, *Antisymmoriakos,* I, p. 183; C. M. Woodhouse, *The Struggle for Greece, 1941–9* (1976), p. 205.
41. FO 371/67131/-, police mission report for May 1947, report by G. Dimoulas, 18 May 1947; Zapheiropoulos, *Antisymmoriakos,* I, pp. 201–2.
42. Nars, 868.00/11-3046, MacVeagh to Secretary of State; FO 371/101818/-, 'The work and achievements of the British Military Mission'.
43. Zapheiropoulos, *Antisymmoriakos,* I, pp. 185–6.
44. Nars, 868.00/11-3046, Athens Embassy to Secretary of State.
45. *USFR, 1945*, VIII, pp. 254; Alexander, *Prelude,* pp. 197, 225, 234, 243, 248.
46. Bruce R. Kuniholm, *The Origins of the Cold War in the Near East* (Princeton, 1980), p. 297; Terry H. Anderson, *The United States, Great Britain, and the Cold War* (Columbia, 1981), p. 112; *USFR, 1946*, VII, p. 235.

47. S. Xydis, *Greece and the Great Powers, 1944–7* (Salonika, 1963), pp. 185–9.
48. Thanasis D. Sfikas, *The British Labour Government and the Greek Civil War* (Keele, 1994), p. 102; Robert Frazier, *Anglo-American Relations with Greece* (New York, 1992), pp. 113–19; Lawrence S. Wittner, *American Intervention in Greece,1943–9* (New York, 1982), pp. 17–19, 22, 25, 37, 42; John O. Iatrides, 'Perceptions of Soviet involvement in the Greek civil war, 1945–9', in Lars Baerentzen, J.O. Iatrides and O.L. Smith, eds, *Studies in the History of the Greek Civil War, 1945–9* (Copenhagen, 1987), p. 232.
49. Wittner, *American Intervention*, pp. 65–80; Frazier, *Anglo-American Relations*, pp. 158–9; Jones, *New Kind of War*, pp. vii–x, 13–15; Yannis P. Roubatis, *Tangled Webs. The U.S. in Greece, 1947–67* (New York, 1987), pp. 32–3.

CHAPTER 8

The Civil War, 1947–50

THE DEMOCRATIC ARMY

By their muted response to Truman's speech, the Greek Communist leaders showed that they failed to appreciate its significance, and proceeded with their war against the government. They decided in February to give priority to the war effort, and then gave increasing support to Markos's attempts to build up the Democratic Army (DSE). By May 1947 it had become apparent, as Wickham the chief of the British police mission told the Greek Minister of Public Order, that 'the authority and security of the State is [*sic*] gravely menaced'.[1]

Despite what seem to have been quite heavy losses caused by enemy aircraft and artillery, by some desertions, and by shortage of facilities for its sick and wounded, the DSE managed to increase its numbers steadily until in the spring of 1948 it reached its peak of 26,000 in Greece, the great majority of them being effective combatants, supported with information and food by many thousands of civilian supporters who under pressure could join the guerrillas. Across the northern frontier were several thousand reservists and wounded. During 1948, the army's geographical reach reached its zenith. In the spring it was active all along the northern frontier and southward along the country's central mountain spine, as well as in the islands of Lesbos, Samos, Ikaria, and Crete, while in the Peloponnese its activities were still expanding. The forces on the mainland, including the Peloponnese, were linked by radio, and could to some extent coordinate their activities. The British police mission reported at this time that a third of rural police stations were abandoned by the government. According to a plausible American estimate, the guerrillas effectively controlled over a third of the rural population and a half of the surface area of the country. Their power in the Peloponnese was discovered the hard way by the BBC correspondent Kenneth Matthews, when he went to Mycenae in October for a weekend, only to be kidnapped and marched for scores of miles across rugged mountains to the Communists' regional HQ near Patras. Here he was surprised to find the hub of an efficient system of communications, supply, and civilian administration, supervising elected councils in more than 400 villages.[2]

While occasionally engaging enemy units of several hundred, the DSE devoted most of its efforts to small-scale, hit-and-run raids with the obvious aim of seizing food and recruits, undermining government authority, and compelling the government's forces to disperse in defence. By frequent attacks on gendarmerie outputs and militia units, the guerrillas intimidated them and captured weapons. There were also terroristic attacks on villages and towns, and a campaign of economic sabotage against targets such as electricity generators, bridges, and water supplies.[3]

Conscripts, who commonly came from villages inclined to sympathize with the revolt, were disciplined and incorporated into the army by typical Leninist methods. The party established an elaborate machinery of indoctrination and surveillance, of which fascinating records came to light in the Myrovleto archive (described above, p. 176). A political commissar was attached to every unit down to a group of about five soldiers, and ordered to organize 'democratic assemblies', which were discussions – daily if possible – of the day's activities, with participation by all members. Commissars at group level were expected to report fortnightly to the party's Military Security Service on their soldiers' morale and political loyalty. The Military Security Service also required all party members to submit autobiographical statements in which they had to confess to possibly incriminating facts such as bourgeois parentage or past breaches of discipline.

The Myrovleto archive depicts the difficulties of maintaining morale in conditions of extreme hardship. A commissar, for example, reported someone for remarking that if he had not been conscripted he might have been leading an easy life in America, instead of which he was starving in the DSE. Another commissar confessed that despite his attempts at 'political enlightenment' of his charges, 'they won't think of anything but food'. A common daily ration was 100 grams of bread – in today's terms about four slices from a machine-sliced loaf. Another reported that 'the problem which preoccupies the men today is that of shoes. They have no shoes and have difficulties during marches. Also they are very tired.' The soldiers had to travel constantly, with heavy loads, through rocky terrain where temperatures were near or below freezing for much of the winter.[4] Later in the war, when the soldiers' hardships and the odds against them increased, their obedience had increasingly to be secured by harsh discipline and the vigilance of commissars. One soldier overheard talking about desertion was tortured into naming accomplices before being executed. Methods like these restricted desertions to a dribble, which although continuous seems to have been largely confined to new recruits driven by hunger. Discipline and offensive spirit remained high, and, except perhaps after crushing defeats, there seem to have been no reports of large-scale collapse of morale, such as repeatedly occurred in the national army.[5]

The capacity of the DSE to sustain large-scale operations increased until shortly before its final defeat in 1949. A training school for officers had by that time turned out 3,460 graduates. The printing presses produced a government gazette, military orders, a daily newspaper, and a monthly military review. Depots of arms, food, and clothes, and hospitals, were established both in the mountain bases near the frontiers, and in Albania, Yugoslavia, and Bulgaria.[6]

There were two especially serious obstacles to the DSE's aims: one imposed by the national army, and one imposed by its foreign patrons. The former was the evacuation of the mountain villages which provided the DSE with food and recruits. By the end of 1947 probably about 300,000 people had been moved and dumped in miserable conditions in or around towns controlled by the government. By early 1949 the total was over 700,000 – a tenth of Greece's population, and probably the bulk of the inhabitants of the mountain ranges north of the Gulf of Corinth. Leading Communists later recorded that this process was the decisive limitation to the DSE's expansion.[7]

Given this difficulty, the Communists could not be selective or lenient in recruitment. According to American military sources, as early as September 1947, their soldiers were generally in poorer physical condition than those of the national army. Most were very young. A quarter of the total were women, only a few of whom rose even to the command of battalions, because of male discrimination. By 1949, it seems that over a third of the total were slavophones, and it was to appease them that Zachariades, in January 1949, adopted once more the pre-war position of support for Macedonian secessionism.[8]

The other limitation was the inability or unwillingness of Tito, Stalin, and other leaders of Communist states to provide more arms, for reasons suggested earlier. The Soviet satellites, under American pressure, declined even to recognize the provisional government established by the Greek Communists in December 1947. The DSE never acquired the tanks and aircraft which its leaders hoped for; and its artillery never amounted to more than about 60 field guns, mainly small, and its small anti-aircraft guns. Its supply of mortars and heavy machine-guns was always meagre: about two of each per battalion, to judge from the Myrovleto archives. With so few heavy weapons, the DSE found it difficult to attack, or defend, fixed positions, or engage large enemy forces.[9]

These weaknesses were shown during 1947 in the army's failure to take the towns of Metsovo in October and Konitsa in December. Metsovo commanded a vital pass over the Pindus range linking Thessaly to Epirus; and Konitsa near the Albanian border was needed as a capital for the projected provisional government. These failures revealed also a shortage of senior commanders, owing to the internment by the government of most of the former professional officers who had served in ELAS. The failure at Konitsa showed that the national army, because of its superiority in transport, could always count on reinforcements by road and air. The nearest approach to an attack on Salonika was a brief bombardment by the crew of one field gun in February 1948.

The DSE did however learn how to overrun, though not to hold, small or medium-sized towns (i.e. with a normal population of 5,000–20,000) that were not strongly defended. Among its most impressive feats were the temporary capture and plunder, in December 1948 to January 1949, of the towns of Karditsa in Thessaly, Karpenision in Sterea Ellada, and Naoussa in western Macedonia. Otherwise the nearest approach by the Communists to positional warfare was the defence of fortified mountains near the northern frontier against powerful attacks by enemy artillery and aircraft. The massif of Grammos on the Albanian frontier was defended in three successive summers in 1947–9, and in 1948 the defence lasted eight weeks. These departures from guerrilla tactics hastened the war's end, because they exposed the Communist forces to the enemy's immensely superior firepower and so resulted in heavy casualties. The new tactics were dictated by the leading party cadres appointed after 1947 by Zachariades to command the army in place of ELAS veterans like Markos Vapheiades. The new commanders had little experience of guerrilla warfare, but had their sights fixed on the goal of winning political power by capturing towns and territory. Like other orthodox Leninists, they assumed that correct political attitudes could overcome physical obstacles. On this assumption they drove their hungry, ragged, and weary troops to astonishing feats of endurance and frequently to sacrificial attacks. But the assumption had the ugly corollary that failure to achieve the impossible was due to political treachery. At least seven officers are known to have been executed, one or more of them after torture, as scapegoats for failures caused by unrealistic orders.[10]

Dependence on Tito would by itself have doomed the DSE, if it had not been already defeated for different reasons. Tito's rift with Stalin – which became public in June 1948 – provoked economic sanctions from the Soviet satellites in 1949, and so made it necessary for Tito to seek American economic aid. He could obtain this only by giving up his support for the Greek Communists, who stayed loyal to Stalin. After gradually reducing aid he closed the frontier with Greece in July 1949, so cutting off 4,000 Greek soldiers recovering from wounds in Yugoslavia.[11] This blow reduced still further the DSE's chances of continuing the conflict.

Stalin's attitude was more complex. In February 1948, while trying to deter the Yugoslav leaders from pursuing a policy which seemed likely to increase their influence, he revealed what was evidently his real view of the Greek Communists' prospects:

> No, they have no prospect of success at all. What do you think, that Great Britain and the United States – the United States, the most powerful state in the world – will permit you to break their line of communication in the Mediterranean Sea! Nonsense. And we have no navy. The uprising in Greece must be stopped as quickly as possible.[12]

Later in the year Stalin evidently saw it as expedient once more to keep the DSE going while detaching it from Tito, because he encouraged Zachariades, when the latter was in Moscow in September, to hope for imminent deliveries of tanks and heavy artillery. The Greek Communists remained pathetically optimistic that Stalin would support them. The last commander of the DSE, Giorgos Vontitsos-Gousias, admitted in his memoirs that it was only in April 1949 that he first doubted Stalin's fidelity, after Stalin had temporarily ordered the cessation of the DSE's activities, when they seemed likely to provoke an invasion of Albania by the national army.[13]

Zachariades's desire to imitate Stalin's style of leadership and ideology in all respects is illustrated by his abrupt announcement in January 1949, without prior consultation with his colleagues, that the Greek Communists' goal was 'proletarian socialist revolution'. Although Zachariades later stated that he had made this decision three years earlier, it was a fundamental departure from the official aims of the provisional government, which were those of EAM during and after the occupation: popular democracy.[14] Zachariades evidently considered it beyond dispute that his party should keep in step with those of the Soviet satellites in eastern Europe. There need be no doubt therefore what was in store for Greece in the event of a Communist victory: a dictatorship on the Stalinist model, with a police terror imposed on the population, and periodic purges of dissidents within the party. It was a prospect of which many among the Communists' own followers were becoming painfully conscious. Several for example of the veterans who contributed to the protracted discussions and reminiscences in the newspaper *Elevtherotypia*, when it published the Myrovleto documents in 1978 and 1986, described the atmosphere of malevolent paranoia and mutual distrust which pervaded the DSE after the party leaders imposed strict party discipline on it from September 1947 onwards. This change cannot be attributed solely to Zachariades, because those responsible for running the Military Security Service – Ioannides, Rousos, and later Vlantas – had been prominent in the wartime resistance.

RIGHT-WING VICTORY

As American money and provisions arrived, they gave increasing heart to government supporters. By the end of 1949, military aid alone amounted to $353.6 million, and included 159,922 small arms weapons and 4,130 mortar and artillery pieces. In the twenty years from 1947, economic and military aid totalled $3,749 million. Even the participants in the DSE, insulated as they were from the outside world, saw that for every mule load of foreign aid reaching themselves, a ship load reached their opponents. At least one soldier was executed for remarking on this contrast. In later years, Vlantas admitted that, largely on account of the contrast, his party in its propaganda failed ever to persuade its opponents that it had a chance of winning, by defeating the national army or capturing cities. The best it could realistically expect was a military stalemate.[15] In time, civilian aid strengthened the government's authority by enabling it to pay its employees, give welfare benefits, and invest in economic recovery. If one counts the burgeoning numbers of government appointees and all those receiving or hoping for agricultural credits, welfare benefits, contracts, and police licences, it is probable that the government influenced the livelihood of most people outside the territories controlled by the DSE. According to an estimate quoted by the American ambassador in October 1948, over 30 per cent of the total population depended on government welfare. With American assistance, Gross National Product returned to the pre-war level in about 1950, although the benefits of recovery were very unequally distributed among the population.[16]

The Americans' style of interventionism contrasted with that of the British in more respects than the financial. They approached their task with crusading zeal and buoyant optimism quite different from the British scepticism and despondency. Their belief in their ideological war against totalitarian Communism harmonized with the security legislation which Greek governments introduced or reintroduced in 1947–8: the new formulation for example of the Idionym Law; the reintroduction of the certificates of sound social opinions; and the introduction for the first time of a loyalty oath for public officials which was modelled on a recent American law. American officials participated in suppressing what remained of left-wing power in the trade union movement. In general, though, they allowed the police and army to continue their campaign against Communism by their accustomed methods. Meanwhile, at the Americans' request, the British maintained their military and police missions, as well as a garrison of 5,000 troops.[17]

While determined to ensure that the Greeks won the war, the US representatives strove to economize on their own citizens' lives and money. The American administration debated whether to commit its own troops to combat and decided against doing so, thus provoking widespread resentment among Greeks that they were being used as cannon fodder. The American representatives also imposed whatever controls were necessary on the Greek administration and army to ensure that US taxpayers got value for money. Thus American officials vetted in detail the decisions of key departments of the Greek government and over several years repeatedly influenced the composition of Greek governments. In September 1947 a senior State Department official, Loy Henderson, remedied a vital weakness, the narrow factionalism of Greek governments since the general election of March 1946, by ordering Tsaldares – who had just become prime minister again as a result of a demand to the king by the chief of general staff Venteres – to resign, and accept office under Sophoules in a coalition of the Populist and Liberal parties. The Americans then used periodic threats to hold this shotgun marriage together, in the face of opposition by right-wingers in parliament. High-handed as it was, this course did something to secure wider public support for the government.[18]

In June 1947 American and British representatives began to take the war out of the inept hands of the politicians, who till then had been trying to run much of it through what amounted to private armies. One result of this policy had been the reorganization of much of the gendarmerie into military battalions by Zervas as minister from January to August. Zervas personally deployed the battalions in the Peloponnese, with the net result that he intensified the white terror and increased the numbers of left-wing guerrillas. Meanwhile other veterans of guerrilla warfare against ELAS during the occupation, Anton Tsaous and Michal Agas, were equipped by the army to reassemble their bands, in a despairing attempt to fight fire with fire. The best that such chieftains could accomplish was to force the left-wing guerrillas to transfer their activities temporarily to other localities. Many other lesser-known veterans of wartime struggles against EAM were organized under army supervision in village militias. Without adequate leadership or discipline, these irregular units appeared to many civilians as a scourge no better than the left-wing guerrillas. By mid-1947 it was apparent to Anglo-American advisers that the Communist revolt could be overcome only if the campaign against it was coordinated on a nation-wide

scale by the regular army, undertaking determined and large-scale offensives.[19]

Thenceforth army commanders assumed increasing authority over the
police and the territorial militias. The police were confined gradually to the
role of destroying what was left of the Communist organization in the large
towns, and collecting information about the DSE's civilian network of
intelligence and supply in the countryside, while helping the military
authorities to comb out Communists among army recruits. The militia
were given the task of watching over suspect civilians and guarding villages
behind the army's lines. Eventually, from the end of 1948, the whole of
the mainland was placed under martial law, which gave the army power to
censor information, control civilian movements, order local authorities to
provide for its needs, and make mass arrests.

In time the Americans also supplied the money needed to increase the
size of the national army to nearly 150,000 (over half as large again as at the
start of 1947), backed by militias totalling about 100,000, besides a navy of
14,300 and an air force of 7,500. By the end of 1948 American representatives finally realized that the older classes of conscripts were so demoralized
that they had 'simply quit' and had to be replaced.[20] They also supplied the
army with the weapons and equipment which it needed for mountain warfare, especially pack animals, mountain artillery, mine detectors, and radios.
After the arrival of an American military mission under General James Van
Fleet, American and British officers for a time accompanied Greek commanders in the field, to instil into them the necessary offensive spirit.
Perhaps the chief value of these advisers was that they protected Greek
officers against the demands by politicians for guards to protect their voters.

The Americans had no inkling in March 1947 of the size of their military task; nor yet did the Greek national army. In April–October, this army
conducted for the first time a coordinated series of operations, after staff
planning to which British officers contributed. The original strategy was to
clear the DSE firstly from northern Thessaly and then from the massifs
along the frontier with Albania and Yugoslavia. The national army managed in the end to kill, wound, or capture several thousand of the DSE,
mainly by achieving surprise in the initial attacks. It also arrested some
thousands of civilian sympathizers, quite apart from its mass evacuation of
mountain villagers (a process which the British and Americans evidently
preferred not to notice). But overall the campaign was a dismal failure.
Most officers still showed little skill in the techniques of catching guerrilla
forces, and the mass of the rank-and-file showed little inclination to learn.
Only a month after the campaign started, the DSE threw the national army
off balance by sending large forces southward to the mountainous regions
of Sterea Ellada. Then in July the DSE thwarted an offensive against the

Grammos massif on the Albanian frontier by filtering a force through the national army's lines and attacking towns far south of them: Ioannina on one side of the Pindus range and Grevena on the other. From October 1947 to March 1948, the majority of the national army was pinned down in defensive duties. The DSE again held the initiative in most regions, and managed in time to send guerrillas back into all of the areas which its opponents had laboriously cleared.[21]

The next series of coordinated operations by the national army began in April 1948, in greater strength than before. This was designed to clear guerrilla forces in successive stages from Sterea Ellada to the frontier region. It culminated in an offensive from June to August by a force of 50,000 against fortifications on Grammos that were defended by 15,000 troops. This was the fiercest battle of the war, costing the national army 6,740 in killed, wounded, or missing, and costing its opponents 4,500 in killed, wounded, and captured. This time the national army captured Grammos, only to be out-manoeuvred once more, as its opponents escaped south-eastwards, using both sides of the Albanian frontier, to the heights of Vitsi, whence in September they launched a surprise offensive which inflicted a humiliating reverse on the national army, and failed only because of the usual shortage of reserves to open a disastrous breach in its lines.[22]

Most of the national army again reverted to the defensive, while the DSE took the initiative in widely separated regions. The capture of Karditsa, Naoussa, and Karpenision in December 1948 to January 1949 was followed in February by an unsuccessful attack on the strategic target of Florina near the Albanian border, and late in March by an approach to Arta in southern Epirus, far from the DSE's usual areas of operation. Early in April Grammos was reoccupied.[23] Meanwhile, during 1948, about 3,500 guerrillas in the Peloponnese, who were virtually cut off from their comrades by the Gulf of Corinth, had opened a new front in the war by extending their activities to many parts of this province.

It was understandable then that Greek, British, and American observers at the end of 1948 should conclude that the military situation on the national side was worse than ever. The DSE was showing a new capacity for large-scale and long-distance operations. The morale of most of the rank-and-file in the national army remained dismally low. There were cases near Vitsi in September–October of battalions which collapsed when attacked or refused to conduct offensives. The view of most Greek officers was that all their efforts hitherto had been for nought and there could be no end to a war of this kind.[24] The nature of the guerrilla activity over much of the country during the previous two years is reflected in the report by the British police mission on the national situation in September 1948:

Meanwhile rebel attacks on communications continue without pause. The mining of roads and railways, attacks on trains and the destruction of telegraphic installations are frequent occurrences, while reservoirs and electric power stations in Western and Central Macedonia have suffered considerable damage. Raids on small towns and villages have been wide-spread [*sic*] and, with the exception of the capital and its environs, no part of the mainland can be said to be completely free of bandits.[25]

In fact the tide of war was quietly turning. The DSE's attacks on towns in the winter of 1948–9 were largely propaganda coups, which had little strategic value and cost it dearly in the lives of experienced soldiers. The army's size was gradually diminishing, because its losses were getting heavier while its rate of recruitment was declining. Meanwhile the national army, without yet having mobilized its full potential, enjoyed a superiority of something like ten to one in combat troops, not counting those engaged in administration and support services. Moreover its leadership was improving as its officers gained experience, and as capable men assumed important posts and incapable ones were replaced. As its power over civilians increased, so did its military intelligence, and hence its ability to achieve surprise. Officers learnt appropriate tactics, especially those of continuous pursuit by forces echeloned in depth to ensure that none of the quarry escaped by going to ground or doubling back.[26]

The decisive steps were taken by several Greek generals, imbued both with high professional ideals and a sense of anti-Communist mission. Some of them we have encountered in the struggles against EAM during the occupation. From December 1948 onwards, they began a series of offensives which galvanized their troops and within only nine months threw the DSE out of Greece for the last time. This revival of the army was not expected by Anglo-American officers, showing how far the war was controlled by their Greek partners. One of the generals was Thrasyvoulos Tsakalotos, the former commander of the Mountain Brigade in Egypt, Italy, and Athens in 1944, who in his eccentricity and aggressiveness proved himself the George Patton of the Greek army. He began a whirlwind offensive in the Peloponnese in December with forces of 40,000. Starting by cutting the telephone lines to Athens and arresting several thousand civilians accused of supplying information and provisions to the guerrillas, Tsakalotos then took advantage of the exceptionally bitter winter which forced guerrilla fighters to seek food and shelter and deprived them of much of their tree cover. By 23 February, out of 3,500 guerrillas in the Peloponnese, over 1,029 had been killed, 1,015 captured and 748 had surrendered, while the rest were wretched fugitives.[27]

In January the post of commander-in-chief was created with quasi-dictatorial powers, and filled by Alexandros Papagos, who had held this position in the Albanian war of 1940–1. Unlike the supreme officers before him, Papagos had the authority to ensure that campaign objectives were fulfilled and politicians were excluded from significant influence. He could also ensure that posts were filled on merit, and among his appointees was Venteres, who had been ousted from the post of chief of general staff by Sophoules, and played a role in the final offensives.

It was now the turn of the national forces north of the Gulf of Corinth to show the new spirit. In February, after handing over responsibility in the Peloponnese to the capable and energetic Thomas Penzopoulos, Tsakalotos pursued the enemy detachments which had occupied Karpenision and penetrated southern Epirus.[28] From March onwards the corps responsible for north-eastern Greece, under Theodoros Gregoropoulos, who had led the Military Hierarchy during the occupation, began a series of decisive offensives which cleared large guerrilla forces from eastern Macedonia and Evros, and threw them on the defensive in western Macedonia. In May and June national forces of 70,000 finally cleared the mountains of Sterea Ellada, immediately north of the Gulf of Corinth, defeating a brilliant, sacrificial campaign by one of the most skilled of the guerrilla leaders, Diamantes, who was killed, his corpse being shown in the national press.[29] By 1 August, nearly all of the 17,000-strong forces of the DSE were arrayed along the northern frontiers, most of them on the heights of Vitsi and Grammos, which were fortified and defended with 54 field guns. These heights were attacked and taken by over 100,000 national forces, with intense bombardment by artillery and aircraft using rockets and napalm. Of the defenders, 2,200 were killed; and after losing Vitsi and being out-flanked on Grammos, the rest, led by Zachariades and his colleagues, retreated in good order to Albanian soil during the night of 29–30 August.[30] This soon turned out to have been a decisive defeat. In September the last large formations of the DSE left eastern Macedonia for Bulgaria, so that there remained no units of more than about 200 in Greece. In October, after finding the Soviet, Albanian, and Bulgarian governments unwilling to support his army any longer, Zachariades announced that large-scale military operations had ended, while small guerrilla raids would continue. While keeping the national army and gendarmerie mobilized in northern regions, these raids could no longer do any damage, because the grip of the national forces over the population was too tight. During the rest of 1949 and 1950 the scale of guerrilla activity steadily declined.[31]

During the final stages of the war probably over 140,000 people fled into exile, the majority of them never to return. The scale of exile was especially large among the slavophones and Koutsovlachs. Those killed on the leftist side during the fighting of 1946–50 seem to have numbered close to

20,000. At the end of 1949 the government admitted that 50,000 people were imprisoned in camps and gaols, although there may have been still more who were not recorded. The casualty list on the government side during the fighting of 1946–50 consisted of 10,600 soldiers and gendarmes killed, 31,500 wounded, 5,400 missing, and 3,500 civilians murdered.

But by comparison with other major civil wars of the early twentieth century – for example the Russian and Spanish – the aftermath of this one was mild. Executions ordered by courts martial ceased temporarily in October 1949, so as not to provoke condemnation by a current session of the United Nations General Assembly. When executions started again in 1951, they provoked much public attention and were very few. The number of political prisoners declined steadily, reaching an official figure of 5,400 by the end of 1955 and almost none just before the military dictatorship of 1967. A general election in which opponents of the right could campaign with considerable freedom, and even socialists could participate to some extent, occurred immediately after the end of hostilities and the lifting of martial law, in March 1950. This time the thugs of the shadow state were kept under control by the police and the army. The degree of electoral freedom was proved by the outcome of the election: a victory for centrist or Liberal politicians, many of whom were distrusted by the army and police for being soft on Communism.

The relative mildness of the war's aftermath was due mainly to the Americans' desire to convince their own people and other countries that they were supporting freedom against totalitarianism. Unlike the Soviet Union they could not veil their clients' repression by censoring information, and in any case wielded such great economic power that they had less need to resort to repression. But their attempt to restore parliamentary life received strong support within Greece because parliamentary politics had a long and widely respected tradition, while dictatorship did not. The holding of relatively free elections led to defeat for right-wing politicians, who evidently provoked widespread revulsion by their patronage of the white terror followed by their inept conduct of the war, during which most of them seem to have sheltered in the cities.

AFTERMATH

Greece emerged from the civil war as an embattled outpost of the American sphere, facing what seemed to be possible invasion from Bulgaria, a satellite with especially close links to the Soviet Union. The outbreak of the Korean War in 1950 intensified Cold War tensions and so prevented much reduction of the Greek armed forces; consequently defence expenditure remained extraordinarily high by western European standards. In the event, though, the Cold War maintained stability in the Balkans, so that Greece's northern frontiers remained undisturbed for over 40 years.

As a result of the civil war, Greece diverged still further than before from the rest of the Balkans. Until the general collapse of Communism in the Soviet sphere in 1989–91, the other four Balkan states remained Communist dictatorships, justifying themselves by Marxist–Leninist ideology and maintaining themselves by arbitrary police repression. Not even the Yugoslav system, which was relatively open and decentralized, allowed any questioning of the Communist Party's monopoly of power. The political and economic systems of all four states, from 1948 or earlier, were modelled on those of the Soviet Union, to whose military command their armies (except that of Yugoslavia) were subordinated. For long periods until the 1980s, Yugoslavia, Albania, and Bulgaria were led by figures who had been prominent in the wartime resistance.

The Greek regime was based on systematic denial of Communism, being characterized by among other things a strong monarchy, a respected national church, and an archaic educational system. Another legacy of the civil war was an ardently anti-Communist army that remained insulated by American intervention from politicians' influence, and enjoyed a close relationship with its American patrons. Former participation in EAM was treated by the police as grounds for suspicion or worse. The Communist Party remained illegal and without a significant organization. However the existence in Greece of a restricted parliamentary system allowed the Greek Communist Party in exile to guide the activities of a revived EAM, the United Democratic Left (EDA), which under police harassment participated in parliamentary elections from 1951 onwards and secured the election of some deputies. After George Papandreou as prime minister and then leader of the opposition, in 1964–7, challenged the privileges of the monarchy and army, a clique of colonels, with American tolerance, established a dictatorship which lasted from 1967 to 1974. The colonels themselves were imbued with the mentality of the civil war, and established a regime similar in ideology to the Metaxas dictatorship. After this dictatorship collapsed in 1974, Greek citizens at last acquired liberties comparable to those of the parliamentary democracies of northern Europe. The fall of the dictatorship also reduced America's already waning influence, and brought Greece closer to the European Economic Community, of which she became a full member in 1981.

Economically the other four Balkan states pursued a socialist course from the late 1940s. Their governments acquired ownership of all the means of production and planned their economies in detail, giving priority to heavy industry. Yugoslavia alone gave up the attempt to collectivize agriculture or guarantee full employment. Like Bulgaria and Romania, however, she tried eventually to provide a comprehensive and free welfare system. The Greek economy, on the other hand, remained based overwhelmingly on free enterprise and retained several of its traditional characteristics. The majority of the population continued to be employed in small farms or businesses, while a few businessmen with powerful connections enjoyed great privileges. Heavy industry was neglected by investors and the state. During the 1950s and 1960s, taxation continued to be grossly inequitable, wages low, and the welfare system meagre.

When combined, however, with a stable currency and generous facilities for foreign investors, such a system allowed for remarkably rapid and sustained economic growth. In the long run, this process improved enormously the living standards of the population, and reduced drastically the rural population, especially that of the mountain villages which had supported guerrilla warfare in the 1940s. After 1974 this prosperity, combined with increased freedom, made possible the introduction of the basic elements of a welfare state.

Today, then, Greek society is closer to the democracies of northern Europe, in habits of consumption and political values, than are other Balkan societies. In consequence, the conditions which made possible the civil conflicts of the 1940s have become a distant memory. But the issues at stake in the conflicts were so profound, and the events so dramatic, that they continue to arouse lively public interest.

NOTES

1. Nars, 868.00/5-1947.
2. Kenneth Matthews, *Memories of a Mountain War* (1972), p. 247.
3. *Foreign Relations of the United States* (henceforth *USFR*), *1948*, IV, pp. 198–9; Demetrios Vlantas, *Emphylios Polemos, 1945–9* (1981), ch. 21, p. 299.
4. *Elevtherotypia*, 25 Jan. 1986, p. 16; 19 Jan. 1986, p. 12; 20 Mar. 1986, p. 19.
5. *Elevtherotypia*, 2 May 1986, p. 17; P. Gregoriades, *Istoria tou Emphyliou Polemou. To Devtero Antartiko* (n.d.), IV, p. 1162.
6. V. Bartziotas, *Demokratikos Stratos* 12 (Dec. 1948), p. 501.
7. KKE, *Episema Keimena* (1987), VI, pp. 329–30; Demetrios Vlantas, *Emphylios Polemos*, ch. 10, p. 187.
8. *Elevtherotypia*, 22 Jan. 1986, p. 13; Vasiles Bartziotas, *O Agonas tou Demokratikou Stratou Elladas* (1981), pp. 77, 82; D.H. Close and T. Veremis, 'The military struggle, 1945–9' in D.H. Close, ed., *The Greek Civil War. Studies of Polarization* (1993), p. 120; Evangelos Kofos, 'The impact of the

Macedonian question on the Greek civil war', unpublished paper delivered at Vilvorde conference, Copenhagen, 3–5 June 1987; Vlantas, *Emphylios Polemos*, ch. 21, p. 297.

9. Close and Veremis in Close, ed., *The Greek Civil War*, p. 102.
10. C. Konstantaras, *Agones kai Diogmoi* (1964), p. 169; *Elevtherotypia*, 12 Jan. 1979, p. 7; 22 May 1986, p. 14; Gregoriades, *Antartiko*, III, p. 927.
11. N. Pappas, 'The Soviet–Yugoslav conflict and the Greek civil war', in W.S. Vucinich, *At the Brink of War and Peace: the Tito–Stalin Split in a Historic Perspective* (New York, 1982), pp. 223–36.
12. Milovan Djilas, *Conversations with Stalin* (Harmondsworth, 1962), pp. 181–2.
13. Giorgos Vontitsos-Gousias, *Oi Aities gia tes Ettes* (1979), I, pp. 440, 507–9, 515–16, 547.
14. Vasiles Bartziotas, *Exenta Chronia Kommounistes* (1986), p. 301.
15. Nars, 868.00/8-1547, R.A. Gibson to Secretary of State; Lawrence S. Wittner, *American Intervention in Greece, 1943–9* (New York, 1982), p. 253; Vlantas, *Emphylios Polemos*, ch. 21, p. 297.
16. *USFR, 1948*, IV, pp. 169, 189; Kostas Vergopoulos, 'The emergence of the new bourgeoisie, 1944–52', in J.O. Iatrides, ed., *Greece in the 1940s. A Nation of Crisis* (1981), p. 311.
17. Nikos Alivizatos, 'The "emergency regime" and civil liberties, 1946–9', in J.O. Iatrides, ed., *Greece in the 1940s*, p. 226; J.O. Iatrides, 'Britain, the United States, and Greece, 1945–9', in Close, ed., *The Greek Civil War*, p. 204.
18. J.O. Iatrides, 'Greece in the Cold War and beyond', *Journal of Hellenic Diaspora* 19, 2 (1993), pp. 19–20; Nars, RG 84, US Embassy Confidential File, 1948, Athens Embassy to Sec. of State, 10 Feb. 1948; Wittner, *American Intervention*, pp. 111–15.
19. D.H. Close, 'The reconstruction of a right-wing state', in Close, ed., *The Greek Civil War*, pp. 173–4.
20. Nars, RG 319, military attaché, 15 Oct. 1948.
21. D. Zapheiropoulos, *O Antisymmoriakos Agon, 1945–9* 2 vols (1956), I, pp. 220, 261; *USFR, 1947*, V, p. 383; Nars, RG 319, military attaché's report, 31 May 1947; PRO, FO 371/ 67104/-, R 11915.
22. Zapheiropoulos, *Antisymmoriakos*, II, pp. 340–1, 414, 522.
23. Gregoriades, *Antartiko*, IV, p. 1278; Vontitsos-Gousias, *Aities*, I, p. 500.
24. Nars, RG 319, P & O 091, Greece TS, Van Fleet, 12 Feb. 1949; Zapheiropoulos, *Antisymmoriakos*, pp. 452–3, 460; FO 371/78393/-, R 713; FO 371/72328/-, R 13961, R 14278; *USFR, 1948*, IV, p. 153.
25. PRO, FO, 371/72317/-; *USFR, 1949*, VI, pp. 242–3.
26. Zapheiropoulos, *Antisymmoriakos*, p. 522.
27. FO 371/78358/-, R 3906.
28. FO 371/78357/-, R 2293; 371/78385/-, R 3086.
29. Gregoriades, *Antartiko*, IV, p. 1290; Theodoros Gregoropoulos, *Apo ten Koryphe tou Lophou* (1966), pp. 410–11.
30. FO 371/78389/-, R 8770, monthly intelligence review, 1 Sept. 1949.
31. Nars, 868.00/10-749.

Bibliography

PRIMARY SOURCES

Published Material

Apostolos Daskalakes, *Istoria tes Ellenikes Chorophylakes* 2 vols (1973). This contains important documentary material on the history of the gendarmerie, and some also on its enemy the Communist Party.

John O. Iatrides, ed., *Ambassador MacVeagh Reports. Greece, 1933–46* (Princeton, 1980)

KKE (Kommounistiko Komma tes Elladas), *Episema Keimena*, vols 4–6 for 1934–49 (1981–7).

KKE, *Deka Chronia Agones, 1935–45* (1977)

Kentrike Epitrope tou KKE, *Keimena tes Ethnikes Antistases* 2 vols (1981)

Ioannes Metaxas, *To Prosopiko tou Emerologio* 8 vols (1951–64). The volumes used, D 1 and 2 for 1933–41, are edited by P. Vranas.

Giannes Papathanasiou, *Gia ton Elleniko Vorra. Makedonia 1941–4. To Anekdoto Emerologio tou Gianne Papathanasiou*, ed. by Parmenionos I. Papathanasiou, 2 vols (1988)

United States Department of State, *Foreign Relations of the United States* (referred to as *USFR*). Annual volumes for 1945–8, Washington, D.C., 1968–76.

Unpublished Material

United States National Archives, Washington D.C. (referred to as Nars). US Department of State Decimal File, RG (Record Group) 59, 868.00 series (1936–48).Athens Embassy papers, RG 84

Department of the Army: RG 319, Army papers; RG 226, Office of Strategic Services papers, which include a copy of the Pericles Report (by Costas G. Couvaras) held in the office of the Department of the Army in the National Archives.

British Public Record Office, Kew, London Foreign Office General Correspondence, 1931–47 (FO 371); Athens Embassy papers, 1945–6 (FO 286)

Benaki Museum, Athens Peltekis Archive, relating to the Special Operations Executive

General State Archives, Athens   Metaxas Papers

Newspapers   *Avge* (Dawn), Athens daily. The issues of 2 Dec. 1979 to 23 Jan. 1980 contain reports and letters by Communist leaders in 1946–7.

Elevtherotypia (Free Press), Athens daily. This contains a series entitled 'Emphylios Polemos', annotated by George Mavros, of documents on the Democratic Army discovered in 1978 at Myrovleto. Their publication elicited many letters from Civil War veterans. All this is to be found in the issues from 11 December 1978 to 13 January 1979, and from 20 January 1986 to some time in August 1986.

Kathemerine (meaning 'daily'), Athens

Elevtheron Vema ('free podium'), daily, Athens

Rizospastes ('the radical'), the Communist Party daily, Athens

Vema (weekly successor to *Elevtheron Vema*), Athens

SECONDARY SOURCES

The works which I found useful for this book include the following. This selection is biased towards English-language works, and omits many of the Greek-language works referred to in the text.

General Works

On the regional background there is Barbara Jelavich, *A History of the Balkans. The Twentieth Century*, 2nd of 2 vols (Cambridge, 1983), and L.P. Morris, *Eastern Europe since 1945* (1984).

General histories of modern Greece include: Richard Clogg, *A Concise History of Modern Greece* (Cambridge, 1992), richly illustrated and with useful tables; John Campbell and Philip Sherrard, *Modern Greece* (1968), which is especially informative on the Metaxas dictatorship. The implications of dependency are discussed, with much useful information about Greek society, by Nikos P. Mouzelis in *Modern Greece. Facets of Underdevelopment* (1978), and *Politics in the Semi-Periphery. Early Parliamentarism and Late Industrialisation in the Balkans and Latin America* (London, 1986).

On the economy there are A.F. Freris, *The Greek Economy in the Twentieth Century* (1986), and Bickham Sweet-Escott, *Greece: a Political and Economic Survey, 1939–53* (1954).

Another essential aspect of Greek history is covered by Theodore A. Couloumbis, John A. Petropoulos, and Harry J. Psomiades, in *Foreign Interference in Greek Politics. An Historical Perspective* (New York, 1976); and Theodore A. Couloumbis and John O. Iatrides, eds, *Greek-American Relations. A Critical Review* (New York, 1980).

On constitutional development, a basic work is Nikos Alivizatos, *Les Institutions Politiques de la Grèce à travers les Crises, 1922–74* (Paris, 1979). A useful discussion is found in Adamantia Pollis, 'The state, the law, and human rights in modern Greece', *Human Rights Quarterly* 9 (1987), pp. 587–614.

On political life, Keith Legg, *Politics in Modern Greece* (Stanford, 1969), is especially useful. There is also an essay by Constantine Tsoucalas, '"Enlightened" concepts in the "dark": power and freedom, politics and society', *Journal of Modern Greek Studies* 9, 1 (May 1991), pp. 1–22. On parliamentary elections there is Elias Nikolakopoulos, *Kommata kai Voulevtikes Ekloges sten Ellada* (1985). On the measures taken to suppress Communism, there is Rousos Koundouros, *E Asphaleia tou Kathestotos* (1978), derived from an English-language M. Phil. dissertation of 1974, Brunel University.

On modern society, see Michael Attalides and Nikos Mouzelis, 'Greece', in Margaret S. Archer and Salvador Giner, eds, *Contemporary Europe. Class, Status, and Power* (1971).

On trade unionism and early socialism, there is Christos Jecchinis, *Trade Unionism in Greece. A Study of Political Paternalism* (Chicago, 1967).

On the Communist Party of Greece (KKE) from 1918 to the 1960s, see D. George Kousoulas, *Revolution and Defeat. The Story of the Greek Communist Party* (Oxford, 1965) – an anti-Communist polemic, but with much information, especially about the persecution of the party. A concise insider's view is Antonio Solaro, *Istoria tou Kommounistikou Kommatos tes Elladas* (1975), first published in Italian in 1973. R.V. Burks wrote valuable analyses: see his 'Statistical profile of the Greek Communist', *Journal of Modern History* 27, 2 (June, 1955), pp. 153–8, and *The Dynamics of Communism in Eastern Europe* (Princeton, 1961).

The Inter-War Period, 1922–40

Of fundamental importance is George T. Mavrogordatos, *Stillborn Republic. Social Coalitions and Party Strategies in Greece, 1922–36* (Berkeley, 1983). Also important on the period 1910–36 are George T. Mavrogordatos and Christos Hadziiossif, eds, *Venizelismos kai Astikos Eksyngchronismos*

(Herakleion, 1988), and Mark Mazower, *Greece and the Inter-War Economic Crisis* (Oxford, 1991).

The history of the Communist Party is set in political and social context by Angelos Elefantes, in *E Epangelia tes Adynates Epanastases. KKE kai Astismos ston Mesopolemo* (1976). A view of the party from below in 1935–6 is Bert Birtles, *Exiles in the Aegean. A Narrative of Greek Politics and Travel* (1938).

Two aspects of the inter-war period are examined in D. Pentzopoulos, *The Balkan Exchange of Minorities and its Impact upon Greece* (Paris, 1962), and (on the army in politics, 1915–35, derived from an Oxford D. Phil. dissertation) Thanos Veremis, *Oi Epemvaseis tou Stratou sten Ellenike Politike* (1983).

On the anti-Venizelist accession to power, and the Metaxas dictatorship in particular, there are: Thanos Veremis and Robin Higham, eds, *Aspects of Greece. The Metaxas Dictatorship 1936–40* (Athens 1993); Hagen Fleischer and Nikos Svoronos, *Praktika tou Diethnous Istorikou Synedriou. E Ellada, 1936–44* (1989); D.H. Close, 'Conservatism, authoritarianism, and fascism in Greece, 1915–45', in Martin Blinkhorn, ed., *Fascists and Conservatives. The Radical Right and the Establishment* (1990); D.H. Close, *The Metaxas Dictatorship. An International Perspective* (Centre of Contemporary Greek Studies, King's College, London, 1990, Occasional Paper no. 3).

One aspect of foreign policy is covered by John S. Koliopoulos, *Greece and the British Connection, 1935–41* (Oxford, 1977). For the Albanian war see Robin Higham, *Diary of a Disaster. British Aid to Greece, 1940–1* (Lexington, 1986), and Mario Cervi, *The Hollow Legions: Mussolini's Blunder in Greece, 1940–1* (1972).

The 1940s

Essays on many aspects of this period are found in John O. Iatrides, ed., *Greece in the 1940s. A Nation in Crisis* (Hanover and London, 1981). More specifically focused is David H. Close, ed., *The Greek Civil War, 1943–50. Studies of Polarization* (London, 1993). John O. Iatrides, ed., *Greece in the 1940s. A Bibliographic Companion* (Hanover and London, 1981), contains a section by Hagen Fleischer, 'Greece in the 1940s. A Bibliographical Survey', and one by Steven Bowman, 'Jews in Wartime Greece: a Select Annotated Bibliography'. This was reprinted in translated and expanded form in Greek as C. Flaiser and S. Booyman, *E Ellada ste Dekaetia 1940–1950. Ena Ethnos se Krise* (1984).

The Axis occupation, 1941–4

Important studies are contained in H. Fleischer and N. Svoronos, eds, *Praktika tou Diethnous Istorikou Synedriou, E Ellada, 1936–44* (1989). A basic work is John L. Hondros, *Occupation and Resistance. The Greek Agony, 1941–4* (New York, 1983), drawing on German and British archives. Important information on the politics of the years 1941–3 is also contained in Hagen Fleischer, *Stemma kai Svastika. E Ellada tes Katoches kai tes Antistases* (1988); this is the version for Greek readers of the earlier part of the same author's *Im Kreuzschatten der Mächte. Griechenland, 1941–4* 2 vols (Frankfurt, 1986). There is also much new material in André Gerolymatos, *Guerrilla Warfare and Espionage in Greece, 1940–4* (New York, 1992), and in Giorgios Margarites, *Apo ten Etta sten Exegerse* (1993), a study of life in the first year of the occupation.

Complementing all these works, and re-creating vividly the feel of life in the occupation, is Mark Mazower, *Inside Hitler's Greece. The Experience of Occupation, 1941–4* (1993).

The history of the Communist Party in the 1940s is studied by Matthias Esche, *Die Kommunistiche Partei Griechenlands, 1941–9* (München and Wien, 1982); John C. Loulis, *The Greek Communist Party, 1940–4* (1982); and Christophe Chiclet, *Les Communistes Grecs dans la Guerre. Histoire du Parti Communiste de Grèce, 1941–9* (Paris, 1987). The work by Haris Vlavianos, *Greece, 1941–9. From Occupation to Resistance to Civil War. The Strategy of the Greek Communist Party* (1992) is valuable for party strategy in 1945–7. An indispensable source on the party in the 1940s – even though it had little contact with the Soviet Union – is Peter J. Stavrakis, *Moscow and Greek Communism, 1944–9* (Ithaca, 1989). There is also Evangelos Kofos, *Nationalism and Communism in Macedonia* (Salonika, 1964).

On the system of government established by EAM there is Leften S. Stavrianos, 'The Greek National Liberation Front (EAM): a study in resistance organization and administration,' *Journal of Modern History* 24, 1 (March, 1952), pp. 42–55; Vasiles Bouras, *E Politike Epitrope Ethnikes Apelevtheroseos* (1983); and Chrestos Tyrovouzes, *Autodioikese kai 'Laike' Dikaiosyne, 1942–5* (1991).

British relations with Greek political groups are studied in depth by Procopis Papastratis, *British Policy towards Greece during the Second World War, 1941–4* (Cambridge, 1984); and George M. Alexander, *The Prelude to the Truman Doctrine. British Policy towards Greece, 1944–7* (Oxford, 1982). There is also Elisabeth Barker, *British Policy in South-Eastern Europe during the Second World War* (1976).

The memoirs of British liaison officers with the resistance are an important

source on British policy and on conditions in Greece. They include
E.C.W. Myers, *Greek Entanglement* (1955); John Mulgan, *Report on
Experience* (1947); Nicholas G.L. Hammond, *Venture into Greece. With
the Guerrillas, 1943–4* (1983); Nigel Clive, *A Greek Experience, 1943–8*
(Salisbury, 1985). C.M. Woodhouse built a fine work of contemporary
history on his experiences: *Apple of Discord. A Survey of Recent Greek
Politics in their International Setting* (London, 1948).

Costas G. Couvaras, *OSS with the Central Committee of EAM* (San
Francisco, 1982), is the journal of an American liaison officer who,
unlike his British counterparts, was on friendly terms with the
Communists.

Greek memoirs of special value for the civil war include, on the anti-
Communist side: Pavlos G. Delaportas, *To Semeiomatario enos Pilatou*
(1977); Theodoros Gregoropoulos, *Apo ten Koryphe tou Lophou* (1966);
Panagiotes Kanellopoulos, *Emerologio. 31 Martiou 1942 – 4 Ianouariou
1945* (1977); Anastasios Pepones, *Prosopike Martyria* (1970); and
Chrestos Zalokostas, *Chroniko tes Sklavias* (n.d.). Important works by a
participant, Komnenos Pyromaglou, are the biography, *O Georgios
Kartalis kai e Epoche tou* (1965), and the history, *E Ethnike Antistase*
(1975).

On the Communist side there are these memoirs, or mixtures of autobi-
ography and history: Lazaros A. Arseniou, *E Thessalia sten Antistase* 2
vols (1977); Giorgios Blanas, *O Emphylios Polemos, 1946–9. Opos ta
Ezesa* (1976); Thanases Chatzes, *E Nikephora Epanastase pou Chatheke* 3
vols (1977–9); Giannes Ioannides, *Anamneseis. Provlemata tes Politikes tou
KKE sten Ethnike Antistase, 1940–5,* ed. Alekos Papapanagiotou (1979);
Thanases Metsopoulos, *To 30 Syntagma tou ELAS* 4th edn (1987); and
Giorgios Vontitsos-Gousias, *Oi Aities gia tes Ettes, te Diaspase tou KKE
kai tes Ellenikes Aristeras* 2 vols (1977).

From liberation to civil war, 1944–7

A collection of useful essays is Lars Baerentzen, Ole L. Smith, and John O.
Iatrides, eds, *Studies in the History of the Greek Civil War, 1945–9*
(Copenhagen, 1987). Papers presented to a conference at Vilvorde, in
June 1987, on the same period are about to appear as John O. Iatrides
and Linda Wrigley, eds, *Greece at the Crossroads, 1944–9. The Civil War
and its Legacy* (Philadelphia). An indispensable history of the civil war
from 1945, by an officer in the national army, is Demetrios
Zapheiropoulos, *O Antisymmoriakos Agon, 1945–9* (1956).

Fascinating and perceptive works were written by British and American
observers: Reginald Leeper, *When Greek Meets Greek* (1950); Kenneth

Matthews, *Memories of a Mountain War* (1972); William H. McNeill, *The Greek Dilemma: War and Aftermath* (New York, 1947); Leften S. Stavrianos, *Greece: American Dilemma and Opportunity* (Chicago, 1952); and Frank Smothers, William and Elizabeth McNeill, *Report on the Greeks* (New York, 1948).

On British and American policy towards Greece in these years there are a number of works: George M. Alexander, *The Prelude to the Truman Doctrine* (Oxford, 1982); Theodore A. Couloumbis and John O. Iatrides, eds, *Greek–American Relations. A Critical Review* (New York, 1980); Robert Frazier, *Anglo-American Relations with Greece: the Coming of the Cold War, 1942–7* (New York, 1991); Howard Jones, *'A New Kind of War': America's Global Strategy and the Truman Doctrine in Greece* (1989); V. Kondes, *E Angloamerikanike Politike kai to Elleniko Provlema, 1945–9* (Salonika, 1984); Bruce R. Kuniholm, *The Origins of the Cold War in the Near East. Great Power Conflict and Diplomacy in Iran, Turkey and Greece* (Princeton, 1980); Heinz Richter, *British Intervention in Greece. From Varkiza to Civil War*, translated by Marion Sarafis (1985); Yannis P. Roubatis, *Tangled Webs. The U.S. in Greece, 1947–67* (New York, 1987); Thanasis D. Sfikas, *The British Labour Government and the Greek Civil War* (Keele, 1994); and Lawrence S. Wittner, *American Intervention in Greece, 1943–9* (New York, 1982).

An enlightening discussion is John O. Iatrides, 'Greece in the Cold War and beyond', *Journal of the Hellenic Diaspora* 19, 2 (1993), pp. 11–48.

Among works mentioned earlier, these are especially relevant to the years 1945–9: Close, ed., *The Greek Civil War*; Stavrakis, *Moscow and Greek Communism*; Iatrides, ed., *Greece in the 1940s*; Vlavianos, *Greece, 1941–9*; and Sfikas, *The British Labour Government and the Greek Civil War*.

Maps

Map 1: Provinces in Greece

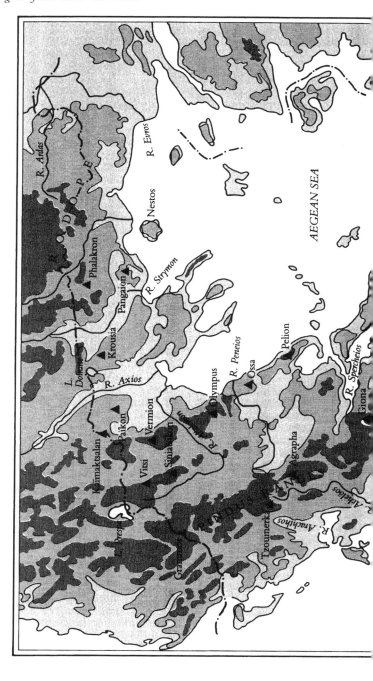

AEGEAN SEA

R. Ardas

R. Evros

R. Nestos

Phalakron

Pangaion

R. Strymon

Krousia

L. Doïran

R. Axios

Paikon

Vermion

Vitsi

Sniatsikon

Olympus

R. Peneios

Ossa

Pelion

R. Spercheios

Giona

Agrapha

Arachthos

R. Acheloos

Tzoumerka

Kalimaktsalan

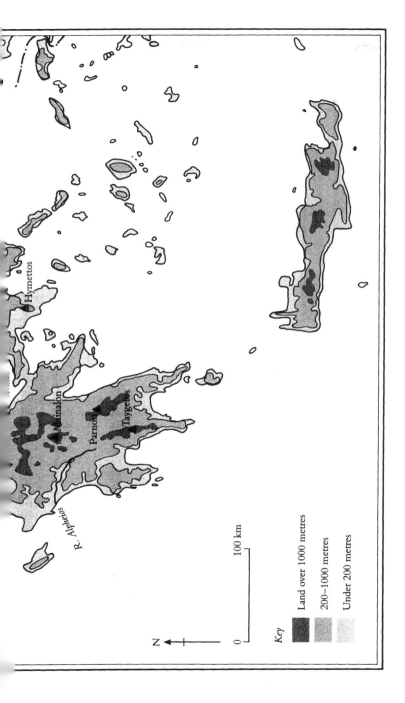

Map 2: Physical features of Greece

Key

■ Land over 1000 metres

▨ 200–1000 metres

□ Under 200 metres

100 km

0

N

R. Alpheios

Kimalon

Parnon

Taygetos

Hymettos

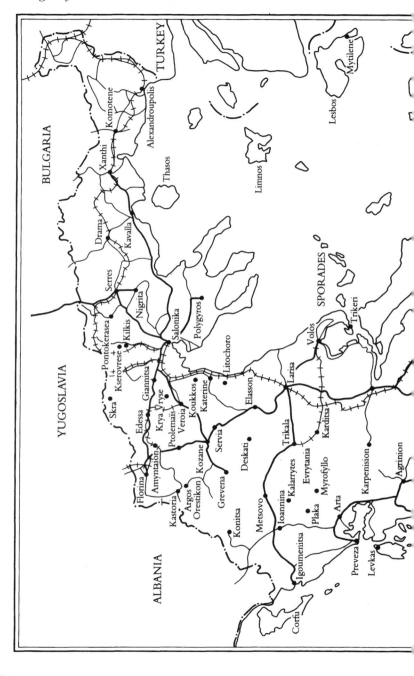

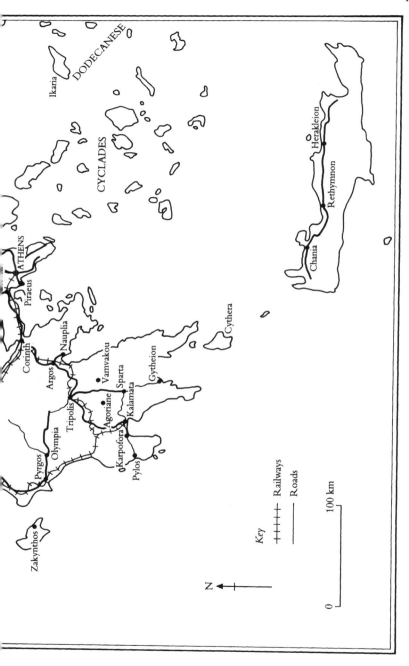

Map 3: Major towns, roads and railways in Greece in the 1940s

Index

and army, 47, 80–1, *see also* ELAS,
DSE
and Britain, 76, 79, 102–13, 129,
132–3, 161, 163–5, 178–9
and EAM, 68–83, 88, 99, 106–13,
128–30, 172, 194
growth of, 35–7, 47–9, 51, 127–31,
134–5
defeat, 141–5
persecuted, 19, 24–7, 38, 41–2,
47–51, 54, 63, 70
power increases, 127–31, 134–5
revival, *see* Zachariades
Communist University for Workers in
the Far East (KUTV), 19–20, 21
Constantine, King, 3
Corfu, 97, 145, 156
Couvaras, Costas, 71
Crawford, General Keith, 200
Crete, 3, 49, 51, 55, 175, 196, 209
and DSE, 196, 209
and EAM, 97, 98, 191
and Venizelists, 34, 36, 157, 191
German occupation, 56, 61, 73
Cyclades, and EAM, 97
Cyprus, 161
Czech Communist Party, 182

Damaskinos, Archbishop, 94, 150, 162
Dangoulas, 91, 115, 119
Daskalakes, Apostolas, 144
Declaration on Liberated Europe, 145,
173, 204
Dedouses, Evthymios, 113
Defenders of Northern Greece (YBE),
64
Demertzes, Konstantinos, 38
Demetratos, Aristides, 45
Democratic Army of Greece, *see* DSE
Democratic Socialist Party, 108
Dertiles, Vasilios, 89
Diakos, Iannes, 42, 66
Diamantes, death of, 219
Dimitrov, Georgi, 142, 182
Drakos, Markos, 55
Drama, 171
Dromazos, Giorgios, 151
DSE, 195–203, 209–14, 216–18

EA (National Solidarity), 68, 71–2

EAM (National Liberation Front), xii,
13, 68–83, 159, 169–73, 189, 190,
191, 194, 218
and Communist Party, 68, 71–8,
80–2, 110, 130, 166, 169–73, 198,
221
and elections, 175–6, 182
and Political Committee of National
Liberation (PEEA), 81, 99–100
defeated, 142–5, 155–6, 158
EAM/ELAS, 90, 96, 97, 101, 115,
143–4, 159, 177, 201
EDA (United Democratic Left), 221
Eden, Sir Anthony, 133, 150
EDES, xii, 74, 91, 93–4, 95, 101–2
and EAM, 113, 128, 129, 143
and ELAS, 73, 101–6, 111, 113–14,
116, 118, 119, 138, 140
Edessa, 114
Educational Association, 17, 19
Egypt, 56, 107, 108
Greek army in exile, 77, 92–3, 101,
102, 107, 109, 132, 176
Greek government in exile, 56, 66,
67–8, 81, 83, 95, 102, 104, 105,
107–9
Greek community in, 130, 157
EKKA, xiii, 93–4, 95, 102, 103, 104,
109, 113
ELAS, xiii, 71, 73, 74, 99–106, 111–13,
115–16, 117–19, 128, 137–42, 180
and British, 73, 76, 80–1, 100, 101,
103–4, 118, 119, 136
and DSE, 195, 196
and EDES, *see* EDES
demobilization of, 128, 131–5,
144–5, 152–3
opponents of, 75, 90–4, 96, 104,
113–14, 115, 143–4, 159, 215
strength, 77, 92, 94, 99, 100, 101,
115, 133, 141, 212
structure, 80–1, 83, 96
elections, general, 33, 37, 38, 175–6,
182, 220
Elephantes, Angelos, 14
Elevsis, 134
Elevtherotypia, 177, 213
ENA (Union of Young Officers), 92
EOK (National Organization of Crete),
98

Mantakas, General Emmanuel, 77, 107, 135
Mao Zedong, 70
Markos Vapheiades, 193, 195–7, 209, 212
Marxism-Leninism, 17, 19, 47, 52, 75, 82
Matthews, Kenneth, 210
Mavrogordatos, George, 174, 175, 190
Mavromichalis, Petros, 157, 192
Mazower, Mark, 62, 90, 137
McNeil, Hector, 163, 203
McNeill, William and Elizabeth, 157, 177
Meligala, 119
Merkoures, Georgios, 62
Merkoures, Stamates, 175
Messenia, 119
Metaxas, Ioannes, 6, 12, 34
  and military, 44, 52–3, 63, 64, 91, 93, 152
  and monarchy, 40–4, 66, 69
  and police, 42–4, 47–9, 52–3, 64, 105, 128, 154–5
  and youth, 46–7, 51, 52, 54, 63
  Communist view of, 69, 71, 107, 130, 179
  regime, 36, 40–56, 60, 65, 69, 74, 94, 151, 152, 158, 221
Metsopoulos, Thanases, 80
Metsovo, 106, 212
Michal Agas, *see* Agas, Michal
Michalakopoulos, Andreas, 24
Mihailovic, Draza, 160
Military Hierarchy, 91, 113, 117, 143, 219
Military League, 38
Military Security Service, 210, 214
Mistra, 119
Mitla, Telemachos, 47
Molotov, Vyacheslav, 181, 182
monarchists, 3, 66, 70, 90, 92, 93, 97, 108, 151, 175, 183–4, 189–93, 192, 201
monarchy, 40–1, 60, 69, 94, 150, 151, 174, 190, 197
  powers of, 32
  restoration of, 37, 92, 105, 173–4
Montgomery, Lord, 203

Mountain Brigade, 93, 109, 131–4, 138–9, 159, 218
Mouzelis, Nikos, 1, 7
Mussolini, 53, 54, 74
Mycenae, 210
Myers, Brigadier E.C.W., 93, 103
Mylonas, Alexandros, 36
Myrofyllo, 106
Myrovleto archives, 177, 210–11, 213

Naoussa, 100, 158, 195, 212, 217
National Action (ED), 91–2, 153
National and Social Liberation, *see* EKKA
National Bands Agreement (1943), 103–5
National Bank, 8, 45, 62, 169
National Confederation of Agricultural Cooperatives, 45
National Council, 100
National Greek Army (EES), 91
National Democratic Greek League, *see* EDES
National Greek Liberation League, *see* PAS
National Guard, 133, 139, 141, 145, 150, 152–7, 161, 164, 171, 174, 179, 194, 199
National Liberation Front, *see* EAM
National Organization of Crete (EOK), 98
National Organization of Youth (EON), 46
National Party of Greece, 175
National Political Union, 175
National Popular Liberation Army, *see* ELAS
National Revolution (EE), 64
National Schism, 3–5, 12, 27, 33, 37, 89
National Solidarity (EA), 68, 71–2
National Workers' Liberation Front (EEAM), 68
Nazi Germany, 35, 39, 53–5
Nazi-Soviet Pact, 48, 69
Nepheloudes, Pavlos, 141
Nepheloudes, Vasiles, 21
Neubacher, Hermann, 61
Nigrita, 102, 120
Nikolakopoulos, Elias, 175, 191